Corporate Trust
Administration
and Management

CORPORATE TRUST
ADMINISTRATION
AND MANAGEMENT

Joseph C. Kennedy

and

Robert I. Landau

Second Edition

NEW YORK UNIVERSITY PRESS   1975

© 1961, 1974 BY NEW YORK UNIVERSITY
LIBRARY OF CONGRESS CATALOG CARD NUMBER: 61-16959
BY ARRANGEMENT WITH WASHINGTON SQUARE PRESS, INC.
MANUFACTURED IN THE UNITED STATES OF AMERICA
ISBN 0-8147-0232-5

Preface to the Revised Edition

FOURTEEN YEARS HAVE ELAPSED since Joseph Kennedy wrote his definitive work on corporate trust administration. During that period many significant developments have taken place in the management of debt financing and the administration of bond indenture contracts, most of which have been incorporated in this revised edition insofar as they are relevant to the purposes this book seeks to serve.

The major developments include the growth in number and volume of direct or private placement contracts, the marketing of public corporate debt issues in all registered form only, the attempts to simplify and standardize indenture provisions through the publication of model provisions and an incorporating indenture, the almost universal adoption of the Uniform Commercial Code, and the increased trend toward special purpose debt financing. These developments and others, together with the changes which have occurred generally in the securities industry and especially in the processing of securities, must be carefully considered and understood not only by bank officers and administrative personnel responsible for such work, but also by those persons engaged in the drafting of debt financing documents and the marketing of bond issues, as well as by those responsible for the establishment and implementation of statutes, rules and regulations applicable to the corporate trust industry.

Many of the problems which are present today have been accentuated by past inflexibility. The future requires not only an alertness to the need for change and the flexibility to meet the requirements of an evolving economy and changing patterns of financing, but also a great deal of imagination and willingness to accept the responsibilities required. It is evident that a sound understanding of basic concepts as well as a thorough knowledge of current practice is an absolute necessity to provide insight into the problems of the future.

Subsequent to the publication of our article, "Recent Developments in Debt Financing and Corporate Trust Administration" [1] and prior to his untimely death in 1972, Joe Kennedy repeatedly urged me to revise this book. The result, for which I am fully responsible including any errors and omissions, is respectfully dedicated to his memory.

In these days of feminine sensitivity to male chauvinism in text books, let it be clear that I have not attempted to revise all of the references to "he" or "his", it being intended that such pronouns are understood to include "she" or "her", as the case may be.

Finally, I wish to express my gratitude to my wife, Carol, for her patience and constant encouragement during the past several months while I was laboring on this work. My appreciation also to my secretary, Miss Christine Gerace, who typed the numerous revisions, most of which from my own rather illegible writing.

Robert I. Landau

1. *The Business Lawyer,* Vol. 22, No. 2 (1967)

A trustee is held to something stricter than the morals of the marketplace. Not honesty alone, but the punctillo of an honor the most sensitive, is then the standard of behavior.

Justice Benjamin N. Cardozo
Meinhard v. *Salmon*
249 N. Y. 458, 464 (1928)

Contents

ix

Corporate Trust
Administration
and Management

1

Some General Principles of Corporate Finance

THE CORPORATE TRUST INDENTURE is undoubtedly the most involved financial document that has been devised. Its administration therefore requires highly skilled and experienced personnel. In the succeeding chapters some of the more important problems and techniques involved in the administration of these indentures will be presented.

While a full discussion of the problems of corporate organization, management, and finance is beyond the scope of this endeavor, a basic knowledge and understanding of their essential features are important even to the beginner in the field. As a preliminary, therefore, this chapter will consider some of the essential concepts involved in the corporate form of business enterprise and the financing thereof.

THE CORPORATE FORM OF BUSINESS ENTERPRISE

The most common form of business enterprise is the individual proprietorship, in which the individual invests his own capital, operates the business alone or with one or more employees, and is entitled to all the profits which are realized or, conversely, suffers the losses. If the business should fail, not only the assets of the business but also all of the personal assets of the proprietor are liable for payment of business creditors. The partnership is similar in content and, in effect, involves only the association of two or more individual proprietors in a common business undertaking. Essential features of both of these forms are the direct participation of the owners in the operation of the business and their unlimited liability for debts of the business.

1

The corporate form of business enterprise is a different matter. A creature of the industrial revolution, it has been essential to the growth and development of the industrialized economies with which we are familiar from the time of the British mercantile companies which were organized for colonial development.

A corporation is a creature of the state and exists only by reason of a charter granted by the state. In the early days of the United States, a corporation could be created only by special legislative enactment. Such a special charter was granted after careful consideration and usually was for a very special and limited purpose. Some corporations still exist with charters so granted. Today, however, all states have general incorporation laws and the organization of a corporation is relatively simple.

Since a corporation is a creature of the state it can exercise only such powers as are specifically granted to it by the state. These powers are enumerated in the corporate charter which is a basic document of every corporation. Incorporators may include in a proposed charter any power not prohibited by law or contrary to public policy. It is therefore the general practice for every charter to include a very broad grant of powers. From the viewpoint of corporate indenture financing, essential powers which must be set forth are the right to borrow money and the right to mortgage and pledge assets of the corporation as security therefor. If a corporation performs or purports to perform an act for which it does not have authority in its charter, such an act is said to be *ultra vires* and this may constitute a defense in a suit against the corporation arising from the act so performed.

A corporation is subject not only to the limitations contained in its charter but also to all laws and regulations which are drafted by the state legislature, or regulatory authority in the state of incorporation, and also by any federal agency having jurisdiction over the corporation.

Another important corporate document is the corporate bylaws. These are essentially rules of procedure which are adopted by the stockholders, and they can be amended at any time by vote of the stockholders. They set forth such things as: the form of the certificates of stock; the frequency and dates of stockholder meetings; procedures for calling special meetings; the scope and functions of the board of directors and the various committees; the powers and duties of the principal officers; and such other basic rules as may be necessary for or pertinent to the continued functioning of the corporate entity.

Stockholders are the owners of the business and as such are entitled to a vote in the management of its affairs in proportion to their ownership of stock. They are also entitled to share in the profits of the corporation—but only through such dividends as may be declared from time to time by the corporate directors. Such rights of ownership, however, differ markedly from those involved in other forms of business enterprises. Stockholders, as such, do not participate directly in the management of the corporate business. They are also protected by the limited liability involved in the corporate form of business. If a venture fails, the stockholder is likely to lose the amount of his investment in the business, but his personal assets are not liable for the payment of corporate debts.

The purchase of stock in a particular corporation usually results from a desire to make a profitable investment of savings or idle funds rather than from a desire to participate in a particular type of business venture. This concept of the pooling of savings of many individuals to make possible the conduct of business on the vast scale we know today, was the great contribution of the corporate form of business enterprise.

Management of a corporation is vested in a board of directors elected by the stockholders. In some cases this board is made up entirely of people who are active officers of the corporation, but it is more common for a percentage of the membership to be drawn from prominent members of the community who are engaged primarily in other professions. The diversity of interests and viewpoints thus brought together is often helpful to the enterprise. Regardless of the composition of the board, however, the directors are primarily responsible for the affairs of the corporation and may become individually liable and accountable for unwarranted acts of the corporation.

Active management of corporate affairs is delegated to an official staff who devote their entire time to the enterprise. These officers are appointed by the board and their functions are set forth in the bylaws or are prescribed by resolutions of the board. Any officer has only such authority as is specifically granted or necessarily implied, and anyone dealing with a corporation should be certain of the authority of the officials with whom he deals and of the proper authorization of any contract or undertaking.

CORPORATE FINANCIAL STATEMENTS

The activities of a corporation are summarized in the records which the corporate officers are required to maintain. Summaries of these records showing the results of operation for designated periods are forwarded periodically to stockholders, creditors, and others. It is customary to have these records audited at least annually by a firm of public accountants who furnish a certificate of their examination. Whenever a corporation issues securities publicly, it must file certified financial statements with the Securities and Exchange Commission. Almost every trust indenture requires the filing of such reports with the corporate trustee.

Regulated industries such as railroads, public utilities, and similar corporations, are required to maintain their records in a uniform manner as prescribed by the particular regulatory authority having jurisdiction over them. Other corporations are not so restricted, so that there may be some differences in detail among various types of companies and even among companies engaged in the same type of business. In general, however, the development of modern accounting techniques and procedures and the requirements of federal tax regulations insure substantial uniformity in the form and content of financial statements.

It is essential for a corporate trust administrator to be familiar with financial statements and to be able to review and analyze them intelligently. Among the more common of such statements are the following.

Balance Sheet

The balance sheet presents the condition of a corporation as of a particular moment in its history. It also may be said to reflect the cumulative results of the company's operations from its inception to the date when the statement is rendered. Exhibit 1 presents comparative balance sheets of a typical manufacturing corporation as of the end of two successive years.

Assets represent the things which the corporation owns, or its investment or use of the funds which have come into its hands. Assets are customarily classified as "current" or "fixed." Current assets include cash and such items as will be converted into cash in the normal operations of the business. Among such items are

EXHIBIT 1. BALANCE SHEET

ABC MANUFACTURING CORPORATION

Balance Sheet

(000 omitted)

	DECEMBER 31, 1974		DECEMBER 31, 1973	INCREASE (DECREASE)
ASSETS				
Cash		$ 6,647	$ 4,250	$ 2,397
U. S. Govt. bonds		12,500	10,000	2,500
Accounts receivable		8,326	9,016	(690)
Inventories				
Raw materials		17,264	14,261	3,003
Finished goods		14,313	12,807	1,506
TOTAL CURRENT ASSETS		$59,050	$50,334	$ 8,716
Fixed property:				
Land		7,600	6,800	800
Manufacturing				
plant	111,342		101,542	
Less depreciation	47,165	64,177	42,427 59,115	5,062
Machinery and				
equipment	52,589		47,289	
Less depreciation	22,438	30,151	19,553 27,736	2,415
Investments (at cost)		15,630	15,630	—
Good will		6,400	6,400	—
Patents, trade-marks, etc.		1,200	1,200	—
Prepaid expenses:				
Insurance		72	96	(24)
Other		30	20	10
TOTAL ASSETS		$184,310	$167,331	$16,979
LIABILITIES AND CAPITAL				
Accounts payable		$ 2,452	$ 2,560	(108)
Accrued taxes		9,468	10,020	(552)
Other accrued expenses		1,390	1,280	110
Bank loan		6,000	10,000	(4,000)
Sinking fund—bonds		750	750	—
—debentures		1,000	—	1,000
TOTAL CURRENT LIABILITIES		$21,060	$24,610	($3,550)
First mortgage bonds—				
6% due 1990		$27,500	$28,250	($ 750)
Debentures—8½% due 1984		14,000	—	14,000
Preferred stock				
4.25% (100 par)		6,000	6,000	—
Common stock—no par				
Stated value $10. Authorized,				
8,000,000 shs.; outstanding,				
4,500,000 shs.		45,000	45,000	—
Excess of proceeds over stated				
value of stock (Also				
called capital surplus)		22,500	22,500	—
Earnings reinvested in the				
business (Also called				
earned surplus or				
undivided profits)		48,250	40,971	7,279
TOTAL LIABILITIES AND CAPITAL		$184,310	$167,331	$16,979

5

temporary investments, receivables (amounts owed by the company's customers), and inventories (either raw materials awaiting processing or finished goods available for sale). Fixed assets include the building and property which the company owns and uses in the conduct of its business; permanent investments which the company may have in other companies; and other types of property which may be necessary or incidental to its operations but which are normally not held for sale. Such things as good will, patents, trade-marks, franchises, etc. are intangibles and may be included as assets if they have a real value. Another term frequently employed is "tangible assets" which include all assets other than good will, patents, and other such intangibles which would have little, if any, value on liquidation of the business.

Assets are offset by an equal amount of liabilities and capital, which represent the source of funds by which the corporate assets were acquired. Current liabilities represent amounts which are due and payable within a specified period of time—usually a year—and which were incurred primarily in connection with normal business operations. Together, current asset and liability accounts are considered the company's working capital accounts, and the excess of current assets over current liabilities is usually referred to as "working capital" or "net current assets." Money which is borrowed for a period longer than one year is usually referred to as funded debt and is shown on the balance sheet as a noncurrent liability, although any portion of funded debt due within one year, either by reason of maturity or a sinking fund obligation, is customarily included as a current liability.

It might be appropriate at this point to distinguish between various forms of borrowing. The ordinary bank loan is usually incurred for working capital purposes and matures within a relatively short time. Since many businesses operate on a cyclical basis during the year, there are periods of heavy inventory accumulation—purchase of raw materials for fabrication or processing. These periods are accompanied by heavy bank borrowing to provide funds for raw materials. During the period of heavy sales, the finished goods are disposed of, inventory decreases, and the resulting increase in cash is used to pay off the bank borrowing. (It is much less expensive to have temporary heavy cash requirements supplied by bank credit than to provide permanent capital sufficient to meet the company's peak cash demands.) All of these transactions, as they occur, are reflected in the company's "working capital" accounts. Funds which are needed for capital or fixed property purposes are borrowed for longer periods of time. It is this type of borrowing with which we will be concerned in our consideration of the trust indenture.

Another type of permanent capital is that supplied by the owners of the business—the stockholders. The net amount invested by the owners—whether representing amounts paid in for purchase of stock or undistributed earnings which have been reinvested in the business—makes up the balance of the liability side of the balance sheet.

Exhibit 2. Income Statement

ABC MANUFACTURING CORPORATION

Income Statement for annual period ending December 31, 1974

(000 omitted)

Sales	$182,538
Cost of goods sold	134,341
	$ 48,197
Selling, general & administrative expense	3,318
Depreciation	7,623
Local and state taxes	5,018
Other expenses	1,341
	$17,300
Net operating income	$30,897
Other income	2,115
	$33,012
Interest	1,738
	$31,274
Federal income taxes	16,540
Net income	$14,734

Statement of Earned Surplus
(December 31, 1974)
(000 omitted)

Balance, December 31, 1973		$40,971
Net earnings—1974		14,734
		$55,705
Dividends paid		
Preferred	$ 255	
Common	7,200	7,455
Balance December 31, 1974		$48,250

Income and Surplus Statements

Exhibit 2 presents the income statement of the ABC Manufacturing Corporation for the year 1974 and a statement of earned surplus as of the year end.

The principal source of the company's income is from the sale of its products, and the first item on the income statement is the amount of the gross sales for the year. From this is deducted the cost of the goods so sold, including the cost of the raw materials and the costs directly chargeable to manufacturing operations. These costs will tend to vary in almost direct proportion to the volume of goods produced. Other costs which are more or less "fixed" without regard to fluctuation in volume of business are the expenses of the sales force, advertising, general office expense, taxes, and other similar charges. These are usually shown separately on the income statement and in such detail as may be appropriate for proper presentation and understanding. Deduction of manufacturing and general expense from gross sales will give the net income resulting from the year's operations.

The charge for "depreciation" is a noncash expense. On the balance sheet (Exhibit 1) only the net value of the manufacturing plant and machinery and equipment was included in assets. This net value was determined by deducting from the gross cost of these assets any depreciation which had accrued. While such assets represent permanent investments, they will in time become worn out as they are used in the manufacturing process and will have to be replaced. It is therefore necessary to charge against each year's income an appropriate amount to represent the deterioration or decrease in value of such fixed assets. This is the depreciation charge. There are a number of ways in which depreciation may be computed, but it is sufficient to understand that, in theory, the charge represents the value of the fixed assets used up in the year's operations.

To the amount of net operating income is added other income which the company may have realized during the year. This may include interest on temporary investments, income from investments in other companies, the excess of proceeds over book value of the sale of fixed assets no longer required in the business, and other similar items. From the total income so shown, any other items of expense not previously included should be deducted. In our typical statement, a deduction for interest on money borrowed is included. This type of charge is frequently, and appropriately, included as an item of general expense. Other items which might be included would be loss on sale of investments or fixed assets, amortization of discount on funded debt obligations sold below par, and so on. The final deduction is the amount of income taxes accrued for the year, and the resulting balance is the net income of the corporation resulting from all activities during the period.

Earned surplus represents the cumulative earnings of the company which have been reinvested in the business rather than being distributed to the stockholders. As indicated by the statement shown, approximately 50 per cent of the corporation's earnings during the year were so retained and reinvested.

Source and Use of Funds Statement

The final example of a common type of financial statement presented here is the Source and Use of Funds statement. Such a statement of our hypothetical corporation for the year 1974 is presented as Exhibit 3.

This type of statement is helpful in considering the financial transactions of a corporation. All corporate transactions are expressed in terms of dollars, but many transactions take place each

EXHIBIT 3. SOURCE AND USE OF FUNDS STATEMENT

ABC MANUFACTURING CORPORATION	
Source and Use of Funds Statement—1974	
(000 omitted)	
SOURCE	
Net income for year	$14,734
Depreciation accrual	7,623
Issuance of debentures	14,000
(Less amount due in one year)	
Miscellaneous (decrease in prepaid expense)	14
	$36,371
USE	
Increase in working capital	$12,266
Plant expansion	15,900
Reduction in bond indebtedness	750
Dividends paid	7,455
	$36,371

day without a concurrent transfer of dollars. Goods are bought to be paid for at a later date. Wages, taxes, and other items of expense accrue which represent requirements for cash outlays in the future. Similarly, sales are made on credit or services are performed to be paid for over a period of time.

Financial officers must plan to provide the cash, when required, to meet the payments called for by the corporate operations. Similarly, anyone extending credit to the company is primarily concerned that funds will be available to meet the service payments on the debt as they become due.

The source and use of funds statement reflects the flow of cash through a company's operations for a stated period. Such a statement can be prepared from the statements previously considered. Of more importance to financial officers is the use of such projected statements as a part of budget preparation so that proper planning may insure that the company's financial obligations will be met promptly.

A single balance sheet provides little information other than the financial condition of the company as of a particular moment. It does not reflect the trend of the business. By a comparative analysis of balance sheets for the beginning and end of a designated period, however, a great deal of information may be disclosed concerning the activities of the corporation during the period. These, combined with the income and surplus statements, provide sufficient information from which a cash flow statement for the period can be constructed.

Assets represent uses of funds and liabilities, sources of funds. An increase in assets or a decrease in liabilities during a period reflects the net use of corporate funds during that period. Similarly, the sum of the decrease in assets and increase in liabilities reflects the net source of corporate funds for the period. Another type of source and use of funds balance sheet can thus be constructed by rearranging the net increase and decrease in assets and liabilities reflected in the change in the balance sheet for the period in question. Of course, there are actually many thousands of sources and uses for any particular accounting period. For an adequate picture of the company's transactions, however, it is usually sufficient to summarize the net effect of all these transactions. While analysis of balance sheets alone would provide such a picture, it would not be as complete as can be obtained by considering also the income accounts for the period. It is also common to regard the working capital accounts (current assets and liabilities) as an entity in any such analysis. Thus, a net increase in working capital represents a use of funds and a net decrease, a source.

By examining the accounts set forth in Exhibits 1 and 2 we see that the company had net income for the year of $14,734,000. This is a source of funds. To this we must add the depreciation charge of $7,623,000. As we have seen, depreciation is a noncash expense and, to the extent that cash income is reduced by such a charge, it is necessary to increase the net income shown by this amount to determine the net *cash receipts* from operations. We have also seen that funded debt was increased by the issuance of $15,000,000 debentures due in ten years. Since $1,000,000 of this amount has to be retired through a sinking fund within one year and is therefore included under current liabilities, only $14,000,000 is shown in our source of funds statement. The final item under "source" is a net decrease in prepaid expenses of $14,000.

Examination of the balance sheets indicates that working capital during the year increased by $12,266,000 (increase in current assets of $8,716,000 and decrease in current liabilities of $3,550,000). This is a use of funds. We note also that $15,900,000 was used to increase the gross value of the investment in fixed property ($800,000 in land, $9,800,000 in manufacturing plant, and $5,300,000 in machinery and equipment). Bonded indebtedness was reduced by a sinking fund payment of $750,000, and dividends in the amount of $7,455,000 were distributed to stockholders.

Financial Ratios

It is not intended to present all of the factors which are important in a complete and thorough financial statement analysis, but the administrator should be familiar with the more commonly used financial ratios, which are referred to below.

Current Ratio.—One of the more frequently used ratios, it indicates the proportion of current assets to current liabilities, and is a measure of liquidity. The 1974 current ratio from the balance sheet in Exhibit 1 is 2.8:1, indicating that current liabilities are covered 2.8 times by current assets.

Interest Coverage.—Strictly speaking, this is not actually a ratio, but it is an important consideration in the extension of credit—particularly long term credit—to a corporation. The purpose of this ratio is to determine how many times the company earns its annual interest charges, and it is computed by taking net earnings before interest and income taxes. If extension of new credit is being contemplated, interest charges on the new debt should also be included. It is customary to take average earnings over a period of years, and if the industry is a cyclical one, to consider earnings during the poorest year. Of importance in connection with extension of long term credit is the company's history of ample coverage of all fixed charges.

Cash Income to Total Debt.—This ratio is related to the next preceding computation and its purpose is to determine what relationship the annual cash flow of the corporation bears to the total debt—both current and funded. Assuming that all cash were applied to liquidating debt, this ratio would give a rough indication of the number of years' operations required for complete liquidation. Cash income is determined by adding depreciation charges to net income.

Working Capital to Funded Debt.—Another measure of current liquidity, it indicates the ratio of net current assets to total funded debt.

Current Assets to Total Debt.—A ratio similar to the preceding one, it is computed by adding current liabilities to funded debt and determining the amount of coverage represented by total current assets. It is a more accurate measure of liquidity than the former.

Tangible Assets to Debt.—The ratio of total tangible assets (all assets, less such intangibles as good will, etc.) to the sum of current liabilities and funded debt. Another variation is the ratio of net tangible assets (tangible assets less current liabilities) to funded debt.

Inventory Turnover.—A measure of the liquidity of the inventory account, computed by dividing the gross inventory into annual sales. It is intended to give a rough indication of the number of times inventory is turned over in the course of a year.

Debt Ratio.—The ratio of funded debt to total capitalization, indicating the percentage of corporate capital supplied by creditors as related to the amount supplied by the owners of the business.

Ratios are useful tools in analyzing financial statements or determining the investment value of a company's securities. There is no magic formula for solving every type of financial problem however and these, as all other, tools must be used with judgment and discretion. Obviously ratios will vary between industries and different types of businesses, and a ratio indicative of a stable condition in one instance may be a signal of a weakening position in another. Finally, ratios are at best no more than imperfect measures, and care should always be taken to see that the particular measure used is appropriate to the measurement desired.

FINANCING CAPITAL NEEDS

Corporate financial officers are continually faced with the problem of how to finance the money needs of the business. This is not a problem which will directly concern the corporate trust administrator under normal circumstances, and it is therefore unnecessary to deal with it in detail. Some understanding of the basic principles involved, however, will be helpful in understanding the whys and wherefores of some of the negotiations involved in the drafting of particular indenture provisions.

We have noted that short term working capital needs are customarily financed by short term bank loans. An additional and important source of short-term funds for companies of strong credit standing is the sale of commercial paper. This refers to short-term promissory notes, generally unsecured, which are typically written in multiples of $5,000. with maturities of from three days to nine months. These notes do not bear interest, as such. Instead, an effective interest rate is established by the sale of the notes at a discount from face amount.

Financing of medium term needs (for example, the purchase of equipment that can be paid for in four to five years) might be done through a bank term loan. Fixed capital requirements are normally supplied from the capital markets through the medium of some form of savings. Since this is the type of financing with which the corporate trustee is concerned, discussion will be confined to an analysis of its elements.

Capital requirements can be financed in any one of four principal ways: through some form of borrowing—the issuance of debt securities; through the issuance of preferred stock—while this is a form of equity or ownership security, the holder is entitled only to a fixed return from the earnings of the company, but has a claim prior to common stockholders in the event of liquidation; through the sale of additional common stock; or finally, through retained earnings. While every conservative management normally retains a portion of earnings for use in the business (and this might be said not to be financing in the true sense), retention of earnings is in effect a forced investment by existing stockholders, and many of the considerations applicable to other types of capital financing are pertinent to the portion of earnings which should be retained, particularly if thought is being given to a change in dividend policy.

Many factors affect a decision as to the type of financing to be used for a particular project. Among the more important are: (1) the nature of the project or expansion to be financed, the extent to which it is speculative, and its relationship in size, cost, and profitability to the existing business of the company; (2) the prospective earnings from the proposed investment and the precision with which it is possible to forecast such earnings; (3) the quality and durability of the existing earnings of the company and the extent to which they are affected by cyclical changes in the general economy; (4) the existing capital structure of the company and the effect which alternative methods would have on such structure; and (5) the cost of the alternate methods of raising the needed capital.

These factors reduce themselves generally to a consideration of the risks involved in relation to the cost. It is assumed that the different types of capital are available at a price. If a particular method of financing is not available by reason of a prohibition in an existing contract, the quality of the company's credit, or for other reasons, the choice is more limited or, in fact, may be nonexistent.

It is axiomatic that the less expensive the method of financing, the more risk is involved. Debt is usually the cheapest form of capital, but there is some risk inherent in every type of debt financing, as it involves fixed commitments which must be met regardless of the earnings of the company at the particular time. From the viewpoint of the common stockholder, preferred stock involves more risk than does additional common stock, as it creates a class of holders with claims ranking prior to their own.

The cost of debt is represented by the rate of interest which must be paid. Since interest is deductible in computing income tax, the actual cost of debt financing is less than half the nominal interest rate under present tax laws. The cost of preferred stock is the fixed dividend rate. Because of lower priority, this rate will usually be higher than the rate on debt for the same company. In addition, and possibly of greater significance, preferred dividends are not deductible for income tax purposes. The cost of common stock is normally computed by determining the rate which must be earned on the price at which the stock can be sold to enable the stockholders to realize the same rate of earnings after the sale as they did before. While circumstances would differ as between companies, on the average in the past preferred stock financing has been two to three times more costly than debt, and common stock financing seven to eight times more costly than debt.

Another factor which is sometimes of considerable importance is the effect on existing capital structure which the proposed financing may have. The maintenance of a proper debt ratio is important, not only because of the safety factor inherent in a sound equity base, but also because of the adverse effect which excessive debt may have on the credit standing of the company. There is no approved ratio which should exist, and each analyst uses a different measurement for every class of industry. A fairly high debt ratio might be appropriate for a particular industry, whereas the same ratio in another would be cause for serious concern. Few companies can justify a debt ratio in excess of 50 per cent, and for most a maximum of 35 per cent would be considered advisable. When the ratio begins to exceed the theoretical ceiling, the company's security rating is affected, and this makes additional debt financing more difficult and more expensive. Thus, it is important that a proper proportion of equity to debt be maintained at all times, and it is advisable to include a certain amount of equity financing while a degree of flexibility remains, so that proper advantage can be taken of changing market conditions.

Corporate finance is a volatile and constantly changing field. The expert of a generation ago would find a strange world today. A number of factors which have been introduced into the economy during the past twenty years have contributed to these changes. One, of course, is the tremendous expansion which has taken place in the economy, and which has created an unprecedented demand for investment funds, including the vast sums which have been borrowed by states and municipalities. Another of equal or greater importance is the consideration which every corporation must give to the impact of the tax laws and regulations on its everyday activities. Big government and particularly, big taxes, are ever present specters, and it is no longer possible to make important decisions based on the economics of the situation alone.

One of the most important trends of recent years that has taken place in the area of debt financing, has been the growth in the number and volume of direct or private placement contracts. This has been a direct result of the concentration of savings in the hands of institutions that has been taking place—not only the growth in savings bank and life insurance assets, but the rapid increase in both private and public pension funds.

While avoidance of the uncertainties and expense of a public offering and compliance with the registration requirements of the Securities Act of 1933 are frequently cited as the motivating factors, an important consideration is the ability to achieve greater flexibility—to tailor each financing to fit the particular circumstances, and the greater ease in securing amendments to the contract which may be necessitated by changing conditions. Some institutional investors prefer this type of investment. They not only secure a somewhat better return but are able to plan investment operations more accurately by making commitments for fixed amounts at negotiated rates.

The private placement, which was an insignificant percentage of total debt financing prior to 1955, has assumed major importance. During the 1960s these placements accounted for approximately 50% of total capital debt financing of corporations. Although during the past few years the percent of the market has decreased somewhat, this form of financing still represents a very significant part.

Direct placement financing has fallen into three broad categories:

(1) Issues which are secured by the traditional form of corporate indenture—either an existing mortgage or a new bond or debenture issue. From the viewpoint of the corporate trustee there is little

change in administrative requirements. Except for the number of holders and the likelihood of a home office payment agreement,[2] such an issue is almost the same as a publicly offered issue in registered form.

(2) Special purpose and third party corporation financing. The variations are legion, and the security is more likely to involve leases, charter hires, through-put agreements, or some other form of contractual arrangement than the more traditional mortgage. In this type of financing, the credit of the obligor issuer is seldom important, since in most cases, it will be a corporation specifically created for the purpose of issuing the debt obligation. The loan is made on the credit of the lessee or other contract party and its agreement to perform under its contract with the obligor issuer.

(3) The third category is a note issue involving a direct unsecured loan without a trustee. Initially, these loans were very similar to bank credit agreements except that they were for longer terms and normally for capital purposes. The borrowers were corporations with high credit ratings and usually with no other funded debt. Frequently, only one institutional lender was involved, and it was exceptional to have more than four or five. The loan agreements were uncomplicated, with few, if any, security covenants.

Inevitably, there was not only an increase in the number of borrowers using this device, but in the variety and purpose of the loans. Credit agreements have become more complicated and there is wider participation in individual loans. Eight to ten investors are fairly common, and there have been a number with as many as twenty-five to fifty participants. In private placement financing, these note agreements have in many instances replaced debenture financing, but without the flexibility, marketability and uniformity of administration provided by the traditional debenture agreement with a competent and experienced corporate trustee.

It might be helpful to note, without extensive discussion, two other significant trends of recent years: (1) The increased popularity and use of unsecured, as opposed to secured, debt financing. This

---

[2] Such agreement provides that in consideration of payments of principal being mailed to the holder without requiring the presentation of the obligation for notation as to the payment, the holder, prior to disposing of the note, will surrender it to the obligor (or its agent) for such notation or issuance of a new note for the unpaid balance thereof.

has been particularly true in the service-type industries such as banks and finance companies. Maturities on these issues have ranged between five and twenty-five years. Such financing has often at times involved use of the convertible debenture and the subordinated debenture. In the former case, when the stock price of the particular corporation is moving upward, this becomes an extra incentive to the investor. (2) The tremendous volume of public financing including not only the continuous financing by the federal government involved in the management of the public debt, but the enormous amount of tax-exempt securities issued by states, state and local authorities and municipalities.

Although not directly a consideration of corporate capital needs, the borrowing of long-term funds by states and municipalities has a very real impact on the ability of the private sector to attract investors at favorable rates.

In the last several years there has been not only an increase in revenue bonds, but the introduction on a broad scale of a relatively new concept in tax-exempt financing. This is the use of industrial development bonds, the primary purpose of which is to attract financing of new plants and/or the construction of pollution control facilities through use of the tax-exempt privilege. Without commenting on the economic merits of this concept, it might be noted that a majority of the states have authorized issuance of this type of obligation by local government units. A second development is creation of state bond banks, which permit smaller municipalities to borrow funds at more favorable rates—through the use of funds raised on the credit of the state agency.

2

The Trust Indenture

THE MODERN TRUST INDENTURE is a device by which a corporation borrows money from the holders of savings—either the general public or the large institutional investors. The indenture provides the terms and conditions on which credit is extended; places restrictions on the activities of the issuing company so long as the indenture securities are outstanding; sets forth remedies available to the security holders should there be a default in payments on the debt or in the terms of the indenture contract; and otherwise defines the rights, duties, and obligations of the obligor company, the security holders, and the trustee or trustees named in the instrument. If the indenture obligations are to be secured, the indenture creates or pledges the security and sets forth the terms and conditions for dealing with such security.

The principle of a mortgage to secure the repayment of money is an ancient one. Likewise, the concept of a "use" or "trust" was developed at an early period in the common law. However, the development of the corporate mortgage, or trust indenture, is of fairly recent origin. It was introduced for the first time around 1830, but until the latter part of the nineteenth century was used infrequently. The reasons for this are many. In the first place, early corporate financing was chiefly by stock rather than by bonds. Also, the earlier corporations were generally created for special purposes and by special charter, and their power to incur debt or mortgage their properties was strictly limited.

The growth and development of trust indentures parallel closely the growth of the corporate form of business enterprise. With the passage of general incorporation laws in most states, organization of corporations became relatively simple, and as a result, use of this form of business organization became a common practice. The latter part of the nineteenth century was also a period of tremendous expansion and growth in the United States. Accordingly, there was a phenomenal increase in both the number and size of business corporations and the amount of capital required for their development.

The transaction of business by these vast enterprises came to involve not only large stock financing but also heavy borrowing. It became impractical to secure this financing through one bank, or even a group of banks, so there was developed a system of borrowing from the public at large through a multitude of small loans, each evidenced by the issuance of bonds of the corporation, and all secured by the same mortgage to one individual or a small group of individuals. The corporate mortgage was at first used primarily, and almost exclusively, by railroad corporations, but with the growth of the corporate form of business enterprise and the development of large corporate systems, the practice was extended until now there are corporations and corporate bond issues for almost every type of business undertaking.

Although the corporate indenture has become a necessary and most important factor in the economic life of the country, there is still a great deal of confusion as to its essential nature. While there have been a great many court decisions construing particular provisions and defining the rights of parties with respect to particular problems that have arisen, there is a lack of uniformity among the courts concerning the over-all significance of the contract. Because the indenture device is little more than a century old, and its real development has been achieved during the past sixty years, there has been no opportunity for a slow and gradual development of legal precedents. Courts have looked for guidance to other cases which had only a superficial similarity to the problems at hand, although the legal relationships appeared to be the same.

The trust indenture is an instrument *sui generis*, combining elements of several other legal relationships but being identical with none. Although most courts now agree that the indenture does not create a trust relationship in the customarily accepted sense, some cases have indicated that the full extent of fiduciary responsibility may be imposed upon the trustee. Indeed, it has been suggested that such measure of responsibility should be imposed by statute, even at the risk of seriously impairing its effective use.

Although every form of indenture has elements of similarity, there are various types, designed for the different kinds of obligations to be issued, each with peculiarities of its own. The title of the indenture usually describes the type of obligations to be issued thereunder and the nature of the security, if any. For example, a mortgage indenture indicates that the security consists primarily of a mortgage on the obligor's fixed property and that the obligations outstanding are mortgage bonds. A first mortgage indicates that the bonds are intended to be a first lien on such properties; a second mortgage a second lien, and so on. Normally, an indenture securing junior lien obligations will contain provisions for refunding the prior lien bonds, and in that event the indenture and the obligations issued thereunder will be called respectively a "refunding mortgage" and "refunding mortgage bonds," terms which sound more attractive than a second or third mortgage. If the obligations should have a first or prior lien on any property at all, the title "first and refunding mortgage" is frequently used. In some jurisdictions the term "trust deed" is preferred to mortgage, although in most cases this is simply a variation in title. A collateral trust agreement usually denotes an indenture under which the obligations have a collateral rather than a direct lien. A debenture agreement usually, although not necessarily, indicates unsecured obligations. There are many other variations, combinations, and different forms of designation depending on the type of obligation, the type of security, and other considerations. Although for most purposes these distinctions do not affect the fundamental nature of the indenture or of the rights and obligations of the parties, they do involve different types of provisions and covenants and undoubtedly account to some extent for the confusion and contradictions existing in the law relating to the subject matter.

The legal relationships of features of which the trust indenture most frequently partakes are mortgage, trust, and contract. It might be well to compare the ways in which they are similar and dissimilar to the commonly accepted meanings of these terms in order to get a better understanding of the true nature of the relationships created.

THE INDENTURE AS A MORTGAGE

Most secured indentures under which bonds are issued involve a mortgage of some kind. The nature and extent of the mortgage security will depend on the particular circumstances of the issue, but it usually involves a mortgage on the fixed property and equipment used by the issuer in its business. The forms used are substantially the same. The property is usually described in detail by metes and bounds in the instrument; great care is exercised in the execution of the document to insure that it conforms to the laws and customs of the jurisdictions where the property is located; and it is then properly filed and recorded. All things are done to insure that the indenture creates the lien that it purports to do. The net effect of all this effort, however, is usually quite different from that which the investor would expect when told that he has a first mortgage security.

In the customary mortgage transaction, borrower and lender are dealing in terms of a security, the value of which both understand. In the absence of extraordinary developments, the property usually has an intrinsic and realizable value more than adequate to cover the amount of the loan; and if there is a default, the lender can proceed to foreclose and realize on such security to make himself whole.

A transaction such as this is entirely different from a mortgage on the property of a large business enterprise. The average investor who purchases bonds has no conception of the value of a large railroad system, for example, although a "mortgage" thereon may constitute his security. Even were he able to make an examination of each separate parcel, he would still be unable to ascertain its value, for in this case the value of the whole may be greater or less than the sum of the values of all its parts. As real estate, a railroad right of way one mile long and thirty feet wide may have little value, although the railroad may have issued "mortgage" bonds to the extent of $300,000 or more per mile. The real value of the property of a business enterprise is the "going concern" value of the enterprise. Considered separate and apart from its use for the purposes of the business, its inadequacy as security is readily apparent. In determining the values of securities, analysts concern themselves with balance sheets, profit and loss statements, competitive conditions, economic trends, and other factors which may influence the business as a "going concern," and only infrequently is the intrinsic value of the security, considered separate and apart, of substantial importance. A proper mortgage position is important, not for the value which may be realized on a possible future foreclosure and sale, but for the prior claim on earnings or preferred position in the event of default and reorganization or receivership.

THE INDENTURE AS A TRUST

There is another important distinction between the trust indenture and the ordinary mortgage. In the latter, the mortgagee is usually the real party in interest, holding the mortgage as security for credit which he has extended. In the indenture, or corporate mortgage, immediately following the granting and *habendum* clauses, is a paragraph beginning with the words "In Trust, Nevertheless," which converts the mortgage into a trust deed and defines the terms and purposes for which the conveyance was made.

The trust so created, however, differs substantially from the usual *inter-vivos* or testamentary trust with which courts and practitioners are more familiar. The fundamental characteristic of the ordinary personal trust is possession by the trustee of a specific trust *res* which he holds and administers for the benefit of designated and usually well-known beneficiaries.

The trustee under a corporate indenture, however, has no possession, or right to possession, of the mortgaged property until after a default occurs, and its rights even then are usually circumscribed and limited. It has no control of the business of the obligor (and if it did, it would be disqualified from acting) nor, except in infrequent and unusual circumstances, any voice in the management of its affairs. Efforts to subject it under these conditions to the same degree of care with respect to the security as is required of an ordinary trustee with respect to a specific trust *res*, would make the position of the indenture trustee untenable and render financing of this type almost impossible. It would be unwise indeed, even if practicable, to endeavor to substitute the judgment of the indenture trustee for that of the management of the issuing corporation.

In the case of an ordinary trust there is usually a close and intimate relationship between the trustee and the beneficiaries. The trustee is normally acquainted with their needs and can pattern his action accordingly. He is normally given substantial discretionary powers by the instrument under which he acts, and his duties arise as much from his relationship with his beneficiaries as from the specific provisions of the trust document. In an extreme or doubtful case he can usually secure the directions of a court before proceeding, or he can consult with all parties in interest and secure their consent or waiver in a given transaction. It is also possible for periodic accountings to be submitted so that administration can be kept more or less current.

An indenture trustee, on the other hand, is in the position of both a stakeholder and trustee. Its administration covers a long period of time, and it is frequently called upon to make important and far-reaching decisions without the possibility of consulting the bondholders or seeking instructions of a court. In the ordinary case, the beneficial owners of the indenture securities may be unknown to it and are changing frequently, so that an effort to secure their unanimous consent to a particular action is extremely difficult. In addition, the indenture trustee normally has no discretionary power and only limited authority. It is entirely without authority to deal with or compromise the debt itself no matter how desirable such a compromise might appear to be.

The trustee of a personal trust is responsible only to the beneficiaries, and his duty is to administer the trust solely in their interests. While the indenture trustee's primary fiduciary responsibility runs to the indenture security holders, it also owes to the obligor important duties of both a practical and fiduciary nature, and in the interests of all parties it must be able to work co-operatively with the obligor.

A final and important distinction lies in the amount of compensation received by the two types of trustee. The fees of the trustee of an ordinary trust are measured by the amount of the trust *res* or the income therefrom. While he is liable to surcharge for a wrongful act or failure to exercise due care, the possible consequences of any particular course of action can normally be estimated with reasonable accuracy. The fees received by the indenture trustee are nominal in relation to the amount of indenture securities outstanding or the value of the trust estate. Were it to be held accountable for the full measure of discretion and fiduciary responsibility common to the ordinary trust, the amount for which it might be potentially liable would be out of all proportion to the compensation received or which the mortgagor company could possibly pay.

THE INDENTURE AS A CONTRACT

While it partakes of the essence of other legal relation-ships, the trust indenture is most of all a contract, and courts have been in almost unanimous agreement in applying contractual principles to the relationship.

The parties to the contract, or the indenture, are the obligor company and the trustee, and it is these only who execute the instrument. However, there is another party, or class of parties, whose participation is essential to make the contract operative, and that is the indenture security holders. It is important to bear in mind that three distinct and separate sets of contractual rights and obligations are created by each indenture: those between the obligor and the trustee; those between the obligor and the indenture security holders; and those between the trustee and the indenture security holders.

It is important to distinguish between the contractual rights, duties, and obligations relating primarily to the debt itself, and those which relate principally to the security for the debt. The indenture provisions which define the principal rights, duties, and obligations of the trustee and its relationship with the obligor company relate primarily to the security for the obligations issued or to be issued, whether it be the specific security conveyed or pledged by the indenture or the "negative" security determined and defined by the indenture covenants. These provisions contain the trustee's authority for dealing with this security and define the limitations and restrictions on such authority. They also place re-strictions on the issuing company in dealing with its property or in the conduct of its business. Since both the obligor company and the trustee have an opportunity to read and examine the indenture before it becomes effective, and both are signatory parties, some of the features of a "true" contract may be said to be present. Many are lacking, however, and it is of particular importance to bear in mind that until the contract is executed, the trustee is acting not as a principal but only as a *prospective* fiduciary. The trustee does not negotiate the substantive terms of the contract, and if it objects to particular provisions, it can only suggest and not demand that they be deleted or amended. Its only recourse is to refuse to act, for it does not and cannot become an active participating party until the contract is actually signed and delivered.

The obligations issued under the indenture run directly to the security holders and not to the trustee, and are looked to primarily to define the relationship between the obligor and the security holders. It is therefore of paramount importance that any provisions of the indenture which modify or affect this relationship, or place limitations on the rights of the holders of these obligations, be set forth or sufficiently described in the bond or debenture which runs to the holder. If there is any conflict or discrepancy between the indenture and the bond or debenture, the terms of the latter will be controlling in any suit by the holder thereof. Since the indenture sets forth in detail the rights, duties, and obligations of the parties (including the security holders) and the limitations on those rights, it is important that the security itself embody those provisions by adequate reference. It is obvious that the whole indenture cannot be fully set forth in the bond, debenture, or note and it is usually sufficient to make specific reference to the indenture in general terms. This is done by including in the bond (or other obligation) language substantially as follows: "This bond is one of a duly authorized issue of bonds, issued and to be issued under, and all equally secured by a Mortgage and Deed of Trust dated as of _____, executed by the _____ Company to the _____ Trust Company as Trustee, to which Indenture reference is hereby made for a description of the properties and franchises mortgaged, the nature and extent of the security, the rights of the holders of said bonds and of the trustee in respect of such security, and the terms and conditions under which the bonds are issued and secured." While language such as this is usually adequate to put the security holder on notice as to the existence of the indenture and to make its provisions binding on him, it is desirable to make specific reference to such provisions as directly affect his rights as the holder of the obligation itself. Such provisions would include redemption provisions, sinking fund, transfer and exchange of securities, any provisions permitting substantial modification of the indenture by less than all security holders, waiver of default, and similar matters.

The substantive provisions of the indenture which must be referred to in the bond are printed on the reverse of the certificate as a continuation of the bond form. An alternative procedure which has been used, made possible by the flexibility provided by Article 8 of the Uniform Commercial Code, has been the printing of summaries of the pertinent indenture provisions in less formal and more easily understood language.

While holders of the indenture securities are parties to the indenture contract and bound by its terms, it is more difficult in their case to find all of the essential elements of a true contractual relationship. Since they cannot exist as such until after the contract has been executed and delivered, it is obvious that they can have had no part in negotiating the terms contained therein, although it might be said that the counsel or underwriting houses which acted for the "purchasers" did so in their behalf. It might also be said that, in respect of the security holders, the indenture is in the nature of a unilateral contract to which they become parties by purchasing their security. Here too, however, the analogy is somewhat strained, as the indenture is seldom read by the investor prior to his purchase. As a matter of fact, except for the institutional or professional class of investors, the indenture is almost never read by the security holders and, if it were, many would not understand it. Nevertheless, for the proper functioning of these financing arrangements, it is essential that contractual principles be applied and that the indenture provisions be binding on the security holders as parties, despite the fact that in dealing with the obligor the individual holder is at a distinct disadvantage should there be a default in payment of the principal or interest on the obligation he holds.

These considerations have led many courts not only to construe indenture provisions strictly against the obligor, but also to try to find some other legal theory or precedent with which to "protect" the interests of the security holders. Such decisions have contributed to much of the confusion that exists in the law, particularly as it relates to the third class of contractual relationship—that existing between the trustee and the security holders. The existence of a "trust" is necessary in order to create and define the trustee's interest in and relation to the security and the contract, but its relationship thereto and to the security holders is essentially contractual rather than fiduciary. Its principal function is to administer the contract in accordance with its terms. It has only the authority and powers granted by the indenture and is subject to all the restrictions and limitations therein contained. Except to the limited extent specified, the trustee has no right or authority to represent or act for the security holders or to substitute its judgment for theirs. The trustee should be held accountable for failure to carry out its duties properly, but there is no basis for holding, as some courts have endeavored to do, that the trustee owes to each individual holder duties or obligations not specifically undertaken by it in the contract.

Where the trustee's obligation with respect to a particular subject matter is spelled out in the contract, no particular difficulty is encountered if the obligation has been carried out. There is danger, however, that where the indenture is silent on a particular point, effort will be made to find an implied obligation either from other indenture provisions or from legal precedents evolved under entirely different circumstances. It is therefore important from the viewpoint of the trustee that the indenture clearly indicate its responsibilities as to all significant matters relating to the security or to the obligations, even if it merely recites that no responsibility exists. For example, in a mortgage indenture it is important that the trustee's obligations, or lack of responsibility, with respect to maintenance, insurance, payment of taxes, and the like be clearly indicated to prevent the possibility of a finding of substantial responsibility in the absence of any provision at all.

USUAL PROVISIONS OF A TYPICAL INDENTURE

While the more important provisions of the indenture will be discussed in later chapters in detail, in order to present a composite picture of the usual scope of a typical indenture, the customary articles contained therein are summarized briefly below. These examples have been taken from a mortgage indenture of an industrial corporation. Provisions of other indentures may differ in various respects, depending on the nature of the company, whether the obligations are secured or unsecured, whether the indenture is qualified under the Trust Indenture Act, and other considerations.

Recitals

Each indenture opens by naming the parties, and usually contains a recital of the various factors which led to its creation. These recitals contain the purpose of the issue and state that all legal requirements and authorizations have been fulfilled or obtained. It is important that such recitals be included because they may constitute an estoppel against a later assertion by the obligor that the mortgage or debt was not properly authorized.

The form of bond, interest coupon (if a bearer bond), and trustee's (and authenticating agent's if any) certificate of authentication are also customarily set forth in full therein. As stated above, it is important that the form of bond contain all of the essentials of the contract, either specifically or by appropriate reference to the indenture. Only obligations conforming substantially to the form prescribed in the indenture should be authenticated by the trustee.

Granting Clauses

Following the recitals come the granting clauses which set forth the specific security for the obligations to be issued. These clauses include a recital of the consideration, a specific grant to the trustee, and a description of the property to be mortgaged in sufficient detail to enable the indenture to be properly recorded as a mortgage. If any securities or other property are to be pledged, they are fully described. The specific property descriptions are usually followed by descriptions of other properties intended to be included in the conveyance in general terms, such as appurtenances, franchises, fixtures, and so on. The indenture should also set forth in detail the extent to which it is intended to become a lien on after-acquired property. It is also customary to enumerate the types or classes of property excepted from the conveyance or any other provisions which might aid in defining the exact nature and scope of the security intended to be granted. The granting clauses conclude with the *habendum* and trust clauses which create the trust relationship and specify the purposes and conditions on which the grant is made.

Definitions

All of the important terms used in the indenture are customarily defined, clearly and carefully, in a separate article. This is not only a convenience for those who will later work with the indenture but it also makes the job of draftsmanship easier.

Amount, Form, Execution, Delivery, Registration, and Exchange of Bonds

Whether under this or a similar heading, these sections contain important mechanical provisions for dealing with the obligations themselves and deserve careful attention at the time of drafting, particularly by representatives of the trustee who will administer them. Included herein are limitations, if any, on the amount of bonds which may be issued, or which may be outstanding at any one time under the indenture; the form of the bonds and coupons (if not included in the recitals) and the form of bonds of subsequent series, or authority for the board of directors to determine the form, and other provisions with respect to each such subsequent series; provisions with respect to the manner in which the bonds are to be executed; who may sign; authorizing use of facsimile seal or facsimile signatures, if permitted by the law of the particular jurisdiction; how coupons are to be authenticated; authorizing temporary bonds in appropriate cases and making provisions for their exchange for definitive bonds; appointing a registrar and authorizing issuance of bonds in registered form or the registration of bonds in coupon form, if desired; establishing the various denominations in which bonds may be issued and prescribing the conditions on which bonds of one denomination may be exchanged for a bond or bonds of other denominations, or for the interchange of bearer and registered bonds; providing for the issuance of bonds in lieu of mutilated, destroyed, lost, or stolen bonds and the evidence and indemnity required; provisions with respect to treasury bonds or bonds reacquired by the obligor; establishing and providing for the negotiability of the bonds and coupons; and similar provisions which may be deemed desirable to authorize and facilitate the efficient servicing of the obligations as long as they remain outstanding.

Since most modern indentures, particularly open-end mortgage indentures, will remain in existence for a long period of time, it is important that these provisions be made as broad and as flexible as possible so that both the obligor and the trustee can take advantage of changing and more efficient methods for processing and handling the indenture securities.

Issuance of Bonds

Included in this section are the terms and conditions on which bonds may be issued under the indenture and the documents which must be furnished to the trustee on the basis of which it is authorized to authenticate and deliver the bonds.

Redemption of Bonds

If the obligor desires to reserve the right to retire the obligations, in whole or in part, prior to their stated maturity, this right must be reserved in the indenture. These provisions are included in a special article and set forth conditions on which bonds may be prepaid; the premium required, if any; the method of giving notice to the holders; and other pertinent requirements.

Sinking Fund

If the obligor is required to provide a sinking fund for retirement of a portion of the outstanding bonds from time to time, this article will set forth the amount of such sinking fund, how it is to be paid, and the manner in which it must be applied by the trustee.

Particular Covenants

Covenants are an important part of each indenture contract and are normally set apart in a separate article. Most indentures, whether secured or unsecured, include covenants of some kind. They are both of an affirmative nature, requiring performance of certain things by the obligor company, either continuously or at specified times, and negative in character, placing restrictions on particular activities of the obligor, such as the incurring of additional debt. These covenants provide additional security to the holders of the indenture securities, and the trustee has particular duties with respect to their enforcement.

Provisions as to Pledged Collateral

If the indenture is in the nature of a collateral trust, where the security consists in whole or in part of securities or similar collateral pledged with the trustee, the indenture must set forth in sufficient detail just how this collateral is to be administered. Such matters should be covered as: the form in which the collateral is to be held (whether bearer or registered, and if registered, in what name or names); collection and disposition of income; voting of stock; disposition of principal collected; enforcement of rights as a holder; action to be taken on default in payment or under the indenture securing bonds or debentures held; release, substitution, replacement, etc.; and any other provisions which may be deemed to be pertinent to proper administration in order to accomplish the purposes for which the pledge was made.

Remedies of Trustee and Bondholders

This article will include the default and remedial provisions. Events which will constitute a default under the indenture must be spelled out in detail, including periods of grace, if any. Since the trustee has only the powers specifically granted by the contract, there must always be included the alternative remedies available on default, with a grant of sufficient authority to pursue such remedies. There will also be included a statement of the rights of security holders under the indenture, individually or collectively, and particularly, any limitation on rights of security holders.

Immunity of Incorporators, Stockholders, Officers, and Directors

Since the obligations are a corporate obligation, a provision is almost always included which specifically grants immunity to the stockholders, directors, officers, etc. with respect to the indenture or the securities to be issued thereunder. A similar provision is usually included in the form of the bond or debenture. While such immunity is now fairly well established as a matter of general law, the provision is intended as a protection against the possible application of some remote statutory or implied liability in a particular jurisdiction. It is doubtful that the protection would be applicable if fraudulent misrepresentations were involved. As a matter of fact, the Securities Act of 1933 includes specific penalties for misrepresentations or misleading statements in a registration statement or prospectus.

Consolidation, Merger, and Sale

This article will set forth the conditions under which the obligor company may sell or lease all or substantially all of its properties, or may merge into or with another corporation. If the company has subsidiary companies, the latter should also be specifically covered in these provisions, as the conditions affecting subsidiaries may be quite different from those applicable to the parent company. In many indentures, particularly debenture agreements, this article is in the nature of an additional negative covenant.

Releases

If the indenture is a secured indenture, and particularly if the security is a mortgage, the company must be permitted to sell and dispose of particular segments of the property as may be required or desirable from time to time. The indenture will set forth the conditions under which such disposition may be made and the documents and consideration which must be furnished to enable the trustee to execute an appropriate release thereof from the indenture.

Possession until Default—Defeasance

Since the trustee's interest in the property is simply a security interest, the obligor is entitled to remain in possession, at least until default, and this article confirms such right. It is also important to provide for a reconveyance to the obligor, and the terms and conditions on which it will be made, if the obligor performs all the terms and conditions of the indenture.

Concerning the Trustee

This is a most important article and will be discussed in detail in the succeeding chapter. The specific duties, responsibilities, and liabilities of the trustee will be set forth in detail, as will appropriate exculpatory and protective provisions.

Reports by the Obligor and the Trustee

These provisions are frequently incorporated in other articles (particularly the covenants and trustee articles), but are sometimes brought together and set up in a separate article. In general, they include particular required provisions of the Trust Indenture Act of 1939 relating to reports which the obligor must furnish to the trustee; the mechanics for developing and maintaining lists of names of holders of the securities; and reports by the trustee to security holders.

Additional Provisions as to Evidence of Compliance with Indenture Provisions and Certificates

The Trust Indenture Act of 1939 requires the inclusion in indentures of general provisions relating to statements or reports which must be furnished the trustee as evidence of compliance with particular types of provisions, and to the contents of certificates and opinions with respect to compliance with conditions and covenants. To avoid the necessity of repetition throughout the indenture, these general provisions are usually set up separately and made applicable to all covenants or conditions in the indenture relating to the specified subject matter. Some draftsmen like to make specific reference to this article in every section to which it is applicable. The desirability of this is questionable, since these requirements are now so familiar to trust administrators that their attention does not have to be specifically drawn to them. Excessive cross-reference in indentures makes administration difficult, and a real problem of construction is presented if such cross-reference is inadvertently omitted from one or more provisions and included in all others.

Supplemental Indentures, Bondholders' Meetings, Bondholders' Acts, Holdings, and Apparent Authority

These provisions set forth the manner in which the indenture contract may be supplemented or amended. Some amendments may be made by the company and trustee without reference to the security holders, and these are usually enumerated. In general, any provision which does not affect a substantive right of the security holders may be added without their consent. Other provisions may be changed with the consent of a specified percentage of the holders, while others require 100 per cent consent. If the consent of the holders is required, the manner in which such consent is to be evidenced will be spelled out, as will the evidence on which the trustee may rely to establish ownership of particular obligations.

Various miscellaneous provisions will be embodied in a final article.

THE TRUST INDENTURE ACT OF 1939

The idea of regulation—particularly by the federal government—has become a fixed and accepted principle in everyday business life and is assuming greater importance each year. Despite this fact, there are still wide differences of opinion as to the proper scope and purpose of such regulation and the limits to which it may properly be extended. In certain areas of activity it undoubtedly performs an important and essential function. This function, however, should normally be limited to the establishment of minimum standards or modes of conduct deemed essential to the public interest, to which all engaged in the particular activity are required to adhere. Its value is in direct proportion to the uniformity of standards which exist, or are capable of existing, in the particular activity.

With respect to trust indentures, the scope and value of government regulation is necessarily limited. Trust indentures do not in themselves constitute a "business," but are simply the instruments by which all types of businesses secure financing necessary to their functioning; and each type of financing produces its own type of indenture.

The trust indenture was developed with few restrictions imposed by governmental authorities. Legislation concerning the sale or distribution of securities was limited to the Blue Sky laws enacted by various states and having to do with the use of fraudulent devices in the sale of securities.

Following the financial collapse of the 1930's, defaults under indentures became numerous, and the savings of many individuals were seriously depleted and sometimes wiped out. The concurrence of the drop in security values with the national depression brought the whole security structure before the public attention. The result was the enactment by Congress of a series of security acts designed for the protection of investors.

The first legislation was the Securities Act of 1933—sometimes called the "truth in securities" act. With certain exceptions, this act requires the filing of a registration statement covering each public issue of securities and the use of a prospectus in connection with their sale and distribution. Stringent penalties are imposed for misrepresentations or misleading statements in either of these documents. The Securities Exchange Act of 1934 was designed for the regulation of national securities exchanges, the listing of securities thereon, and the purchase and sale of securities through the facilities of such exchanges. This act also created the Securities and Exchange Commission for administration of this, and the earlier, securities act. Section 211 of the Securities Exchange Act directed the commission to "make a study and investigation of the work, activities, personnel, and functions of protective and reorganization committees in connection with the reorganization, readjustment, rehabilitation, liquidation, or consolidation of persons and properties and to report the result of its studies and investigations and its recommendations to the Congress." As a part of this study, the commission included a report on the activities of trustees under indentures.

Because of this report the so-called Barkley bill was introduced in the Senate in 1937 and was referred to a subcommittee of the Committee on Banking and Currency. Although the measure was favorably reported by the committee, the Senate did not vote on it at this session. A similar bill was introduced in the House of Representatives in 1938, and in both the House and Senate in 1939. The latest bill was enacted by Congress as the "Trust Indenture Act of 1939" and became effective on February 3, 1940.

The Trust Indenture Act of 1939 was the first attempt by the federal government to regulate the indentures under which securities are issued. In its report the Securities and Exchange Commission recommended extremely stringent provisions, including continuous supervisory administration by the commission, and the initial bill introduced embodied these provisions. The legislation enacted was worked out by the commission and a special committee of the American Bankers Association after extended hearings before the committees of the House and Senate. The act, as enacted, differs substantially from the original recommendations, and does not do violence to the basic concept of the trust indenture as a special financing contract among the parties.

The Trust Indenture Act was enacted as Title III to the Securities Act of 1933, and its administrative provisions were drafted to dovetail with the commission's administration of the securities act. In general, it requires that all indentures, with specified exceptions, be submitted to the commission for "qualification" along with the issuer's registration statement under the securities act. The actual "regulation" provided by the act consists solely in the qualification of the indenture. Once the indenture is qualified, the commission, with one minor exception, has no further jurisdiction over the indenture or over the obligor, the trustee, or the security holders. And once executed, the indenture is a contract enforceable only by the parties thereto. The essential purpose of the act and the qualification of indentures thereunder is to insure that every indenture contains the minimum standards imposed by the act and conforms to the requirements of the act.

In general, the legislation was intended to accomplish three basic purposes: (1) The establishment of certain minimum standards with respect to specified acts and duties of the obligor and trustee to which all indentures must conform. This is accomplished by requiring the inclusion of specified provisions in each qualified indenture which become an essential part of the contract. (2) The inclusion of minimum standards of responsibility and accountability for trustees under indentures, and the elimination of the very broad exculpatory provisions which had been included formerly. (3) The elimination of conflicting relationships between the trustee and the obligor, and between the trustee and underwriters for the obligor.

While the act has not eliminated the occurrence of defaults or losses to investors, it has not proved to be the burden which many trust companies had feared. It has been in effect since 1940 and is now accepted as part of the normal routine of indenture administration. While the prescribed provisions are required only in indentures qualified under the act, a majority of them have come to be accepted as reasonable standards for all indenture administration and are now included in practically all indentures, whether or not qualification is required. The standards of conduct imposed had been accepted and followed by the more responsible trust companies for a long time prior to enactment of the legislation, so that no abrupt or sudden change was effected. Some problems have arisen, due primarily to the adoption of new modes of debt financing, but so far these have been resolved without necessitating any change in the concept or content of the act.

UNIFORM COMMERCIAL CODE

The Uniform Commercial Code was adopted in New York in 1962 and became effective on September 27, 1964. The Code has now been adopted in forty-nine states, the District of Columbia and Virgin Islands. The only exception is Louisiana. Although the Code deals with all facets of commercial practice, Articles 8 and 9 are of particular importance in the corporate trust field.[3]

Article 8 deals with investment securities and confirms or establishes certain basic principles:

[3] For a detailed analysis of Article 8, see Israels and Gutman, Modern Securities Transfers (rev. ed. 1971, Supp. 1974)

1. It makes all investment securities negotiable. This makes possible increased flexibility in the form of these instruments without fear of creating problems of negotiability.

2. It broadens the application of the rules relating to fiduciary transfers, placing responsibility on the fiduciary rather than the transfer agent, and in effect penalizes the transfer agent which requires excessive documentation.

3. It defines the responsibilities of an authenticating trustee, transfer agent and registrar.

4. It imposes direct and independent responsibility and liability on the transfer agent or registrar for their acts. It is no defense to show that such action was strictly in accord with a principal's direction.

5. It establishes guides for issuers and transfer agents in dealing with adverse claims.

Article 9 deals with secured transactions, and its impact on commercial transactions is probably more extensive then that of any other Code Article. Unlike Article 8, which deals specifically with investment securities, Article 9 was not drafted with corporate indentures primarily in mind. It is nevertheless of importance in this area since it establishes uniform rules relating to all security transactions involving personal property, regardless of the form of the particular transaction or the security documents. The present trend toward the more special purpose secured financing where contract rights, equipment leases, receivables, chattel paper or the like constitute the principal security, makes an understanding of the basic purposes and principles of the Article particularly desirable.

In addition to providing a single body of law for security transactions affecting personal property, the Code made significant changes or clarifications in four important areas:

1. It provides statutory authority and rules for accounts receivable financing.

2. It specifically authorizes and makes effective arrangements for subjecting after-acquired property to a security agreement and for the making of future advances under the agreement without the necessity of preparation, signing and recording or filing of supplemental agreements. This greatly facilitates security arrangements involving property which is constantly being disposed of and replaced, such as inventory.

3. It repeals the troublesome rule enunciated in *Benedict* v. *Ratner* [4] and permits the debtor to mortgage his inventory, stock in trade or similar property and continue to operate his business in a normal manner, and in accordance with the understanding and agreement of the parties, without the necessity of cumbersome provisions for the flow of proceeds. A necessary corollary is the protection of those who deal with the debtor in the normal course of business.

4. It recognizes and provides for the special status of the purchase money security interest.

Most corporate mortgages secure obligations which will be outstanding for many years. Some railroad bonds have maturities extending for a hundred years or more, and many corporate mortgages, particularly those of public utilities and railroads, are in the nature of open-end indentures, designed to serve as permanent financing media. As security, the obligor customarily mortgages all land, plants, equipment, machinery, fixtures, franchises, and all other items of property, real, personal or mixed, then owned or thereafter acquired, which generally constitute its fixed plant and property account, permanent investments, and other classes of property exclusive of cash, receivables, merchandise and the like.

While in the normal commercial financing arrangement the intrinsic value of the collateral is readily measurable and adequate to secure the loan, the real security underlying a corporate mortgage is the "going concern" value of the business itself rather than the specific value of the individual items of property. The importance of the security interest is the priority claim against the capital assets of the business necessary to its continuance as a going concern. Since the specific items of property are constantly being replaced or otherwise changing, the effectiveness of the after-acquired property clause is of paramount importance.

Prior to enactment of the Code, the law in most jurisdictions had so evolved that no particular problems were encountered in entering into those long term security arrangements and in making effective the security interests intended. Public utility and railroad mortgages in particular had been accorded a special status. In many jurisdictions recording of the indenture as a real estate mortgage was all that was required to perfect the security interest as to both

[4] 268 U.S. 353 (1925)

the real estate and chattels. The effectiveness of the lien as to after-acquired property was recognized without the necessity of re-recording or re-filing. In other states, and more commonly as to other types of obligors, an equitable lien on after-acquired property was recognized, which was periodically perfected by recording a supplemental indenture, frequently in connection with additional financing under the indenture. Only rarely were obligors or corporate trustees concerned with statutes dealing with interests in personal property only. Property descriptions in the case of public utility and railroad obligors, and less frequently for industrial companies, were necessarily general although no particular problems were encountered.

While the Code excludes real property and interests flowing from real property from its scope, it does cover all security interests in personal property and in fixtures. Since every corporate mortgage involves security interests in fixtures and various types of personal property, Article 9 cast some doubt on the effectiveness of the pre-code financing arrangements and created problems of compliance, particularly in states which had no provision for central filing for this type of security interest.

Most railroads and utilities operate in a great many jurisdictions. The requirement for the filing of the security interest with respect to fixtures in each jurisdiction where real estate is located presented a dual problem: filing and refiling of financing statements in each such jurisdiction and providing an adequate description of the real estate involved.

A special problem in the case of railroad rolling stock is involved. While the customary equipment trust is filed under Section 20 (c) of the Interstate Commerce Act and is exempt from the Code filing requirements because of the existence of the Federal statute, all railroad general mortgages also cover rolling stock. It had never been the practice to record general railroad mortgages with the Interstate Commerce Commission although they indicated that they would accept corporate railroad mortgages for filing under Section 20 (c). The obligor may state that the mortgage covers any rolling stock then owned or thereafter to be acquired, subject to equipment trust obligations, although technically such filing does not comply with the regulations relating thereto.[5]

[5] 49 C.F.R. Sec. 57.1 to 57.5 (1963)

The problems referred to above have been dealt with to some extent by several of the states. In New York, a mortgage covering both real and personal property recorded as a real estate mortgage after the effective date of the Code required only the filing of a financing statement in the department of state with respect to the fixtures and personal property, and it was unnecessary to include a description of the real estate in such financing statement.

Special efforts have been made to secure adoption of appropriate amendments to the Code in all states. The alternatives suggested have been to (1) either exempt all public utility and railroad mortgages—and possibly all corporate mortgages—from the filing requirements of the Code or (2) to provide for central filing as under the New York statute and as recommended by the Association of American Railroads. It would also be desirable to eliminate the necessity of refiling a financing statement every five years. Since the corporate mortgage secures obligations which will be outstanding for many years, and the date of maturity can be shown on the statement, no real purpose is served by the requirement for periodic refiling.

While no further action is required to continue the perfected status of the security interest in personal property covered by a corporate mortgage of real and personal property recorded prior to the effective date of the Code, it is not clear as to the action, if any, which should be taken with respect to personal property acquired after such effective date. If a supplemental mortgage is executed and filed, or if there is additional financing under the mortgage, the requisite financing statement should be filed in the department of state.

If the obligor has outstanding more than one mortgage covering its property and there is additional financing under a junior or refunding mortgage, financing statements under all mortgages should be prepared and filed in the proper order of priority because of the "first to file" rule.

Where partial releases of personal property are executed under a corporate mortgage, it would seem unnecessary to make any filing with respect to such partial release unless it involves the release of all such property in the jurisdiction. If necessary to protect the purchaser of the property released, execution of the release on the bill of sale should be all that is required.

Despite repeal of the *Benedict* v. *Ratner* rule, draftsman of corporate indentures should avoid the temptation to extend the scope of security coverage of the corporate indenture unnecessarily. Little will be added to the value of the security in the usual case and a great many problems may be created, particularly with respect to an indenture qualified under the Trust Indenture Act of 1939. A different question is presented, of course, if a principal purpose of the transaction is the financing of "working capital." In such a situation the security must be tailored to the requirements of the particular arrangement.

While a few ambiguities still exist and some problems have been created, the Code on the whole represented a constructive contribution to our body of commercial law, but realization of the full potential offered requires intelligent and realistic implementation by both attorneys and judges. The basic purposes and policies should always be kept in mind, as well as the express admonitions that the Code is to be liberally construed and applied to promote these purposes and policies.

MODEL INDENTURES

Since the indenture was first used approximately 150 years ago, it has developed into the largest and, in many respects, the most complex of legal documents. Language was added through the years in response to frequent court decisions interpreting particular provisions, but until 1962, little effort had been made to reduce the excess verbiage.

In that year, the American Bar Foundation announced the adoption of a "Corporate Debt Financing Project—A Project to Develop a Model Form of Corporate Debenture Indenture and Mortgage with Annotations and Comment." [6] The basic format adopted after extended discussions by the Project committees, consists of two documents. One document called "Model Provisions" consists solely of the traditional "boiler plate" provisions common to most corporate debt indentures. The second document, sometimes called the "Incorporating Indenture," incorporates by reference the Model Provisions, or as many thereof as are agreed to by the parties to the particular financing, and also contains the

[6] For a detailed discussion of the background of this project, see Churchill Rodgers, *The Corporate Trust Indenture Project* 20 Bus. Law 551 (1965).

so-called "negotiated provisions" which usually include the dollar amount, the interest rate, the stated maturity and the terms of redemption of the debenture issue, certain particular covenants and other special provisions, all as negotiated by the parties. These two documents were published in a book entitled "American Bar Foundation Corporate Debt Financing Project—Sample Incorporating Indenture—Model Debenture Indenture Provisions—1965." They were the result of many meetings and discussions participated in by counsel who had frequently represented issuers or investors or investment bankers, a representative group of corporate trust officers, the Securities and Exchange Commission (with particular reference to conformity with the Trust Indenture Act of 1939), the Stock List Department of the New York Stock Exchange and an Ad Hoc Consultative Committee of the American Institute of Certified Public Accountants. The final product inevitably represented many compromises. Nevertheless, it represented an important contribution by simplifying those provisions which were generally subject to negotiation in the drafting of indentures and providing standardized "boiler plate" for non-negotiated provisions.

The use of the Model Provisions 1965 (which provided for both coupon debentures and fully registered debentures) was limited by the fact that by the time of publication a majority of new issues were being offered in registered form only. In the latter part of 1964, while the Model Provisions 1965 were still in the drafting stage, the corporate trust group urged the Project Directorate to undertake the preparation of Model Debenture Indenture Provisions for "all-registered" issues. This corporate trust group undertook the task of securing general agreement on the basic procedures which should be incorporated in such Model Provisions and early in 1966 the group published its "Recommended Procedures." [7] The result of this cooperative effort was the preparation by the Project Directorate of the "American Bar Foundation Model Debenture Indenture Provisions—All-Registered Issues—1967".

The Model Provisions do not constitute an instrument, but are intended as an exhibit to be attached to an indenture in the form recommended by the Sample Incorporating Indenture. It is, therefore, possible in the incorporating indenture to express specific

---

[7] "Recommended Procedures For Registered Bond Issues," Corporate Trust Activities Committee, American Bankers Association (1966).

deviations from the Model Provisions or to omit certain provisions entirely by not incorporating them in the Indenture.

The practice recommended by the Project of incorporating the Model Provisions in the indenture by reference has not met with widespread acceptance, although the Model Provisions are very often used as part of the modern indenture and are seldom modified or changed.

The publication of the "Commentaries on Indentures" in 1972 marked the third major step in accomplishing the Project's objectives. The Commentaries were intended to accomplish a number of things: to outline the Model Provisions and how they were to be used, to explain why the particular form used was adopted and why certain traditional, but outmoded provisions could be safely eliminated, to deal with the theories underlying the negotiable positions of the indenture and to offer sample alternative provisions which might be suited to particular requirements.[8]

With the planned publication in 1975 of the Model Mortgage Indenture Provisions and Sample Incorporating Indenture, the Project will substantially complete its objectives established thirteen years earlier. The sum total of these efforts has produced an important and valuable addition in the field of corporate finance, and particularly in the simplification of the corporate trust indenture.

---

[8] This publication should be of significant benefit to lawyers engaged in negotiating and drafting indentures, and to bankers involved in the corporate trust function.

3

The Corporate Trustee

DEVELOPMENT OF THE TRUSTEE CONCEPT

AS MIGHT BE EXPECTED, the development of a firm concept of the duties and responsibilities of the indenture trustee has closely paralleled the growth and development of the trust indenture itself. In the very early history of corporate mortgages there are cases where the mortgage ran directly to the bondholders themselves, without a trustee being named. The difficulties presented by such an arrangement became apparent when the first default under such a mortgage occurred. The court ruled that in order for the mortgage to be foreclosed, all bondholders had to join in the petition. Consequently, the practice of using a trustee to whom the mortgage would run for the benefit of all the bondholders was developed at an early date.

In the early years of this development, the trustee was usually a single individual, and was frequently an officer of the issuing corporation. Although his interests were obviously adverse to those of the bondholders, it made little practical difference, as the trustee at that time was simply a convenience for the mortgagor and had few, if any, actual duties to perform. He was in almost every sense of the word a mere stakeholder.

With the growth in the number of indentures and the gradually increasing intricacies of corporate borrowing, criticism began to be directed at this officer-trustee device and it soon became impractical. The next step was the designation of an independent individual as trustee. To give added status to the issue, individuals selected were usually outstanding citizens in the community.

45

The first instance of a bank's being designated as an indenture trustee occurred in 1839, but the use of the institutional, as opposed to the individual, trustee did not become general practice until the latter part of the 19th century. The initial reason for the change was undoubtedly avoidance of the problems presented by the death or incapacity of the individual trustee. After initial authentication of the bonds, there were still few duties to be performed, and responsibilities were not onerous.

As the use of the corporate indenture became more common and numerous problems were presented as a result of defaults, it was inevitable that greater powers should be placed in the hands of the corporate trustee. As corporations grew and the size of their bond issues increased, it became difficult for bondholders themselves, either individually or collectively, to enforce their security in the event of default. Consequently, more and more restrictions were placed on suits by individual holders, and most rights of action were concentrated in the trustee. It was much easier to create an appearance of protection, however, than it was to provide remedies adequate in fact. Several factors tended to impede an orderly growth and development of the trustee's duties and responsibilities.

Corporate trusteeships were regarded by many banks as being in the nature of escrows and were accepted, usually without compensation, as a service to corporate banking customers. *Laissez faire* was the guiding economic theory of the day, and it is not surprising that in this, as in other areas of corporate practice, a real sense of responsibility was slow in developing.

The growth in the trustee's duties was accompanied by an equivalent growth in the number and scope of exculpatory clauses. Early efforts to improve fees for trustee services met with stubborn resistance, and the resulting reluctance of the trustee to undertake lengthy, expensive, and time-consuming legal proceedings was understandable.

As has been indicated previously, there was an absence of clearcut legal precedents and considerable confusion in the minds of courts as to the exact nature of the indenture and the legal responsibility of the trustee for preserving and enforcing the security. Reliance by courts on different precedents and concepts led to many conflicting opinions and to the introduction of new and unusual provisions into each indenture. After each court decision, indenture draftsmen devised new language for the protection of the mortgagor and the trustee. As a result, the corporate indenture developed rapidly into the most complex of all legal documents, without offering a real solution to the basic problem of how to provide reasonable protection to security holders without exposing the trustee to undue and unwarranted liability.

A start had been made, however. Many of the more responsible banks began to evidence concern over the losses suffered by bondholders and the apparent ineffectiveness of remedies after default. The volume of corporate trust business was now sufficient to warrant the establishment of separate corporate trust units in the larger institutions, and this led to a re-examination of policies and practices. The sense of responsibility grew, and more attention was paid to all phases of corporate trust activity. Even among the older indentures, which contained little more than the basic mortgage provisions, advantage was taken of the "further assurance" clauses to secure continuing up-to-date information as to the status of the security and the condition of the obligor's affairs. In newly drafted indentures, trustees began to insist on the inclusion of additional protective provisions and covenants. A new pattern of responsibility rapidly emerged, and by the late 1920's the corporate trustee had begun to be recognized as an important party to these financial transactions.

The pattern thus established by the more responsible institutions was not universal, however, and the practice still followed in a number of cases brought continued criticism by courts and recognized authorities in the field. The financial collapse of 1929 and the ensuing depression resulted in an increasing number of defaults and led to a critical examination of all phases of security practice. While the broad generalities embodied in the conclusions and recommendations of the Securities and Exchange Commission report of 1936 were neither impartial nor fair, no serious student of the subject could question the desirability of the establishment of minimum standards to which the trust indentures and the conduct of corporate trustees should conform. The Trust Indenture Act of 1939, in effect, codified the more important practices which had been developed and were already being followed by the leading corporate trust departments. As has been indicated, the essential provisions of this act are now fairly standard for all corporate indentures whether required to be qualified under the act or not.

While by 1940 the practice of using an individual as opposed to institutional trustees was practically obsolete, the act required the designation of an institutional corporate trustee meeting certain minimum standards of eligibility under all indentures to be qualified under the act.

ESSENTIAL FUNCTION OF THE CORPORATE TRUSTEE

In succeeding chapters consideration will be given to the duties of the trustee with reference to typical specific indenture provisions and the issuance and servicing of the indenture securities. It might facilitate an understanding of the trustee function, however, to consider briefly the principal areas of the trustee's responsibility.

As indicated in the preceding chapter, the essential function of a trustee is the administration of the security provisions of a contract between the issuing corporation and the holders of the indenture securities. There are three principal areas of responsibility.

In the first place, if the issue is secured in any way, the trustee holds and deals with the security. If the security consists in whole or in part of a mortgage on corporate properties, the trustee is the mortgagee and must concern itself with problems related to maintenance, insurance, taxes, release and replacement and, within the scope of the powers granted, must see that the security is provided and maintained in the agreed manner.

Secondly, as administrator of the contract, the trustee has the responsibility of making sure that the covenants and other indenture provisions are performed in the agreed manner. This it does in large part through examining reports and certificates which it receives from the obligor corporation or independent accountants, engineers, or other experts.

Finally, in the event of a default, the trustee has a primary responsibility for enforcing the remedial provisions of the contract. As will be discussed in greater detail in a later chapter, the nature of this responsibility has been substantially changed by the enactment of federal and state laws dealing with bankruptcy and creditors' rights.

In addition to the performance of specifically enumerated duties, the modern corporate trustee contributes a great deal more to the relationship. Most of the larger institutions now have a trained staff experienced in the handling of many types of indentures and the innumerable problems concerning them which have arisen over the years. By reason of this experience, corporate trust officers make substantial contributions during the indenture drafting process and frequently suggest an appropriate course of action whenever difficulty arises. These staffs are also continually devising new and more efficient methods for handling the many mechanical details involved in the processing and servicing of securities, which result in substantial savings to both issuers and holders.

During the past decade there has been an increasing number of "direct placement" contracts whereby an issuer sells long term debt obligations to a limited number of institutional investors. This practice eliminates the necessity of registering such securities under the securities act or of qualifying an indenture. Occasionally, such securities are issued under purchase contracts with the separate investors, and no indenture or trustee is involved. Such a procedure is quite proper in an appropriate case. Where security is involved, however, or where more than a few investors purchase a single issue, or where complicated sinking fund or similar provisions are involved, or, again, where the terms of the contract are unusual or require frequent checking, the use of a trustee is recommended. From the point of view of the investor, the activities of the trustee supplement rather than supersede those of the investor institution. From the point of view of the obligor, the convenience and service obtained usually outweigh the fairly nominal fees involved.

The terms of these issues are set usually in consultation with an investment banking firm and after discussion with one or more of the principal prospective purchasers. Special counsel appointed by the issuer to represent the purchaser usually drafts the financing documents. While the flexibility available as a result of direct negotiations between issuer and purchaser is regarded as a major advantage of private placements, patterns of inflexibility have developed as the major institutional investors establish their own set of required covenants, sometimes without regard to the needs of a particular case. As a result, most note purchase agreements now follow a more or less rigid pattern, which is not always in the best interest of either issuer or investor. For public and many private issues, an experienced corporate trustee, familiar with all types of financing arrangements, constitutes an important addition to the team of experts which work out the details of the financing documents. A similar contribution could be made in the case of privately placed note issues.

The use of a corporate trustee for such issues would also contribute to the solution of other problems which now exist, including:

(1) Uniform administration of the security provisions of the contract.

(2) Identification of holders of notes entitled to the benefits of the contract provided through the trustee's authentication of the notes issued.

(3) Improved marketability of the obligations. To qualify for exemption from the registration requirements of the Securities Act of 1933 the notes must be purchased for investment and not for distribution. Nevertheless, an essential requirement for eligibility as an institutional investment is that any obligation purchased be marketable, and an increasing volume of obligations originally placed privately is being sold by the original investors. Obvious problems are being created, not only in consummating these transactions, but in determining rights of the transferees in the absence of an indenture and uniform provisions governing transfers or assignments.

(4) Improve marketability should also tend to reduce the interest cost to obligors. Institutional investors usually insist on a premium of ten to twenty basis points in the rate of interest paid on notes acquired in a private placement because of limited marketability. Anything which would tend to improve marketability should reduce this spread.

(5) Efficient servicing of the debt obligations, particularly application of the amortization formula to assure continuation of the relative interests of the investors in the total debt. Many issuers now employ a bank as agent to render these services.

(6) Each investor now receives a complete set of all documents delivered at each note closing, although it is difficult to understand what real purpose is served by this volume of paper. If a complete set of documents were provided the trustee acting on behalf of all investors, all that any investor should require would be the note itself, a copy of the purchase agreement and opinion of its special counsel. This should represent a considerable saving in expense to most institutional investors as well as to issuers.

ELIGIBILTY REQUIREMENTS

The indenture normally contains a section setting forth the conditions which the institution must meet in order to be eligible to serve. Section 310(a) of the Trust Indenture Act requires certain minimum standards for qualified indentures. The institutional trustee must be a corporation organized and doing business under the laws of the United States or of any state or territory or the District of Columbia, which is authorized under such laws to exercise corporate trust powers and is subject to supervision or examination by federal, state, territorial, or District of Columbia authority. It must have at all times a combined capital and surplus of not less than $150,000.

These minimum requirements are very light, and enable almost any banking institution normally exercising trust powers to act. Most indentures securing sizable issues impose much more stringent requirements. A customary minimum capital and surplus requirement in such cases is $5,000,000. It is also frequently required that the corporate trustee have its principal office in one of the large financial centers, such as New York City. This requirement is no longer of major importance, as many institutions throughout the country are now fully qualified to act under most indentures, although the actual experience and qualifications of the prospective trustee are important factors which should always be considered carefully. On some types of issues, investment bankers insist, quite properly, on limiting the area from which a trustee may be chosen. A typical example of this would be a large issue of a quasi-public corporation, the proceeds of which are to be used for construction of a major project. Selection of a trustee from outside the area of the project avoids the possibility of a conflict of interest or of the use of political pressures in connection with administration of the trusts. Administration of such an indenture also involves many technical problems of major importance with which most of the smaller institutions are not familiar.

Since the trustee will have been selected and will be acting at the time of the execution and delivery of the indenture, the purpose of the eligibility provision is to govern the selection of a successor trustee in the event the original trustee resigns or becomes incapable of acting. Because this is a substantive provision, a successor trustee who does not meet the specified standards cannot be named without the consent of all the security holders or a specified percentage thereof. In the unlikely event that no other trustee meeting the requirements of the indenture and willing to act can be found, it has been held that a trustee not meeting such requirements can be appointed and can exercise all the rights and powers granted by the indenture. If such a situation should develop, however, it is recommended that judicial sanction for such an appointment first be obtained.

PROHIBITION OF CONFLICTING INTERESTS— QUALIFICATION OF THE TRUSTEE

The problem of conflicting interests is a troublesome one, and one of which the trustee should always be conscious. Under normal circumstances, an issuing corporation will select one of its principal banks to act as indenture trustee. The familiarity which such an institution has with the corporation's affairs and the close, confidential, continuing relationship, as a practical matter, will enable such an institution to do a more thorough job for the security holders, as well as for the issuing corporation. The administrative officers should familiarize themselves thoroughly with all relationships between their bank and the obligor corporation, and insure that no possibility arises for the fairness and impartiality of the trustee's acts to be questioned.

One of the innovations introduced by the Trust Indenture Act was the setting down of certain "rules of thumb" which would disqualify an institution from acting as trustee under a qualified indenture. These provisions are set forth in Section 310(b) and must be incorporated in all qualified indentures. This section, however, does not cover the whole field of conflicts or prohibit any interest which might possibly be a conflict. The trustee is deemed to have a conflicting interest if it has one or more of nine different relationships. For the purpose of discussion, these relationships will be considered from the viewpoint of the general interests or affiliations which are prohibited.

Trusteeship under More Than One Indenture

Section 310(b)(1) prohibits the same trustee from acting under more than one indenture of the same obligor. Two situations are excepted from this prohibition. The first occurs where the indenture to be qualified is a collateral indenture, with the only collateral consisting of obligations issued under the other indenture. The second exception is where both issues are unsecured and confer upon the holders substantially the same rights. It is required, however, that the indenture to be qualified specifically refer to the obligations under the other indenture. No problem is presented where the second indenture is to be qualified under the act. Where the initial indenture is qualified, however, and the second is not, a special application must be made by the obligor to the Securities and Exchange Commission for permission to designate the same trustee. This is a very simple form of application and requires little effort or expense. It is made under a provision of the act which authorizes the commission to permit trusteeship under more than one indenture if it finds that such trusteeship is not likely to involve a material conflict of interest.

The importance of having separate trustees for separate indentures is apparent. Although prior to default the trustee might act under two indentures of the same obligor without encountering particular difficulty, the happening of an event of default will usually create a conflict and prevent the trustee from adequately representing holders under both indentures, since their interests are quite likely to be adverse. The importance of having independent representation in proceedings after default was recognized in an 1895 decision of the federal court in New York, which permitted intervention of individual bondholders in a foreclosure suit where the trustee was acting under several indentures. Also, it was suggested that the trustee should be subjected to a higher standard of care where it was acting under more than one indenture.

The term "obligor" is defined in the act as every person who is liable on the indenture securities. Trusteeship under indentures of affiliated companies is permissible provided the same company is not liable on the indenture securities issued under more than one of such indentures.

Where one corporation guarantees the securities issued by another, it is clear that the guaranty makes the former an "obligor" to bring it within the prohibitions of the section. A somewhat different and more difficult question is presented where no guaranty in fact exists, but where the credit of one corporation is the primary security for obligations issued by another. Such a situation would arise, for example, if corporation A issued securities for the construction of certain facilities to be leased to corporation B, the rental payments being sufficient to service the securities and the lease, and the right to receive the rents being pledged under the indenture. These facts alone are not sufficient to constitute corporation B an "obligor" on the securities, but great care should be exercised in such a situation, and all the facts surrounding the proposed transaction should be considered to determine if an actual, as distinguished from a technical, conflict is likely to arise.

Ownership of Securities

Subdivisions (5) to (9) of Section 310(b) set down certain rules for the disqualification of the trustee based on affiliations through security ownership. Disqualification under these subdivisions does not depend on the existence of actual control or of any conflicting interest in fact, but beneficial ownership of the specified percentage of securities is required to be made a conflicting interest as a part of the contract between the parties. A conflicting interest is deemed to exist, and the trustee will be disqualified from acting as such, if any of the following situations exist:

(1) Ten per cent or more of the voting securities of the trustee is beneficially owned either by an obligor or by any director, partner, or executive officer of an obligor; 20 per cent or more of such voting securities is owned, collectively, by any two or more of such persons; or 10 per cent or more of such voting securities is beneficially owned either by an underwriter for any such obligor or by any director, partner, or executive officer thereof, or is beneficially owned, collectively, by any two or more such persons.

(2) Beneficial ownership by the trustee or the holding by the trustee as collateral security to an obligation which is in default as to principal for thirty days or more of

(a) 5 per cent or more of the voting securities of the obligor;

(b) 10 per cent or more of any other class of security of the obligor, excluding all securities issued under an indenture for which the trustee is acting as trustee;

(c) 5 per cent or more of the voting securities of a person who, to the knowledge of the trustee, owns 10 per cent or more of the voting securities of, or controls directly or indirectly, or is under direct or indirect common control with, an obligor;

(d) 10 per cent or more of any class of security of a person who, to the knowledge of the trustee, owns 50 per cent or more of the voting securities of an obligor; or

(e) 10 per cent or more of any class of security of an underwriter for an obligor.

Since a conflicting interest by reason of the trustee's ownership of the above percentage of securities is predicated on the existence of an adverse interest in the trustee, ownership of securities issued under the particular indenture in question, or under any other indenture for which the trustee also acts as trustee, has been excluded.

(3) Ownership by the trustee of securities in a fiduciary capacity. The trustee is required to make a check of its holdings, as of May 15 in each year, of the types of securities enumerated above in its capacity as executor, administrator, testamentary, or *inter-vivos* trustee, guardian, committee, conservator, or any similar capacity. A conflicting interest is deemed to exist if, on such date, the trustee holds in such capacities, an aggregate of 25 per cent or more of any class of security, the beneficial ownership of a specified percentage of which would constitute a conflict. In order to eliminate the possibility of an inadvertent conflict arising by reason of acquisition of securities in new estates, the act provides that the conflict provisions will not apply, for a period not to exceed two years from the date of such acquisition, to the extent that such securities do not exceed 25 per cent or more of the particular class outstanding.

In the event that there is a default in the payment of principal or interest under an indenture which continues for thirty days, the trustee is required to make a prompt check of its fiduciary holdings, and thereafter any ownership in such capacity of securities over which it has sole or joint control is to be deemed beneficial ownership for the purpose of determining whether or not a conflict exists.

Excluded from the operation of subdivisions (6) to (9) of Section 310(b) is any security held by the trustee as collateral security to an obligation not in default; held as collateral security under the indenture; and held by it in the capacity of custodian, escrow agent, depositary, agent for collection, or any similar representative capacity.

Other Affiliations between Trustee and
Obligor or Underwriters

Three other situations are specified in Section 310(b), the existence of any one of which will constitute a conflict of interest.

First, a conflicting interest will exist if the trustee or any of its directors or executive officers is an obligor upon the indenture securities or an underwriter for such an obligor.

Second, a conflict will also exist if the trustee or any of its directors or executive officers is a director, officer, partner, employee, appointee, or representative of an obligor or of an underwriter for an obligor. One individual may be a director and/or executive officer of the trustee and a director and/or executive officer of an obligor, provided he is not at the same time an executive officer of both. Also, if, and so long as, the number of directors of the trustee in office is more than nine, one additional individual may be a director and/or executive officer of the trustee and a director of such obligor.

Finally, a conflict of interest will exist if the trustee directly or indirectly controls, is directly or indirectly controlled by, or is under direct or indirect common control with, an obligor or an underwriter for an obligor. The control referred to here is actual control, whether or not it involves ownership of a prohibited percentage of the securities referred to above. The question of whether or not actual control exists must be determined by the circumstances of each case.

With the advent of the bank holding company and the creation of subsidiaries engaged in the underwriting of securities outside the United States, a conflict will exist if such subsidiary underwrites a new debt issue and the bank affiliate of the holding company is a trustee for another issue of the same issuer. Such underwriting will also preclude the particular bank from acting as trustee for the issuer (or the company which guarantees the issue) for a period of three years.

A qualified indenture must provide that, if a conflict of interest, as outlined above, exists or develops, the trustee, within 90 days after ascertaining that it has such conflict, much either eliminate such conflict or resign. The trustee should therefore establish such procedures and checks that will bring to light any conflict that develops. No established routine is required, but the trustee should be in a position to establish that it has exercised reasonable care, and it must affirmatively state annually that it has continued to be eligible and qualified to serve. As indicated, an annual check of fiduciary holdings is mandatory. It is recommended that an annual report be obtained from the obligor as to the latter's holding of trustee securities, if any; as to the outstanding securities of such obligor; and as to firms which have acted as underwriters for such obligor within the preceding three years. Such internal procedures within the trustee's office should be established as will insure the prompt reporting of such security holdings as might constitute a conflict.

PROBLEMS OF QUALIFICATION IN FOREIGN STATES

A corporation is a creature of the state in which it is incorporated, but it is a foreign entity insofar as other states are concerned. While it is regarded as a "person" for many purposes of the law, it is not entitled to the protection of the "privileges and immunities" clause of the United States Constitution. Accordingly, with certain exceptions relating to interstate or foreign commerce, a state may exclude a corporation of another state from doing business within its borders, and from suing in its courts with respect to any prohibited transactions or otherwise engaging in activities over which the state has jurisdiction; or it may impose such terms and conditions as it deems proper for the granting of permission to do business within its borders. Most states have general statutes, whether on a basis of reciprocity or otherwise, relating to the conduct of business by foreign corporations. Banking corporations are not permitted to do general banking business in other states, but the exercise of trust powers may, or may not, be permitted. Some states permit the exercise of such powers under specified conditions; a few have specific prohibitions; but most have no statute relating to the matter at all.

This presents a special problem for the corporate trustee. Most of the larger corporations do business and own property in a number of different states. Where such a corporation wishes to execute a mortgage on its fixed properties to secure a bond issue, the question arises as to whether or not the designated trustee may properly hold a security interest in property in all of the states in which such property is located. It is impossible to set down a general rule as a guide in these situations because the law differs from state to state. The following may be taken as a general guide: (1) where there is a specific statute prescribing conditions for the exercise of trust powers by foreign banking corporations, the trustee should qualify under such a statute before accepting a mortgage or security interest in fixed property within that state; (2) where there is no statutory provision, the trustee may normally hold such a security interest unless such act contravenes the general "doing of business" statutes; (3) where there is a specific prohibition against the exercise of trust powers by a foreign bank, the trustee should not undertake to hold a security interest in property in such a state. These are suggested as general guides only, however, as the statutes, and judicial interpretation of statutes, vary from state to state. Counsel should therefore be certain of the proper authority of the corporate trustee in each such situation.

If a corporate trustee undertakes to act without authority, it may not only subject itself to heavy penalties, but from the viewpoint of its fiduciary responsibility, it may also be denied access to the courts of the state for enforcement of the security if such becomes necessary.

The usual solution to this problem is the designation of an individual to act as a cotrustee under the indenture. Where only one state is in question, it would also be appropriate to designate a banking corporation in that state as a cotrustee. Under the federal constitution, an individual citizen of a state is entitled to all the privileges and immunities of citizens of other states, and cannot be excluded from holding property or doing business as can a foreign corporation. In any situation in which there is a question as to the authority of the corporate trustee, an individual cotrustee should be named.

Care must be exercised in drafting the appropriate indenture provisions. The usual provision, and a requirement of the Trust Indenture Act for qualified indentures, is that all rights, powers, duties, and obligations conferred or imposed upon the trustees shall be conferred or imposed upon and exercised by the institutional corporate trustee, or the institutional trustee and the cotrustee jointly, except to the extent that under any law of any jurisdiction in which any act or acts are to be performed, such institutional trustee is incompetent or unqualified to perform such act or acts, in which event such rights, powers, duties, and obligations shall be exercised and performed by the cotrustee.

Since all rights, powers, and duties are to be performed by the corporate trustee, except only such functions as it is incapable of performing, the corporate trustee is usually given the right, either alone or jointly with the obligor, to remove the designated individual trustee at any time and to appoint another individual to act. It is also a common practice to reserve to the corporate trustee and obligor the right to designate a cotrustee, or an additional cotrustee, at any time in the event such designation is necessary or desirable for the carrying out of any specific duty. This is done even though in the first instance a cotrustee may not be required, since it avoids the possibility of a situation's arising where the corporate trustee could not act and no mechanics were available for resolving the difficulty.

While any individual citizen may be designated as cotrustee the usual practice is for an officer of the corporate trustee to be designated as the individual cotrustee. This facilitates the exercise of powers or the performance of duties, such as the execution of releases or supplemental indentures, which the trustees are required to perform jointly.

Two states (Florida and Missouri) prohibit the exercise of trust powers by other than a corporation or individual citizen of such state. While such statutes probably do not exclude an individual citizen of another state from holding or enforcing a security interest in property, it is advisable to comply with the letter of the law and designate an individual or a bank in such a state as the cotrustee.

The problems outlined above do not arise in the case of an unsecured debenture or note agreement, or in other indentures where no property is mortgaged or pledged, as the trustee normally performs no acts outside its principal office.

SPECIAL PROVISIONS RELATING TO TRUSTEE

In addition to the matters previously discussed, there are certain general provisions relating to the trustee which should be incorporated in all indentures. These are usually found in the separate "Trustee" article.

First, is the acceptance by the trustee of the trusts and obligations imposed upon it by the indenture. While the act of execution would undoubtedly constitute a sufficient acceptance, it is customary to include an affirmative statement to this effect in the indenture.

Second, a provision should also be included relating to the compensation and expenses of the trustee. Rather than setting specific rates of compensation, the common practice is to provide that the trustee shall be entitled to reasonable compensation which shall not be limited by any statutory provision governing compensation of trustees. The latter is to avoid the possibility that statutes which exist in many states fixing maximum compensation for executors and trustees of testamentary or inter-vivos trusts, would be held applicable to these agreements. It is also desirable for the trustee to have included a provision by which the obligor will indemnify it with respect to any liability incurred or damage suffered by it resulting from other than its own negligence. The trustee should also be permitted, but not required, to make advances to preserve the mortgaged property, pay taxes, or for other purposes. All of these items, including all expenses and disbursements made by the trustee, should be payable by the obligor on demand (with interest in the case of any funds advanced by the trustee), and if the indenture is a secured indenture, the trustee is usually given a lien on the security (prior to that of the indenture securities) to assure payment of its compensation, expenses, advances, and liabilities. This is desirable, although one would be hard pressed to find a case in which the full implications of such priority of lien had been upheld.

Third, the trustee should be given authority to act through agents or attorneys in carrying out its duties, and it is customarily provided that the trustee will not be liable for the acts of such agents or attorneys if reasonable care is exercised in their selection.

Finally, the indenture should contain appropriate provisions relative to the resignation or removal of the trustee. As has been indicated, a conflict of interest may develop requiring the trustee's resignation. It should also be permitted to submit its resignation at any time for any reason it deems sufficient, or for no reason if it no longer wishes to act. The indenture should provide appropriate mechanics for such resignation and for the appointment of a successor, which must be eligible and qualified to act. A majority of the holders of the indenture securities are usually given the absolute right to designate the successor trustee, but until such right is exercised, any successor appointed by the obligor has full authority and power to act. As a practical matter, a successor trustee is usually appointed by the obligor and seldom by the bondholders. If the trustee is involved in a merger or consolidation with another institution, it is usually provided that the surviving corporation will automatically succeed to the trusteeship without further act, if it is eligible and qualified.

A majority of the indenture security holders are customarily given the absolute right, at any time and with or without cause, to remove the trustee. Since the latter is supposed to serve their interests, it is quite appropriate that they have the power, by majority action, to remove the trustee and substitute another if for any reason they believe their interests are not being served properly. The obligor, however, should never be given the right by unilateral action to remove the trustee.

If the trustee submits its resignation because of a disqualification and no successor is appointed within a reasonable time, the trustee or any security holder may petition a court for appointment of a successor, and an institution so appointed will be qualified to act.

EXCULPATORY PROVISIONS

Among the provisions which were the subject of a great amount of comment, criticism, and controversy in pre-Trust Indenture Act days were the so-called "exculpatory clauses" which had come to be more or less standard in all indentures. The general legal effect of these provisions was to exempt the trustee from liability for any act or failure to act, short of willful misconduct or gross negligence. A great deal could be written pro and con on this matter, as these clauses tended to be enlarged and expanded over a lengthy period. This development was due in no small part to the misunderstanding on the part of security holders and courts concerning the essential nature of the trustee function and to efforts which were made to hold the trustee accountable in some way for every unfortunate and unwise investment. Under these conditions it was essential for even the conscientious trustees and their counsel to endeavor to protect themselves. Regardless of the arguments which could be, and were, made in favor of these provisions, they had two unfortunate results. They provided protection even to the trustee who was indifferent to its fiduciary responsibility, and they subjected all trustees to criticism, even those who were diligent and conscientious in the performance of their duty, and these latter represented a great majority of trustees.

One result of the enactment of the Trust Indenture Act was the prohibition of such broad immunity provisions. A qualified indenture may not contain any provisions relieving the trustee of liability for its own negligent action, its own negligent failure to act, or its own willful misconduct, although it may provide that the trustee shall be protected from liability for any error of judgment made in good faith by a responsible officer, where the trustee was not negligent in ascertaining the pertinent facts. This has become the accepted practice for almost all modern indentures, whether or not they are qualified.

Certain exculpatory provisions are still perfectly proper and permissible if they do not contravene the foregoing prohibition. Trustees should endeavor to have them included to prevent the possibility of a court's reading into an indenture an implied covenant or duty on the part of the trustee when none in fact was intended. In the absence of any express duty in the indenture, or only to the extent of any duty specifically imposed, the following are provisions which should be included:

(1) The trustee has no obligation or duty to record the indenture.

(2) The trustee has no responsibility for the truth or accuracy of the recitals in the indenture.

(3) The trustee has no responsibility as to the application of the proceeds of any bonds, or as to the use or application of any property or monies released or paid out in accordance with indenture provisions.

(4) The trustee may advise with counsel and shall be protected for anything done, in good faith, in accordance with the opinion of such counsel.

(5) The trustee is not responsible for the validity of the indenture

or of any securities issued thereunder, or for the obligor's title to, or the value of, the security held.

(6) In the absence of bad faith, the trustee may rely on any certificates, opinions, documents, or other papers furnished to it and believed by it to be genuine and to be signed by the proper party or parties; the trustee is under a duty, however, to examine any such instruments furnished to it in accordance with an indenture provision to make sure that it complies with such provision.

(7) The trustee shall not be liable for any action taken on the request or direction of holders of a majority of the indenture securities.

PRESCRIBED STANDARDS OF CONDUCT

What should be the prescribed standard of conduct for an indenture trustee? A clear distinction should be made between the duties prior to a default and those existing after a default occurs, when the security holder's investment is in jeopardy. In the normal case, the obligor will perform its obligations and covenants, and the investor's principal concern is in receiving his interest and principal when due. Under these circumstances, the duties of the trustee are largely administrative. It is important, however, that the interests of the security holders be protected at all times, no matter how solvent or secure the obligor may appear. An active and vigilant administration by the trustee is necessary at all times to insure, if possible, that there will be no default, or if default occurs, that the bondholders will have the security for which they bargained for recovery.

The nature and extent of the duties of the trustee will vary with each indenture, depending on its terms. Since it constitutes a contract between the obligor and trustee, it not only prescribes rules of conduct for the former, but also defines the limits of the trustee's authority, and the latter may do only what the indenture either in express terms or by necessary implication authorizes it to do.

It is customary to provide in modern indentures, as authorized by the Trust Indenture Act, that prior to default: (1) the trustee shall be liable only for the performance of such duties as are specifically set forth in the indenture; (2) that the extent of such duties shall be determined solely by the express provisions of the indenture; and (3) that no implied duties or covenants on the part of the trustee shall be read into the indenture.

Presumably this language will be construed to mean what it says, although it has not yet been interpreted by the courts. Most court decisions on this question relate to indentures which did not contain this language, but many courts found implied duties not expressly set forth, and frequently based their decision on the nature of the agreement itself. The majority of indentures still contain language from which it might be possible to infer such a duty. For example, it is usually provided that a trustee may on its own initiative make independent investigations or require further evidence as to the performance by the obligor of its covenants. Such a provision is highly desirable, but it is recommended that an express qualification be inserted that the trustee is under no duty to do so. Some courts have indicated that the trustee is under an implied duty to do whatever may be necessary to preserve the trust estate, and that to this extent such duty cannot be abridged even by agreement.

A real problem exists whenever the trustee deems it necessary to act beyond the scope of its express duties and powers. It is quite possible that an even higher standard of care may be imposed with respect to any such action, and the trustee may lose the benefit of the exculpatory clauses. While situations sometimes arise where it is imperative that action be taken, every effort should be made to find an indenture provision on which to base such action.

The Trust Indenture Act requires that upon the occurrence of an event of default, the trustee shall exercise such of the rights and powers vested in it by the indenture, and shall use the same degree of care and skill in their exercise, as a prudent man would exercise or use under the circumstances in the conduct of his own affairs. This provision will be considered in more detail in considering events of default and remedies available to the trustee.

OTHER RELATIONS BETWEEN TRUSTEE AND OBLIGOR

A trustee is normally selected from among the banks with which the obligor conducts a general banking business. This is perfectly proper, and the indenture usually contains provisions specifically permitting all other normal and customary relationships. The trustee, in its individual capacity, may own indenture securities and, as such holder, has the same rights and privileges as other holders. It may act as depositary, custodian, transfer agent, registrar, paying agent, fiscal agent, escrow agent, or in any similar capacity. Subject to the qualification provisions of the indenture, it may also act as trustee for the obligor, whether under an indenture or otherwise.

The existence of a creditor relationship between the obligor and the trustee is not a conflict of interest, except to the extent that ownership by the trustee of a specified percentage of the securities of the obligor is prohibited. It is obvious, however, that the bank as creditor of an obligor may be in a position adverse to the bank as trustee for security holders of the obligor whenever the obligor's financial position becomes difficult and it faces insolvency. Creditor relationships have never been prohibited, and courts have been fairly uniform in holding that the trustee bank, as creditor, is chargeable with notice of provisions in an indenture under which it acts as trustee, and may be liable if it acts without regard to the rights of the indenture security holders.

In its 1936 report, the Securities and Exchange Commission recommended that creditor relationships between trustees and obligors be prohibited, citing several cases in which it appeared that the trustee had protected its position as creditor without regard to the interests of indenture security holders. The Congress wisely concluded, however, that such a prohibition would be unwise. The more important and experienced trust institutions are also large commercial banks and have important credit arrangements with corporate obligors. If extension of credit were prohibited, these institutions would unquestionably surrender their corporate trust relations with these obligors. Instead of benefiting security holders, such a step would provide them with a less experienced and capable trustee.

An effort was made, therefore, to solve the problem in a different way. Section 311 of the Trust Indenture Act requires the inclusion in the indenture of a provision that if the trustee shall be, or shall become, a creditor, directly or indirectly, of an obligor upon the indenture securities within four months prior to a default in the payment of principal or interest on the indenture securities, it may not enforce any preferential collection of its claim against the obligor except on the conditions therein specified. The indenture must require the trustee bank under these circumstances to set aside, in a special account, for the benefit of itself and the indenture security holders (1) an amount equal to any and all reductions in the amount due and owing upon any claim as such creditor with respect to principal and interest effected after the beginning of such four months' period, and (2) all property received in respect of any claim as such creditor, either as security therefor or in satisfaction or composition thereof, after the beginning of such four months' period, or an amount equal to the proceeds of such property if it shall have been disposed of.

The trustee bank is entitled: (1) to exercise any right of setoff which it could have exercised if a petition in bankruptcy had been filed by or against such obligor upon the date of the default; (2) to retain for its own account payments made on account of its claim by a third person, and/or distributions made in cash, securities, or other property in respect of claims filed against such obligor in bankruptcy or receivership or in proceedings for reorganization pursuant to the Bankruptcy Act or applicable state law; (3) to realize for its own account on any property held as collateral security to such claim prior to the beginning of the four months' period; (4) to realize for its own account on any property received as security simultaneously with the creation of such claim if the trustee bank became a creditor after the beginning of such four months' period and had no reasonable cause to believe that a default would occur; and (5) to receive payment on any claim against the release of any property held as security therefor to the extent of the fair value of such property. Property substituted after the beginning of the four months' period has the same status as property released to the extent of the fair value of the latter, and any renewal effected after the beginning of such period has the same status as the pre-existing claim.

The language of the act relative to the disposition of any funds or property segregated in such a special account is somewhat laborious. It appears that the property in the account cannot be apportioned until the obligor has gone through bankruptcy, receivership, or reorganization proceedings. The court having jurisdiction of such proceedings is given the right to apportion the property in accordance with the indenture provisions corresponding to Section 311(a) of the act or, in lieu of such apportionment, to give due consideration to such provisions in determining the fairness of the distributions to be made to the security holders and the trustee bank in such proceedings.

The formula according to which the property in the account is to be distributed is quite simple. Secured portions of the claims of both the security holders and the trustee bank are to be disregarded, and the respective claims are to be reduced to the extent of distributions with respect to such portions. The funds in the special account are then to be so allocated that the security holders and the trustee bank will receive the same proportion of the unsecured portions of their claims from such account and from dividends paid from the obligor's estate with respect to such unsecured portions. The problem will be one of applying the formula. Anyone familiar with reorganization proceedings will appreciate the difficulty of even approximating the value of any particular lien position or of the securities and interests distributed in reorganization. The ascertainment of such values to the extent necessary to permit an allocation of a fund according to an exact mathematical formula is all but impossible.

If the trustee resigns or is removed after the beginning of the four months' period, it is still subject to these provisions. If the resignation or removal was prior to such period, the trustee bank is subject to such provisions only if the receipt of property or reduction of claim occurred after the beginning of such four months' period, and within four months after such resignation or removal.

Certain creditor relationships may be excluded from the operation of this section. These consist of creditor relationships arising from: (1) the ownership or acquisition of securities issued under an indenture, or any security having a maturity of one year or more at the time of its acquisition by the trustee; (2) advances for the purpose of preserving the trust estate or discharging taxes, prior liens, etc. authorized by the indenture or by a bankruptcy or receivership court, if notice of such advance is given as provided in the indenture; (3) disbursements made in the ordinary course of business as trustee under an indenture, transfer agent, registrar, custodian, paying agent, fiscal agent, depositary, or similar capacity; (4) indebtedness created as a result of services rendered or premises rented, or as a result of goods or securities sold in a cash transaction; (5) the ownership of stock or of other securities of a corporation organized under the provisions of Section 25(a) of the Federal Reserve Act, as amended, which is directly or indirectly a creditor of the obligor; or (6) the acquisition, ownership, acceptance, or negotiation of any drafts, bills of exchange, acceptances, or obligations which fall within the classification of self-liquidating paper.

The increased use of the subordinated debenture issue raises special problems for a bank which is also a creditor of the issuer. In relation to other creditors, the subordinated debenture holder has much the same status as a preferred stockholder. As a matter of fact, a number of such issues have been created to refund preferred stock issues to take advantage of the tax deductibility of interest as opposed to dividends. In addition to prior funded indebtedness, these issues are usually made subordinate to all existing bank indebtedness and all future bank indebtedness up to specified amounts.

What is the status of a trustee bank which is or becomes the holder of preferred indebtedness to which the debentures issued under the indenture are specifically subordinated? The intent is clear but an ambiguity is created by the inclusion in the indenture of a provision corresponding to Section 311 of the act, unless such provision specifically excepts from its operation the preferred indebtedness to which the debentures are subordinate. Indebtedness to the bank with a maturity in excess of one year at the time of its creation, is undoubtedly exempt from this provision since a note is a "security" within the meaning of the Trust Indenture Act, and securities having a maturity in excess of one year are exempt from the provisions of Section 311. As to shorter term indebtedness, a court might well take into consideration the expressed intent of the parties in making an allocation in a bankruptcy or reorganization proceeding, although there is no assurance that this would be done.

Although the Securities and Exchange Commission has not conceded that the Section is not operative, they do permit the inclusion of a proviso qualifying the preferential collection of claims provisions to the extent that the trustee is entitled to all of the rights (in the indenture) with respect to any senior indebtedness at any time held by it to the same extent as any other holder of senior indebtedness and that no other section of the indenture should be construed to deprive the trustee of any of its rights as such holder.

Despite the inequity of the possibility of treatment on a basis different than that accorded other holders of the same indebtedness, until this question has been clarified by statutory amendment or judicial decision, trustees would be well advised to assume that they will be required to account in accordance with Section 311 even though they hold an obligation which by its terms is superior to the indenture securities. If they are unwilling to continue on the basis of such an assumption, the alternative is to refuse an appointment as trustee under a subordinated indenture.

4

Preparation, Execution, and Recording
of Indenture

CORPORATE FINANCIAL OFFICERS have a difficult and responsible task. They must secure the funds for the expansion and operation of the corporate enterprise, and these funds must be provided in the amounts and at the times they are required. To the extent that such funds are not generated from operations of the business itself, they must be obtained in a highly competitive market, and an effort must be made to secure the most economical terms with the fewest possible restrictions being placed on the company's freedom of action.

There are many reasons why capital financing has to be undertaken. The most common is the providing of new facilities in the form of plant and equipment for the expanded needs of the business. It may be desired to construct a new office building to house the executive and administrative staffs. Additional working capital may be required. Conditions may be appropriate for refunding existing indebtedness on more favorable terms, or funds may be needed to meet an existing maturity. Since capital financing is an expensive operation even for mature corporations with a high credit rating, careful planning is required so that there will be no necessity for too frequent recourse to the capital markets. Many companies resort to their commercial banks for interim financing, with the understanding that at periodic intervals or within an agreed period, funded debt will be issued and the bank loans paid off.

Many factors enter into determination of the form and method of financing, including the purpose of the loan, the credit standing of the issuer, existing capital structure, availability of investment funds, market conditions, and so on. While the exact terms will be · determined by negotiation, the corporate officials, usually with the assistance of qualified financial advisers, will normally make a preliminary determination of the amount of the issue, whether it will be secured or unsecured, the approximate amount that can be repaid annually by way of a sinking fund, the restrictive provisions that will be permitted, and the ultimate maturity date. Decision must then be made as to how the issue will be marketed or distributed. There are three principal ways in which this is done.

In a negotiated transaction, an investment banking firm is selected to underwrite the issue, and the substantive terms of the issue are negotiated with this firm. Where this method of marketing is used, the investment bankers usually, although not necessarily, act for all issues of the particular company and are thoroughly familiar with the corporation's financial affairs and programs. In addition to underwriting the company's public offerings, this firm is normally used as a general financial consultant and is able to render substantial valuable collateral services to the corporate officials. The investment bankers would probably have participated in discussions from the earliest date, and their familiarity with security markets as well as the company's affairs will enable them to tailor the issue to meet the company's requirements as well as current market conditions. Compensation of the underwriters is provided by the "spread" between the wholesale price they pay for the entire issue and the retail price at which the securities are sold to the investors. Usually the principal underwriter will associate a number of other firms with it in marketing the issue, each being responsible for, and assuming the risk involved in, a percentage of the total issue. The amount of the underwriter's "spread" will vary, but it is calculated to provide a reasonable profit based on the work involved and the risk assumed in the particular case.

Another method of marketing is through a public invitation for bids. All companies which are subject to the jurisdiction of the Securities and Exchange Commission under the Public Utility Holding Company Act are required to sell their securities in this manner unless specifically exempted. Other public bodies having jurisdiction over regulated industries may or may not prescribe or influence the manner in which securities are offered, but they must approve the method selected and the terms of sale. Under the method of public bidding, the issuing corporation will engage an independent firm of counsel, experienced in the field, to represent the prospective purchasers of the securities, and the terms and details of the offering will be negotiated between the company and such firm, except for the price which will be determined by the public bids. Occasionally the company will retain a firm of investment bankers as advisers who will work for a fee and who will not participate in the bidding. Usually the company and counsel will know the investment houses which will head the various syndicates that will participate in the bidding, and these firms may be consulted in advance as to some of the proposed terms of the issue. Since market conditions determine the price at which securities can be offered successfully, most bids are very close, and competition revolves around the amount of the underwriter's commission. There are certain advantages and disadvantages to the use of public bids as opposed to the negotiated method. Some regulatory bodies feel that the corporation obtains a better price through public bids, although experts differ on this matter. The disadvantages can be measured against the value placed on a continuing relationship and the advisory service received from selected investment bankers.

A third method, which is frequently used by the more mature companies with a high credit rating, is the direct placement. Under this method the issue is not underwritten at all, but negotiations are conducted with a group of institutional investors who are the actual purchasers of the securities. The company usually retains an investment house as an agent to find interested purchasers and negotiate the terms, although it may elect to do this itself. Such an issue does not have to be registered under the securities act, and the indenture is not qualified. In some instances where the issue is unsecured, where only a few purchasers are involved, and where the terms are not complicated, no indenture and no trustee are used. The company will execute separate but identical agreements with each purchaser, embodying all the terms of the contract.

While the three methods outlined are the principal ones used in distributing debt securities, others are sometimes used. Mention has been made of the offering of convertible debentures, which may or may not be underwritten, to existing stockholders. Mergers, acquisitions, recapitalizations, reorganizations, and similar transactions usually involve the offering of securities to existing security holders either of the issuing or of a different corporation. The corporation itself may elect to market its securities publicly without the assistance of an underwriting firm, although this practice is rare.

PREPARATION OF THE INDENTURE

Since the indenture, when executed, becomes a contract binding on the security holders as well as the trustee, and setting limitations on the rights of both, it follows that the preparation of the indenture is one of the most important steps in the whole process. It is here that the security holders stand in the greatest need of protection, and it is here that they frequently lack adequate representation. The substantive terms are established by agreement between the issuer and the underwriter, or counsel appointed to represent the underwriter. While some protection is afforded by this process—since the leading investment houses feel some moral responsibility for issues which they sponsor—the underwriter's primary concern is in securing terms which will make the issue readily marketable and not necessarily the terms which a security holder, in retrospect, might have considered desirable.

There have been a number of developments in recent years, however, which have substantially resolved this problem, with the result that the typical modern indenture is a fairly sound financial document with reasonably adequate safeguards designed to protect the investor. Among such developments are the following:

(1) The increasing influence of the institutional investor. While the direct placement contract involves the only situation in which the investors actually negotiate the terms of an issue, the institutional purchaser is important even in publicly distributed issues, and both issuers and underwriters endeavor to style the issue and the terms of the contract so as to attract the professional investor.

(2) The minimum standards of the Trust Indenture Act. Where an indenture is required to be qualified, which is the case with most public issues, the act requires the inclusion of specified provisions in the indenture designed for the protection of the investor. These provisions have come to be more or less accepted as standard and are now found in most indentures whether qualified or not.

(3) The disclosure provisions of the Securities Act of 1933. Most public issues of securities are required to be registered under this act which requires full disclosure not only of the history and current financial condition of the issuer but also of all important terms and

provisions of the indenture and the securities to be issued. This information, or appropriate summaries thereof, is required to be set forth in a prospectus which must be furnished to all prospective investors. Thus, the investor has available to him all pertinent information, and the decision to invest is his to make. If he fails to take advantage of the information so furnished, he has no one to blame but himself.

(4) The regulatory powers of the Securities and Exchange Commission and other regulatory agencies. Regulatory agencies, and particularly the Securities and Exchange Commission, have certain minimum standards which they require in cases where they have the authority to approve or prescribe the terms and conditions of proposed financing.

(5) The patterns for typical indentures which have become established among investment houses, institutional investors, and bond counsel.[9]

(6) The influence of the more experienced corporate trustees.

Once the essential terms of the indenture have been agreed upon, the process of draftsmanship is relatively simple. A prior indenture, frequently of the same obligor, is selected as a pattern. Many of the provisions will remain exactly the same. Clauses which are not appropriate to the current transaction or which experience has shown to be troublesome or difficult will be eliminated; and the new provisions which embody the terms of the contract will be added, as well as any new clauses which the evolutionary process has revealed as beneficial or desirable. Once an initial draft of the new indenture is ready, copies are distributed to all interested parties, and the document is modified and refined until all parties are reasonably satisfied.

FUNCTION OF THE TRUSTEE

At some point the corporate trustee must be selected. This should be done at the earliest possible moment, as the trustee can make important contributions to the process of finalizing the terms of the indenture. While it has no responsibility for the substantive provisions of the contract and, under normal circumstances, should never undertake to alter the terms of the basic contract, it is the party which will have to administer the agreement

---

[9] See p. 44 *supra*

and is therefore entitled to participate fully in all discussions relative to translating the contract into indenture language.

By reason of the importance of all phases of the indenture preparation process, the trustee should always be represented by legal counsel and should work closely with such counsel until the indenture has been executed and the initial bonds delivered. Some corporate trustees follow the practice of relinquishing to counsel the conduct of all matters during this preliminary process. This is inadvisable. A number of practical as well as legal considerations are involved, and the trustee cannot delegate, and should not permit counsel to usurp, its responsibility for decision making, although it should consult with counsel on all legal questions.

It would be difficult to set down in detail the exact procedure which the trustee should follow in its examination and review of the terms of the proposed indenture. A number of general principles may be suggested:

(1) As the recitals constitute no part of the substantive contract and the trustee has no responsibility with respect thereto, there is a tendency to skip over these clauses. It is important, however, that the due authorization by the obligor of all acts relating to creation of the indenture, issuance of the securities, and mortgaging or pledging of property be stated. While appropriate evidence of such authorization should be obtained and examined, the recitals may constitute an estoppel against the company should it at a later date claim lack of proper authorization.

(2) The form of bond as set forth in the indenture should be examined closely. As the bonds, when executed, become separate instruments and constitute separate contracts and obligations running directly to the holders thereof, they should contain specific reference to the indenture and should also set forth in sufficient detail any provision of the indenture which modifies or affects the obligation contained in the bond or imposes any limitations upon the rights of the holder. In any suit by a bondholder, if the provisions of the indenture conflict with the provisions of the bond itself, the latter are controlling.

(3) The adequacy of the granting clauses to convey the property and create the lien which is intended is a legal matter and should be a concern primarily for counsel. The trustee should secure appropriate opinions covering these points. A detailed examination of the property descriptions would serve no purpose, as the trustee

usually has nothing against which to check or compare such descriptions and must rely on the company and its counsel. The trustee should make sure, however, that it is qualified to hold property as mortgagee in the various jurisdictions in which the property is located. If there is any question, consideration should be given to appointment of a cotrustee so qualified. Where the ownership of franchises, rights, or permits is essential to the carrying on of the obligor's business, the trustee should make certain that these are included among the mortgaged property. The same care should apply to any important leases, easements, contracts, rights of way, etc., the purpose being to insure that the lien covers the obligor's property as a "going concern." If any important franchises, leases, contracts, etc. expire before the maturity date of the securities to be issued, investigation should be made concerning any renewal privileges or the securing of alternative rights to avoid the possibility of a substantial diminution of security or of a default. If an after-acquired property clause is included, the trustee should insure that it expresses clearly the intent as to what subsequently acquired property is to be covered. If any property is to be assigned or pledged, proper record should be made so that an executed assignment or physical delivery of such property is secured at the closing. If any part of such property is in the possession of another trustee, proper notification should be given to such other trustee and a tickler record prepared to obtain possession of such property on satisfaction of the other lien. If any leasehold estate is mortgaged, the last day of the term of each such lease should be specifically excluded. This avoids the creation for the trustee of an estate identical with that of the obligor-lessee, and the possibility of a claim that the trustee is liable for performance of the lessee's obligations under the lease. Finally, consideration should be given to the possible applicability of any special laws or regulations in the jurisdictions in which the property is located or the mortgage contract executed and delivered.

(4) While the trustee has no responsibility for the substantive provisions of the contract, or for the covenants that may be included, it should review these provisions carefully to make certain that they are clear and unambiguous and adequately set forth the intent of the parties.

(5) The trustee should examine carefully the evidence which it is to receive as to compliance by the obligor with the various inden-

ture covenants to assure its adequacy. For specific types of covenants, it is difficult to devise an appropriate compliance certificate, and it is therefore suggested that a general certificate to the effect that the obligor has complied with all covenants and is not in default be obtained at least annually. This would be in addition to specific evidence as to the more important covenants.

(6) It is the obligor's and not the trustee's responsibility to see that an indenture to be qualified complies with the Trust Indenture Act. If there is a variance, the commission is likely to take exception. A diligent trustee, however, will see that the required provisions are included and give consideration to the desirability of the permissive provisions. If the trustee is acting as trustee under another indenture of the same obligor, it should insure that such other indenture and the obligations outstanding thereunder are specifically mentioned and excepted in the qualification provisions inserted.

(7) The trustee has a particular responsibility for the mechanical provisions which relate to the servicing of the indenture securities. It should verify that they are workable and not in conflict with its established practices and procedures. The greatest degree of flexibility consistent with clarity should be retained. Whenever possible, the manner in which a particular operation is to be conducted should be left to the discretion of the trustee rather than being set forth in detail. This permits a change in procedure to conform with evolving and more efficient methods, and is not only proper but also desirable so long as substantive rights are not affected.

(8) Particular attention should be given to the remedial provisions and to the trustee article. The rights, powers, duties, and responsibilities of the trustee, and any limitation on its rights and powers, will be governed by the general provision of these articles. The trustee should ascertain that it has all requisite power and authority to carry out its duties. It should also be careful to see that appropriate exculpatory and protective provisions are included, as the potential liability is substantial.

(9) Finally, after appropriate attention has been given to each separate section, the contract should be considered as an entity. It is important that the various provisions and covenants be consistent, as the indenture must be considered and construed as a single document. The trustee should have a clear understanding of the essential purpose and intent of the transaction, and the provisions

of the indenture, considered together, should clearly express and carry out this purpose and intent.

THE REGISTRATION STATEMENT
AND QUALIFICATION OF THE INDENTURE

Issuance of securities is not only a delicate marketing operation but also a matter of careful planning and timing. The many different transactions which together constitute a unified operation must be initiated at the appropriate time so that everything will be completed on the date set for delivery of the securities. Time is usually of the essence, and the customary procedure is to select a date for sale of the securities and to relate all other activities to such date.

Where securities are to be distributed publicly, they must be registered under the Securities Act of 1933. It takes four to six weeks for a registration to be cleared and to become effective. A copy of the indenture has to be filed as an exhibit to the registration, and the indenture should be in as complete and final form as is possible in order to minimize the number of amendments which have to be filed.

The contents of the registration statement and the prospectus are the responsibility of the obligor and not the trustee. It is advisable for the latter to review copies of these documents, however, to insure that no information is disclosed therein which might affect its rights or obligations or which might be contrary to its understanding of the transaction. In particular, the sections which summarize indenture provisions should be reviewed.

The Trust Indenture Act requires the filing with each registration statement of such information and documents as the commission may prescribe in order to enable it to determine whether any person designated to act as trustee is eligible and qualified. The commission has prescribed the form in which this information is to be furnished. Form T-1 is required for institutional trustees and Form T-2, for individual trustees. Form T-1 requires the filing of the trustee's most recent report of condition, a copy of its articles of association and certificate of authority to commence business, a copy of its bylaws, and the consent of the trustee that copies of reports of examination by federal, state, territorial or district authorities may be furnished to the commission. Both Forms T-1 and T-2 provide for information sufficient to enable the commission to determine whether or not there exists a conflict of interest as defined in Section 310(b) of the act.

Form T-1 must be prepared and signed by the trustee. In order that it may be in a position to supply the requisite information, one of the first steps which the trustee should take after being advised of its appointment is to secure all necessary information from the obligor and its underwriters and make the necessary check of its qualification. Form T-1 requires the filing of information as to conflicts with underwriters who have acted as such for any securities of the obligor within the preceding three years, and also with respect to the underwriters for the securities to be issued. Where public bids are requested, these underwriters are unknown at the time the statement is filed. As to these matters, the trustee may answer the pertinent Form T-1 questions in the negative and include an undertaking to file an appropriate amendment if a subsequent check would require a different answer. The usual procedure is for the obligor to require from all members of underwriting syndicates formed to bid on the securities statements which include the necessary information for the trustee to determine its qualification. These statements should of course be reviewed by the trustee.

In certain cases an indenture is required to be qualified even though the indenture securities do not have to be registered. In such case, a special form of application for such qualification must be filed by the obligor, accompanied by Forms T-1 and/or T-2, executed by the trustee(s).

EXECUTION, DELIVERY, AND RECORDING
OF THE INDENTURE

As soon as the registration statement has become effective and all other authorizations and approvals have been obtained, the indenture may be executed and the securities delivered. The trustee should make certain that the officers of the obligor company who execute the indenture have been authorized to do so. The trustee is also usually requested to furnish an appropriate certificate as to the authority of its officers who join in the execution of the indenture.

The indenture customarily contains an express statement that the laws of a particular state will apply as to all questions which may arise in its interpretation. This is important, as the laws of different states may vary substantially in important respects. It is desirable, although not essential, that the state specified be that in which the office of the trustee is located, since its laws are the ones with which it is presumably most familiar. In the absence of an express provision, the law applied will be that of the state in which the contract is executed and delivered. As delivery usually takes place at the office of the trustee, there is no problem. Where the laws which are to govern are those of another state, an effort should be made to have execution and delivery of the indenture take place in such state. While the express indenture provision would undoubtedly be controlling, such a procedure avoids the possibility of any question being raised.

At the time of the delivery of the indenture, the trustee should receive documents sufficient to establish the due authorization of all proceedings in connection with the indenture and the securities. Counsel should be consulted as to the documents required and the form and content thereof. For convenience, Exhibit 4 sets forth a typical list of documents customarily requested.

EXHIBIT   4. LIST OF DOCUMENTS USUALLY REQUIRED WHEN
             ACCEPTING APPOINTMENT AS TRUSTEE UNDER
             CORPORATE INDENTURES

1. Certificate of Secretary of State of state of incorporation of the Company, under recent date, certifying good standing or subsistence of Company (including payment of franchise taxes) and listing all of charter documents on file.
2. Copies of charter documents listed in Item 1, above, certified as true copies by Secretary of State of state of incorporation, under recent date.
    (Note: Items 1 and 2 may be consolidated in certain states.)
3. Certificate of Secretary of Company, as of closing date, that the Company's charter has not been amended since the date of certification referred to above in Item 1.
4. Copy of by-laws as amended to closing date, certified as of the closing date by the Secretary of the Company as a true copy and as including all amendments.
    Note: If a supplemental Indenture is being executed, we should receive Items 1 and 3, any subsequent charter amendments certified as in Item 2 and currently cer-

tified copy of the by-laws or certificate of Secretary of the Company as to any changes since the previous date of certification of by-laws.

5. Secretary's certificate, dated closing date, certifying the incumbency and specimen signatures of the presently acting officers of the Company who have signed or may thereafter sign obligations or documents submitted to the Trustee.

6. Resolutions of Board of Directors certified by Secretary of Company as of the closing date (a) authorizing the execution and delivery of the Indenture and the obligations, approving the forms thereof, *etc.*; (b) if the obligations are convertible, reserving the maximum number of shares of stock issuable on conversion and authorizing the issuance of said shares upon requisition by the conversion agent to the transfer agent; and (c) designating an office or agency for presentations, demands, *etc.*, and appointing a paying agent and registrar and, if the obligations are convertible, a conversion agent.

7. Stockholders' resolutions or consents, similarly certified with appropriate evidence of the filing thereof (if filing is required), unless the opinion of counsel referred to below in Item 13 specifically states that stockholders' action is not required by the law of the State of Incorporation or by the charter or the by-laws.

8. Copy of Indenture as approved by the Board of Directors, similarly certified.

9. Specimen certificates of each authorized denomination, similarly certified.

10. Copies, certified by the proper public officials, of orders of any public authorities having jurisdiction.

11. If applicable, duplicate original or certified copy of the S.E.C. order(s) establishing effective date of registration statement and qualification under Trust Indenture Act and/or declaration under Public Utility Holding Company Act.

12. If applicable, copy of "no stop-order" telegram as of the close of business on the business day preceding the closing, from the S.E.C.

13. Opinion by Company's counsel stating in substance that:
    (a) The Company is a duly organized and existing corporation, that all requisite corporate action has been duly taken by it (including consent or action by stockholders, if applicable)

to authorize the execution and delivery of the Indenture and the issuance of the obligations, that the Indenture has been duly executed and delivered and is a valid and subsisting agreement of the Company with the Trustee enforceable in accordance with its terms and that the obligations have been duly executed by the Company and, when authenticated by the Trustee and delivered for value, will be valid and subsisting obligations of the Company enforceable in accordance with their terms;

(b)   The approval of public authorities (including courts), if any, having jurisdiction in the premises has been obtained, or stating that no public authority has jurisdiction;

(c)   The execution and delivery of the Indenture, the execution, issuance and delivery of the obligations and (if applicable) issuance of stock upon conversion of the obligations do not and will not conflict with or result in a breach of the terms, conditions or provisions of, or constitute a default under, the charter or by-laws of the Company, any order or decree of any court, or public authority having jurisdiction, or any other indenture, contract, agreement or undertaking to which the Company is a party or by which it is bound;

(d)   The Registration Statement under the Securities Act of 1933, as amended, is effective, or that no registration is required under the Act;

(e)   The Indenture is qualified under the Trust Indenture Act of 1939, or that no qualification is required under the Act;

If the Indenture mortgages or pledges or creates a security interest in any property, also:

(f)   The Company lawfully owns or has the interest specified in the property described in the Indenture as mortgaged or pledged, or as subject to security interest, subject only to exceptions and encumbrances stated in the Indenture, and that the Indenture gives or, when all required recording and filing have been completed, will give the lien which it and the obligations issued under it purport to create;

(g)   The amount of mortgage recording tax or other taxes, if any, payable upon the transaction, the recording of the Indenture or the filing of financing statements, or stating that no such taxes are payable;

(h)   Stating in detail the recording or filing of the Indenture and/or financing statements which is necessary and whether or not, and if so what, necessity exists for any periodic rerecording or refiling to maintain the lien of the Indenture or the perfection of the security interest;

(i) Upon completion of recording and filing, a supplemental opinion stating that all proper recording and filing have been done so as to make effective the lien and security interests intended to be created by the Indenture and reciting the details of such action.

If the obligations are by their terms convertible, also:

(j) The maximum number of shares of stock of the Company issuable on conversion have been reserved for that purpose;

(k) The shares issuable on conversion have been validly authorized, and when issued in accordance with the terms of the obligations and the Indenture, will be validly issued, fully paid and nonassessable;

(l) The shares issuable on conversion have been registered under the Securities Act of 1933, as amended, or that no such registration is required; and

(m) No approval or authorization of the issuance of said shares upon conversion is required by any governmental authority, or that any such approval or authorization has been duly obtained.

14. Order of Company for authentication and delivery of obligations. If all or a substantial amount of the obligations are in registered form, order should refer to specific instructions from underwriter as to registration information.

15. Receipt for authenticated obligations.

16. Evidence of payment of any mortgage and/or other tax imposed by law, preferably in the form of a receipt by the proper public official or evidence that provision for such payment has been made.

17. At or after the closing, counterparts of the Indenture bearing recorders' notations and a filing counterpart of each financing statement showing filing data (if recording or filing is required), and, if appropriate, the agreement of each paying agent to hold funds in trust, *etc.*

18. After the closing, we should receive 12 conformed counterparts of the Indenture.

Proofs in triplicate of the Indenture and relative papers should be submitted to the Trustee as early as possible to facilitate its consideration thereof.

The documents listed should be received at or prior to the first issue of securities under the indenture. With each additional issue, new documents should be received or those on file brought up to date. In addition to the above, the specific papers and certificates set forth in the pertinent indenture section are required.

If the indenture grants a mortgage or lien on any property, one of the first steps to be taken after it has been executed is to have it recorded in all jurisdictions in which the property is located. Sometimes this is done before or simultaneously with delivery of the securities, but it is usually sufficient if done promptly thereafter. While the contract is binding on the obligor when delivered, the importance of recording is to give public notice of the lien and prevent a third party from obtaining a lien prior to that of the trustee. Recording is the responsibility of counsel to the company. If a number of jurisdictions are involved, local counsel familiar with the laws of each jurisdiction are used to insure strict adherence to recording requirements.

If the indenture creates a security interest in real estate, including a lease or rents thereunder, *and* in any personal property or fixtures, the filing provisions of Article 9 of the Uniform Commercial Code will be applicable to perfect the security interest in the personal property. The appropriate filing must be done even though the mortgage or supplemental mortgage creating the lien on real and personal property is properly recorded as a real estate mortgage. If, however, the mortgage or supplement creating such lien was properly recorded as a mortgage of real property *prior* to the effective date of the Code, no filing is necessary.

If all the collateral under an indenture is in the possession of the trustee, that alone will perfect the security interest, and no filing is necessary. In the usual collateral trust indenture, this will consist of negotiable instruments or securities such as stocks and bonds.

Where filing is necessary, the Code prescribes the formal requisites for the financing statement; most states have adopted a standard form for this purpose. Completion is merely a matter of filling in the blank spaces, and having it signed by the obligor company (the debtor) and the trustee (the secured party). Although the indenture itself may be filed if it meets the particular state's requirements, as a practical matter it is simpler to use the prescribed form for this purpose.

The trustee should obtain appropriate evidence as to such recording and/or filing. The recorded counterparts of the indenture and/or a filing counterpart of each financing statement, showing the recording or filing data are usually returned to and retained by the trustee.

In addition, the trustee should receive a legal opinion or opinions as to the sufficiency of such recording and/or filing. There should be included in the indenture an appropriate covenant as to the furnishing of such opinions. This covenant should provide that the obligor will furnish the trustee (1) promptly after the execution and delivery of the indenture and of each indenture supplemental thereto, an opinion of counsel either stating that in the opinion of such counsel the indenture has been properly recorded and/or filed so as to make effective the lien or security interest intended to be created thereby, and reciting the details of such action, or stating that, in the opinion of such counsel, no action is necessary to make such lien or security interest effective; and (2) at least annually thereafter an opinion of counsel either stating that in the opinion of such counsel such action has been taken with respect to the recording, filing, re-recording, and refiling of the indenture and of each supplement as is necessary to maintain the lien or security interest of such indenture, and reciting the details of such action, or stating that in the opinion of such counsel no such action is necessary to maintain such lien or security interest.

It should be noted that although a mortgage of real property usually need not be re-recorded to maintain the lien, a financing statement perfecting a security interest in personal property will lapse after five years from the filing date unless a continuation statement is filed within sixty days after the five-year period. Upon timely filing of continuation statements, the effectiveness of the original statement can be continued for successive five year periods.

One of the first actions which should be taken by the trustee after execution and delivery of the indenture is to make a complete review of the indenture provisions and establish an appropriate tickler record as to all action which the obligor or trustee has to take in connection with administration of the indenture. This would include such things as dates on which the sinking fund is to operate, the date when certificates and opinions are required to be filed, and so on. No particular form of record is required, provided the form used is adequate to insure that appropriate timely reminders will be brought to the attention of the administrative officers.

SUPPLEMENTAL INDENTURES

In addition to the original indenture, supplemental indentures may be executed from time to time for various purposes. They may provide the terms of additional series of securities to be issued under the indenture; they may convey additional property or pledge additional security; they may modify or amend provisions of the original contract; they may impose additional restrictions on the obligor; or other reasons may require that the original contract be supplemented.

The same care as to the proper authorization, execution, and delivery and recording of these instruments should be exercised as in the case of the original indenture. The trustee should also insure that each such supplement is consistent with and is authorized, either explicitly or by necessary implication, by the original indenture.

Once the supplement has been executed and delivered, it constitutes a part of the contract, and the original indenture and all supplemental indentures must be read together to determine the rights, duties, and obligations of the parties.

To facilitate the work of the administrator, it is helpful to prepare check lists to serve as a guide on all important transactions. Exhibit 5 is a typical guide for use in reviewing new and additional security issues under indentures.

Exhibit　5. Guide for Use in Reviewing New and Additional Issues Under Indentures

Obligor _____

Guarantors and/or Joint Issuers (if any) _____

Title of Indenture _____

Date Executed _____ Closing Date _____

Issue of $ _____ Under Art. _____ Sec. _____

Description _____

Authorized Issue under Indenture　$_____　under this section $ _____

Total Issue to date, under Indenture
(including this issue)　　　　$_____　under this Section $ _____

Balance Unissued under Indenture $_____　under this Section $ _____

Indenture qualified
under Trust Indenture Act _____　Indenture subject to Streit Act _____

Company's Counsel _____　Trustee's Counsel _____

Underwriters' (Purchasers') Counsel _____

Check each item as completed. If inapplicable or pending, so indicate.

I. *Prior to Closing*

_____A.　Obtain three copies of draft of indenture for review. Send one copy to counsel.

_____B.　Memorandum to Banking Department and Credit Files of new issue, and whether indenture is to be qualified under Trust Indenture Act.

_____C.　Complete conflict check and execute Form T-1 if indenture is to be qualified.

_____D.　If a ship mortgage, execute and file required certificate, affidavit and most recently published financial report with Secretary, Maritime Commission.

_____E.　Determine dates for information meeting (if any), opening of bids, bond signing, preliminary and final closings; reserve conference rooms.

_____F.　Determine schedule for receipt of bonds and lists from underwriters. If issue is entirely or substantially fully registered, determine quantities of each denomination and prefixes.

_____G.　Check qualification to act in all states in which property is located. (Applicable only to issues where an interest in real or personal property having a situs in the state is involved and there is no individual trustee.) NOTE: If Florida or Missouri property involved, co-trustee or individual trustee in these states must be designated.

_____H.　Prepare list of supporting documents required for closing and review drafts. (Exhibit 4 and pertinent indenture sections.)

_____I.　Review proofs and specimens of each denomination and check signatures.

_____J.　Prepare instructions to operating section:
1. To receive and examine bonds;
2. To authenticate and deliver bonds and to record total issue authorized by indenture;
3. To record and prepare fully registered bonds after list obtained from underwriters;
4. To make bonds available to underwriters for examination and packaging.

_____K.　Consider necessity of obtaining County Clerk's certificates on notarial acknowledgment.

_____L. Prepare Document Executed Slip(s) covering execution of indenture and, if indicated, any supporting documents.

_____M. Distribution of _____ executed counterparts of indenture:

_____   _____

_____N. Prepare Trustee's Authentication Certificate and appropriate receipts for closing.

_____O. Determine whether certified copies of the Bank's by-laws, signing resolutions or other documents will be required and, if so, obtain them from Office of Secretary.

_____P. Determine disposition of funds (clearing house or federal) to be received at closing and arrange for receipt, clearance and/or deposit or transfer.

_____Q. If new indenture is involved, make sure that appropriate fee arrangements have been made .

_____R. Consider with counsel applicability of Uniform Commercial Code and, if indicated, arrange for completing and filing of financing statement promptly after closing.

II. *At Closing*

_____A. Obtain all supporting documents.

_____B. If collateral is to be pledged, ascertain that it is in negotiable form and that trustee holds title thereto.
1. Open account in trust department.
2. Prepare instructions covering statements and disposition of income.
3. Control collateral and prepare deposit instructions.
4. Ticklerize maturity of obligations.
5. Consider necessity for reporting income under applicable revenue acts.

_____C. If cash is deposited, open account and prepare instructions covering statements and disposition of income.

_____D. Obtain receipt for bonds from obligor.

III. *After Closing*

_____A. Obtain opinion of counsel covering documents, execution of indenture or supplement and issuance of bonds.

_____B. Prepare memorandum covering attendance and action at closing, and distribute.

_____C. Write to obligor, if necessary, for:
1. Date fiscal year ends if indenture requires knowledge by trustee;
2. Appointment as fiscal agent and withholding agent;
3. Appointment as destruction agent if not specifically covered by indenture;
4. Undertaking pursuant to provisions of indenture conforming to Section 317(b) of Trust Indenture Act if obligor appoints a paying agent other than the trustee;
5. Directions as to charges for exchanges and transfers if not specifically covered by indenture;
6. Preparation of ownership certificates and remittance of tax if company subject to Pennsylvania Corporate Loan Tax;
7. Lost security replacement procedure.

_____D. Determine if issue subject to Original Issue Discount Tax. Make arrangements for filing 1099-OID.

_____E. Prepare following office records:
1. Account summary cards;
2. State of incorporation file and mortgage file;
3. Authorities file;
4. Instruction sheets;

             5. Address book (obligor and co-agents);
             6. Instructions for payment of short interest.

_____F. If there is an individual trustee obtain undated resignation and power of attorney.

_____G. Write prior lien trustees:
1. Send copy of indenture;
2. Call attention to our lien on collateral held by them or restriction of our indenture upon issuance of their bonds, etc;
3. Obtain copy of their mortgages for document file;
4. Send other notices as may be required or as counsel may advise.

_____H. If indenture qualified under Trust Indenture Act enter record date for annual report in conflict file. If indenture subject to Streit Act enter name of obligor in conflict file and write memo for Streit Act file.

_____I. Make sure fee letter has been or is being prepared (unless covered by Item I.Q.).

_____J. Prepare tickler register sheet and cards. Consider sending list to obligor.

_____K. If issue is listed or to be listed, prepare required forms for Stock Exchange (usually at request of obligor).

_____L. In case of supplemental indentures annotate reference copies of original indenture with respect to any modifications.

_____M. Document closing papers.

_____N. Obtain sufficient supply of conformed copies of indenture.

_____O. Obtain all recorded originals of indenture or evidence of recording or filing of financing statement.
1. Obtain opinion of company's counsel regarding the sufficiency of recording and/or filing and payment of all recording or filing fees.
2. Prepare ledger record showing recording data.
3. File recorded counterparts of indenture in vault.

	Prepared	Checked	Approved
Date_____	By_____	By_____	By_____

5

Issuance of Indenture Securities

SINCE THE WHOLE PURPOSE of the indenture is to provide security for the outstanding securities and to set forth the terms and conditions upon which they can be issued, the proceedings surrounding the authentication and delivery of the indenture securities are among the more important responsibilities of the trustee. Securities can be issued only in accordance with the indenture provisions, and it is the trustee's responsibility to see that the necessary conditions precedent have been fulfilled. Where the trustee receives the documents called for by the indenture, it is entitled to rely thereon and is not required to make an independent examination of the facts certified. If it acts in good faith it will be protected even though it develops that such certificates were false. Where the requisite conditions precedent do not exist and the trustee fails to receive the requisite documents, or where the documents are not in the required form, or where they disclose facts which put the trustee on notice that the requisite conditions precedent do not exist, the trustee may be held liable by the security holders. The measure of liability has been held to be that which would be required to put the security holders in the same position as they would be if the requisite conditions had been performed.

All securities issued under the indenture are required to be authenticated by the trustee. This is accomplished by the trustee's signature to a certificate affixed to each separate bond or debenture. The form of this certificate seldom varies from standard phraseology which is substantially as follows: "This bond is one of the bonds, of the series designated therein, described in the within mentioned indenture." The bond should provide that it will not become valid for any purpose until this certificate has been executed by the trustee.

The basic purpose of the authentication certificate is to enable the trustee to control the amount of the issue and to prevent an overissue. It insures that the obligor corporation cannot sell bonds in excess of the amount authorized. The authentication certificate is not a guaranty nor is it an implied warranty as to the sufficiency of the security or the regularity of the obligor's conduct in issuing bonds. The trustee should be careful that the certificate contains no representation, or it may be held to be under a duty to ascertain the accuracy of the facts represented. For example, a certificate stating that this is a "First Mortgage Sinking Fund Bond" may be held to be a representation by the trustee. While a diligent trustee will to the best of its ability ascertain that all representations made by the obligor are accurate, it is seldom in a position to make an absolute check of all facts, and a representation that it has done so is neither required nor advisable.

FORM AND CONTENT OF SECURITIES

Since the trustee is authorized to authenticate only the securities provided for in the indenture, it is under a duty to see that the securities do conform with the indenture provisions. The indenture will set forth the form and text of the securities authorized, and the trustee should carefully compare the text of the security itself with the text set forth in the indenture. Minor variations in detail are permissible, but each such variation should be noted and reviewed. To avoid possible embarrassment, the trustee should arrange to examine proofs of all securities before they are prepared in final form. As a practical matter, bank note companies which prepare these securities generally require approval by the trustee before they will prepare the final securities. Despite this preliminary check, a final comparison should be made of one bond of each denomination before the securities are released.

Not only should the text be compared but the securities must also be in the form required by the indenture. The various requirements as to form will be set forth in substantial detail and will be designed to comply with stock exchange regulations or with general usage. The New York Stock Exchange has probably the most detailed regulations of any national exchange as to the form of securities; the purpose of which is to guard against duplication or forgery. These requirements are that the border, vignette, denomination or "money" boxes, the promise to pay clause, and certain other standard provisions of the bond be engraved. Variable parts of the text, including those which appear on the reverse side of a corporate fully registered bond, may be lithographed or printed.

Prior to 1963, most corporate debt securities were issued in bearer form as they were the only ones which constituted a good delivery when sold. The indenture usually provided that the holder could have the bond registered as to principal, in which case, it could only be transferred by assignment of the registered holder. It was also customarily provided that bonds could be issued in fully registered form, without coupons, whereby both principal and interest were payable only to a registered holder. As the institutional investors became more important, a number of corporate trustees urged issuers to liberalize exchange provisions to encourage increased holding of large registered pieces by these investors. As the result of such efforts and the cooperation of the underwriters and dealers, as well as the increased awareness on the part of the investing public of the advantages involved, the number of issues sold in fully registered form only has steadily grown each year. During the past few years well over 90 per cent of the new issues marketed have been in such form. (The major exception to this change has involved the sale of debt securities by domestic corporations to non-resident alien investors, the so-called "Eurobond" issues. Because of the reluctance of such investors to hold these debt obligations in registered form, all of these issues have been sold in bearer form, with coupons.)

The indenture will set forth the denominations in which the securities may be issued, and no other denominations are authorized or should be authenticated by the trustee. The customary and recommended practice is to authorize these in $1,000 denominations and any denomination which is a multiple of $1,000.

The tremendous increase in the volume of all registered issues and the greater utilization of machine equipment to process the certificates, as well as the ever present storage problem, dictated the need for the use of the uniform "stock certificate" size (8" by 12"). As discussed before, the substantive provisions of the indenture or summaries of the pertinent provisions are printed on the reverse of the certificates as a continuation of the bond form. The use of certificates with preprinted denominations is also very desirable as well as "blank" or unspecified denomination certificates. In addition to the standard $1,000 denomination certificate, both $5,000 and $10,000 certificates should be prepared for issues in excess of $10 million. For issues in excess of $75 million, a preprinted denomination of $50,000 or $100,000 is also recommended.

For a "good delivery" of certificates of issues which are listed on the New York Stock Exchange, the denomination amount should be engraved in both upper corners of the face of the certificate, the bond number being printed directly below. "Blank" denomination certificates up to $100,000. are also acceptable, provided the numeric amount is macerated on the certificate. Such blank certificates need only have the numeric dollar amount recorded in the upper right corner, the upper left corner being used for the bond number. For unlisted issues, the same requirements are also recommended.[10]

The indenture will also specify the manner in which the bonds are to be executed by the obligor, and the trustee should see that this provision is adhered to strictly. All signatures should appear on the face of the certificate and whenever possible, those of the obligor should be facsimile. The trustee's authentication should never be other than a manual signature, however. The corporate seal on the bond is usually a facsimile, but this also should be specifically authorized by the indenture.

Not only should the trustee compare the text of the bonds of each denomination with that set forth in the indenture, but each individual bond should also be examined by the trustee to see that it is properly signed and sealed; that the text on both face and reverse is complete (to guard against a mechanical printing failure); that the bonds are numbered consecutively; and that the aggregate amount of bonds so executed is the amount authorized to be authenticated.

It is the trustee's responsibility to control the amount of bonds authenticated and delivered, and appropriate records should be set

[10] For specific recommendations on certificate format and paper quality standards, see "Recommended Certificate Standards For Registered Bond Issues" Corporate Trust Activities Committee, American Bankers Association (1974).

up so that this can be done. A proper notation should be made of each bond received, authenticated, delivered, cancelled, or otherwise dealt with by the trustee so that it will be in a position to certify the bonds outstanding at any time.

DISPOSITION OF BOND PROCEEDS

In the absence of express provisions in the indenture, the trustee is under no duty to see to the application of the proceeds of bonds, and the indenture will usually so provide. There have been a few cases where courts have found an implied duty even in the face of an express provision to the contrary. These cases have all involved situations where a specific use was set forth and the facts indicated that the trustee had actual knowledge of misapplication.

Generally, where the indenture provides for proceeds of bonds to be applied to a specific purpose, it should require the furnishing of appropriate evidence to the trustee of such application. In such cases the trustee should be authorized to retain possession of the bond proceeds and disburse them as required upon receipt of proper certificates. A typical example would be where the bond issue is authorized for construction of a specific project. In the case of a newly formed corporation which has no substantial property, or where the proposed expenditure is substantial in relation to the net worth of the company, such protective provisions are essential, and a trustee should not accept an appointment unless they are included. In the normal case, however, where all conditions precedent to the authentication and delivery of bonds have been fulfilled, the trustee should not concern itself as to the actual use made of the specific proceeds.

TYPICAL PROVISIONS GOVERNING THE ISSUANCE
OF BONDS

The indenture must set forth specifically the terms and conditions pursuant to which the indenture securities may be issued. The usual debenture or note agreement providing for the issuance of unsecured obligations will provide for issuance of all authorized securities initially, so that each issue of such obligations will be covered by a separate agreement or indenture. This is not always the case, however, and it is perfectly proper for such an indenture to provide for the creation and issuance of additional series of obligations, provided that such obligations are of the same class. The conditions precedent to the issuance of additional obligations under such an agreement will usually be the existence of no default, and if the indenture requires maintenance of specified financial ratios, such required ratios must exist after the additional obligations have been issued.

As distinguished from a debenture or note agreement, the usual bond indenture is open end, and is designed to provide not only for the current financing, but also for all future bond financing of the corporation. The reasons for this are obvious. Not only would the creation of a separate indenture for each financing be expensive, but use of a single mortgage indenture is the only way in which secured obligations, ranking *pari passu*, can be issued from time to time over a period of years. Since a first mortgage obligation will normally command a better price and be more readily marketable than one having a junior lien position, it is desirable to provide a vehicle under which senior securities can continue to be issued.

Such an indenture will set forth the detailed provisions of the first series of bonds to be issued and will provide the manner in which the terms and provisions of later series are to be established. This is done either by a resolution of the board of directors of the corporation or by a supplemental indenture, or usually by both, since such supplement must be approved by the board. It is recommended that a supplemental indenture always be used. Recording of the original indenture will give public notice only of the initial series of bonds. While the lien created will probably be effective until specifically discharged, it is desirable that public notice of additional debt secured be given, particularly if the maturity date of the later series extends beyond that of the initial series. Such notice will be given by the proper execution and recording of a supplemental indenture.

The indenture will authorize the authentication and delivery of a specified principal amount of bonds initially. These bonds will usually be authorized to be authenticated and delivered upon request of specified officers of the corporation, without compliance by the corporation with any other conditions other than execution and delivery of the indenture and the furnishing of the requisite documents and authorities to support such execution and delivery.

Additional issuance can be secured, however, only after specified conditions have been met. Bondholders contract for specific security coverage for their obligations as a condition to the extension of credit. Each additional creation of debt, ranking equally with that outstanding, will automatically deplete the security interest of each bondholder in the property existing at that time. The purpose of the detailed provisions governing the creation of additional indebtedness is to insure that such security interest is not reduced proportionately (as related to the aggregate value of the property) below the minimum contracted for in the indenture. This is the basic concept which the trustee should have in mind in reviewing these sections of every proposed secured indenture.

No attempt will be made to describe every purpose for which additional bonds might be authorized. The more common and customary purposes will be described briefly.

(1) To provide funds for the construction of property additions or to reimburse the company for expenditures made in such construction.

Property additions should always be specifically defined, but they normally include any type of property which is properly includable in the company's fixed property accounts in accordance with accepted accounting practices. All property owned by the corporation at the date of the indenture (or frequently as of the end of the fiscal period next preceding or next succeeding such date) is regarded as "funded" and is not available for use as a basis for the issuance of additional bonds or for any other purpose under the indenture. Property acquired after such date can be so used. Under an after-acquired property clause, such property becomes subject to the lien of the indenture as acquired but remains "unfunded" until it has been used for a specific purpose under the indenture, at which time its character changes to that of being funded.

An active corporation is almost continuously adding property and retiring property that has become worn out or obsolete. In order that the proper security may be maintained, only "net property additions" should be taken into account when considering the amount of property that can be bonded (i.e., used to support the issuance of additional bonds). At times the computations to determine this become quite involved, as frequently other indenture provisions and the use of property thereunder have to be taken into account. The general purport, however, is to take the gross amount of all unfunded property additions and deduct therefrom the book value of all property retired to determine net property additions. The value at which the gross property additions may be taken into the account is the lesser of the cost to the company, or the fair value as of the date of the certification.

When the net value of property additions has been determined, it is then necessary to compute the amount of bonds which can be issued on the basis thereof. Rarely are companies permitted to issue bonds to the full value of such property. The importance of the debt ratio has been previously mentioned, and bondholders should always insist on a reasonable margin of security. A frequent percentage found in current utility mortgages, for example, is 60 per cent, which means that for each $1,000 of net value added to the fixed property account, a maximum of $600 of additional secured indebtedness is permitted.

(2) To retire prior lien obligations. Where prior liens exist on all or any part of the property mortgaged, provision should always be made for their retirement. Even though no such liens exist at the time of the creation of the indenture, consideration should be given to this problem, as additional property is often acquired which is subject to a lien at the time of acquisition. If such additional property is used as a basis for the issuance of bonds, the amount of the prior lien should first be deducted from the *bondable* value of the property. It is then appropriate to permit refunding of the prior lien by the issuance of additional bonds under the indenture.

This is one of the situations in which the trustee is responsible for the proper application of bond proceeds. A frequent requirement is the surrender to the trustee of the prior lien obligations as a condition for the issuance of the bonds. Such is usually the case where the prior lien is only partially retired, and quite often the prior lien obligations are required to be held alive by the trustee. The desirability of such a provision is questionable, as it is unlikely that the trustee could claim a position *pari passu* with the remaining holders of prior lien obligations to the extent of such obligations held by it. A certificate of the prior lien trustee as to cancellation of a specified amount of prior lien obligations would seem to afford the same protection as the delivery thereof to the trustee, and an indenture provision to this effect should be acceptable.

Where the prior lien is to be retired in whole, the trustee should be protected in paying over the proceeds to the prior lien trustee or to the company if it receives a duly executed and recorded counterpart of the satisfaction of the prior lien obligation.

(3) Refunding of outstanding indenture securities. This is obviously a proper purpose, as it results in the mere substitution of one indenture obligation for another. Where bonds are acquired by the obligor company by purchase or otherwise, their surrender to the trustee for cancellation is a sufficient basis for the authentication and delivery of an equivalent amount of bonds of another series. Where a preceding series is to be redeemed in whole or in part, it is sufficient if the trustee holds in trust funds sufficient to effect such redemption and is authorized to take the necessary steps required. Any premium or interest payable on the redemption must be supplied separately by the obligor.

Frequently, previously issued bonds will be retired or redeemed without the concurrent issuance of additional bonds, but the obligor will wish to reserve the right to issue bonds on the basis of such retirement. This is perfectly proper, and it is unnecessary to require that such previously issued bonds be held alive in the company's treasury in order to preserve this right.

Bonds retired through operation of a sinking fund or similar provisions normally should not be permitted to be made the basis for the issuance of additional bonds under the indenture. This would result in an indirect depletion of the bondholders' security.

(4) Issuance of bonds against deposit of cash. A common indenture provision permits the issuance of bonds against the deposit with the trustee of an equivalent amount of cash. The cash so deposited is subject to withdrawal upon the company's establishing its right to the authentication and delivery of an equivalent amount of bonds under other provisions of the indenture. Each separate bond financing is expensive. Where a company contemplates a substantial expansion program or where such a program and a refunding may be under consideration, it may take down its estimated total requirements through one issue against deposit of cash with the trustee. As property additions are completed, it makes the necessary certifications to the trustee and withdraws cash in an amount equal to the principal amount of bonds it could issue on the basis of such property. The net result is the same. This is a frequently used provision, although it is also common for corporations to resort to interim bank financing to finance construction programs, deferring permanent bond financing until the program is substantially completed. This practice tends to reduce interest

costs. Bond financing rather than interim bank credit might be more advantageous during a period of a favorable bond market with low interest rates.

One final point should be noted. Should a default occur after bonds have been issued under such a provision and before the cash is withdrawn, such cash is part of the general trust estate securing all bonds outstanding, and cannot be set apart for the benefit of the holders of the specific series issued against its deposit. In the absence of express and specific provisions to the contrary, all indenture securities are on a parity as to their claims against the trust estate and the obligor.

EVIDENCE REQUIRED BY TRUSTEE AS TO
COMPLIANCE WITH CONDITIONS PRECEDENT

The indenture will specify the particular documents to be delivered to the trustee to establish the company's right to the authentication and delivery of the bonds requested. The trustee is under a duty to examine all such documents carefully to see that they establish compliance with all conditions precedent, and it must also make sure that the documents are in the form required by the indenture. Because of the importance of these transactions, the trustee should always have such documents reviewed by counsel.

The documents received will be determined by the particular purpose for which the bonds are to be issued. Three documents should be received in all cases, however. These include: a resolution of the board of directors of the company authorizing the issuance of the bonds, setting forth the purpose for which they are to be issued, directing the execution of the bonds by specified officers, providing for execution and delivery of necessary documents to the trustee, and requesting authentication and delivery of the bonds by the trustee. The trustee should also receive a certificate executed by authorized officers of the company to the effect that there is no default under the indenture and that all conditions precedent to the authentication and delivery of the bonds requested have been performed. This should be accompanied by an opinion of counsel that all such conditions precedent have been fulfilled.

Where authentication and delivery of bonds is on the basis of property additions, these property additions should be certified to the trustee in sufficient detail by authorized officers to enable their identification. Such certification should also include an appropriate computation of the net bondable value of such property to establish the company's right to the issuance of the bonds requested. The certificate should be accompanied by a separate certificate of an engineer, appraiser, or other expert as to the value of the property additions. Under certain circumstances such engineer's certificate must be executed by an independent engineer or appraiser not under the obligor's control.

Frequently, an earnings requirement is included as a condition precedent. The customary form of such a condition is that for a specified period, the net earnings of the company available for interest (or the average earnings if the period is in excess of a year) must be so many times the interest charges on all indebtedness including the bonds to be issued. Compliance with this condition should be established by an accountant's certificate, which under certain conditions must be a certificate of an independent public accountant.

Where property additions are made the basis for the issuance of bonds, the trustee should receive an opinion of counsel as to the instruments of conveyance required to subject such property to the lien of the indenture, or assurance that no such instruments are necessary. As previously indicated, if the bonds to be issued are a new series, a supplemental indenture is desirable. A specific conveyance of the property is customarily included in the same supplement.

In the event that authorization of any regulatory agency or public body is required, evidence of such authorization should be secured. If the bonds are to be issued publicly, registration requirements under the securities act must be completed, including the filing of a new Form T-1.

In addition to the documents specifically required by the pertinent indenture provisions, the trustee should receive all the documents outlined in Exhibit 4 or have such documents brought up-to-date.

For the convenience of the administrator, it is helpful to use a guide sheet for each new issue of securities, as outlined in Exhibit 5. This guide sheet calls attention to the various matters that should be considered, or actions to be taken, and when completed can be added to the bond issue documents for historical reference.

6

Sinking Fund and Maintenance Provisions

A COMMON TYPE of covenant found in indentures is the sinking fund provision. This is a device for amortization of the debt, or a part thereof, over the life of the issue and, being essentially a security provision, is most important. It is almost always found in an unsecured debenture or note agreement, but is also quite common to bond indentures. If an issue is created for the construction or purchase of certain fixed property or facilities, the holders' security will tend to be depleted unless the amount of the debt is reduced proportionately to the depreciation or loss in value of the property as it is used in the business. One of the frequent uses for cash generated by the depreciation charge is reduction of debt incurred to purchase the property. Even though unrelated to specific property or security, a sinking fund is a convenient device for reducing corporate funded debt.

In mortgage indentures, particularly those of utility and railroad corporations, a maintenance covenant is frequently included in lieu of, and sometimes in addition to, a sinking fund provision. The type of covenant referred to is not the simple maintenance covenant which constitutes an undertaking by the obligor to keep the mortgaged property in good working order and condition, which should be in all mortgage indentures, but is more in the nature of an undertaking to expend a stated amount of money for renewal and replacement of the property. The theory of such a covenant is that, in lieu of retiring debt as the value of the property depreciates, the company will maintain the security by expending an equivalent amount for the construction or acquisition of additional property.

The operation and purpose of these covenants can be illustrated by a simple example. Let us suppose that a corporation acquires a new plant for $25,000,000 with an estimated productive economic life of twenty-five years. For convenience it will be assumed that the value will depreciate on a level basis, or at the rate of $1,000,000 per year. The plant is financed with $10,000,000 of equity money and $15,000,000 of bonds, secured by a mortgage on the property. It is obvious that for the bondholders to maintain their margin of security, $600,000 in bonds would have to be retired each year. This would be done through operation of a sinking fund. An alternate method would be for the company to maintain the security at $25,000,000. This could be done by mortgaging entirely new facilities, by additions to the existing plant, or by the replacement of portions of the plant as they become old or worn out. Such an alternate undertaking would be set forth in a maintenance or a renewal and replacement covenant.

THE SINKING FUND COVENANT

A sinking fund covenant may take any of a different number of forms, and the exact terms included will result from the negotiations leading up to the issue. Some indentures will not contain a sinking fund, although investors are coming more and more to insist upon the inclusion of an orderly procedure for retirement of debt. This is particularly true in the case of the unsecured debenture or note issue, and it is now very rare for an agreement of this kind not to include a sinking fund. An alternate method would be to provide for the securities issued to mature serially—that is, so many each year—rather than have all come due at the same time. Serial issues are common in the case of state and municipal bonds. Purchasers of corporate bonds, however, prefer term bonds with a sinking fund rather than serial maturities and, consequently, the latter are not often found in issues of industrial companies.

The trustee has substantial duties and responsibilities for the proper operation of the sinking fund. The indenture provisions should receive its careful attention during the drafting of the indenture and in connection with each sinking fund operation since, if it misapplies the funds it may incur substantial liability. This may be true even though the funds are applied to retirement of indenture securities if they are used otherwise than is required by the indenture.

Method of Computation

A sinking fund may be required to operate annually, semi-annually, or even at more frequent intervals. Since each separate operation may be quite expensive, it is inadvisable to provide for a separate operation more frequently than is required to carry out the basic purpose of the contract. There are many different ways in which computation of each sinking fund payment might be made, and there is no particular preference or advantage for one method over another, the one selected being the one best suited to obtain the desired result. (See Exhibit 7 for Check Sheet.)

The more commonly used methods are: (1) payment of a fixed dollar amount; (2) payment of an amount calculated as a percentage of the maximum amount of securities which have been at any time authenticated and outstanding; or (3) payment of an amount sufficient to retire a fixed percentage of such bonds. The latter might be a preferred method in any case where a redemption premium on a declining scale is involved in any sinking fund operation, as it insures retirement of a level rather than a variable amount of bonds.

While most sinking funds are fixed in some definite amount or according to a specified formula, a variable sinking fund is often used. Such a sinking fund might be measured by a percentage of net earnings, either of the total earnings of the company or from a specified source. There might also be a combination of several factors; for example, a minimum fixed sinking fund might be provided, to which was to be added a percentage of net earnings over a specified amount. This type might be particularly desirable in the case of a company whose earnings tend to fluctuate substantially with cyclical changes in the economy, insuring excess retirement of debt during good years and providing some measure of protection in other years.

It is also common for the amount of the fixed sinking fund payment to vary from year to year. Provision might be made for retirement of a smaller percentage of bonds during the earlier years and an increasing percentage during later years. This method is almost always used where the principal security is a lease or contract obligation. Level amortization payments are provided to cover both interest and sinking fund. The amount required for interest decreases with each payment, leaving a greater amount available for retirement of principal.

Where several series of bonds are outstanding under the same indenture, different procedures may be followed. A separate sinking fund may be created for each series and a number of separate payments will be made, either at the same or different times, and each will involve an entirely separate operation related to the securities of the particular series involved. On the other hand, a single sinking fund may be set up which can be applied to the bonds of any or all series. The only change taking place when a new series is created is that the amount of each such sinking fund is usually increased.

Where a single sinking fund payment is made for bonds of different series having different interest rates and maturity dates, the trustee should exercise special care in the application of such monies and should always endeavor to see that the indenture spells out the exact procedure to be followed. The usual provision requires the retirement of bonds which, computed on the basis of the price to be paid, provide the highest yield to maturity. Such application is the most advantageous to the obligor company and results in the greatest reduction in annual fixed charges, and in that way might be said to be the most beneficial to the trust estate. While the usual effect is to eliminate certain series of bonds from any participation in the sinking fund, and so might be said to be unfair in this respect, it should be borne in mind that it is part of their contract and, theoretically at least, the holders of such series could have bargained for a separate sinking fund allocable to their series of bonds had they so desired.

The trustee should make certain that the indenture is clear as to how the interest and premium (if any) required to be paid in connection with any sinking fund retirement are to be provided. It may be evident from the manner in which the sinking fund is computed, but if such is not the case, language should be included specifying whether the company is to provide these amounts separately or whether they are chargeable against the sinking fund.

Since bonds can usually be retired through operation of a sinking fund without premium, or at a lower premium than for optional redemption, the obligor company has no right to increase the amount of a sinking fund or to anticipate sinking fund payments unless such right is specifically reserved. If the indenture includes such reservation, there should also be no doubt as to whether or not the obligor is entitled to a credit against subsequent sinking fund payments of any amounts so anticipated or paid beyond normal requirements.

Method of Application of Sinking Fund Monies

The trustee should insure that the method for application of sinking fund monies is clearly set forth in the indenture and, if alternate methods are provided, the order in which such alternate methods are to be used or the conditions which determine selection of the particular method.

Once specific bonds have been selected for purchase or redemption by the sinking fund, and all steps necessary to effect the purchase or redemption taken except the actual surrender of the bonds, the funds in the hands of the trustee cease to be general trust estate funds and become specifically allocated to the particular bond or bonds so selected. In the event of a subsequent default, the holder is entitled to payment upon surrender of his bond, regardless of what may be realized by other indenture security holders.

A more difficult problem is presented, however, where a default occurs before there has been any application of such monies or before all steps necessary for the retirement of specific bonds have been concluded. The problem is complicated further if the sinking fund payment was made with respect to a particular series of bonds, or if the trustee has selected specific bonds for retirement but has not mailed the notice of redemption.

The law applicable to such a situation is not clear, and the trustee's action should be guided by counsel. As a general rule it is suggested that all further action be suspended, that any preliminary steps which may have been taken be revoked, and that the funds be retained by the trustee without application until the default has been cured or waived or until the trustee receives judicial direction as to disposition of the funds. Even where only one series of bonds is involved, application of funds to retirement of specific bonds with knowledge of a default might involve participation by the trustee in an unlawful preference for which it might be held liable. Aside from the question of the trustee's liability, such an application would be obviously unfair if, as a result of the default, the remaining security holders received less than their full claim.

The obligor company is frequently given the right to receive credit against its sinking fund obligation for any bonds which it surrenders to the trustee for cancellation.[11] This enables the obligor company to acquire bonds throughout the year in the open market, taking advantage of favorable market conditions; and some companies satisfy their entire sinking fund obligations continuously in this manner. The amount of the credit which the company receives for bonds so surrendered may be the par value of the bonds, or the actual cost of the bonds to the company not in excess of the par value or current sinking fund redemption price, if more than par.

In the absence of a specific right to surrender bonds against credit or in lieu of a sinking fund payment, a question arises as to the trustee's right to acquire or purchase bonds held by the obligor company in its treasury in applying sinking fund monies. It is preferable to have such right specifically set forth, although it is followed as a more or less accepted practice and, in the absence of an express prohibition, would seem to be entirely in order. Care should be used, however, that any such acquisition is at or below the price at which equivalent bonds could be obtained by purchase from other holders.

The trustee may be directed to apply sinking fund monies to the purchase of bonds in the open market at a price not in excess of the current redemption price. If the bonds are noncallable, a more or less arbitrary price is fixed by the indenture. Interest and commission paid on such purchases are usually, although not necessarily, separately reimbursed by the obligor. If not, then such amounts should be considered in computing the maximum price which can be offered. A time limit is customarily set for this method of operation and, if the funds cannot be exhausted within such time, a different method must be followed as to the remaining funds.

Another method of operation is for the trustee to invite tenders of bonds. This is regarded by some as a fairer method of operation, although it usually results in payment of a higher average price than would be the case in an open-market operation. Where the current market price is in excess of the maximum price at which tenders can be accepted (which is usually the sinking fund redemption price), an invitation for tenders is a more or less idle gesture and, where the

---

[11] Debentures which have been converted may also be used to partially or fully satisfy a sinking fund requirement.

trustee has discretion as to the method to be followed, this fact should be considered.

The procedure to be followed in the case of an invitation of tenders is relatively simple but it still requires the exercise of care. A date is selected for the submission of tenders, with both the hour as well as the day specified. The invitation is then mailed in accordance with indenture provisions to all registered holders of securities. (If bearer bonds are outstanding, the notice must be published and copies mailed to all holders who may have filed their names with the trustee for the purpose of receiving reports and notices.) It is desirable to request submission of sealed tenders, and all other conditions should be clearly set forth in the notice. The right to reject tenders in whole or in part should always be specifically reserved. To avoid error it is recommended that some form of dual control be established for all tenders received. As they are received, a record of receipt should be made and the tenders deposited in a locked container. If any are received unsealed, they should be examined to see that all necessary information is included and then immediately sealed and deposited. No record of prices should be made and, until the tenders have been opened and examined at the appointed time, no information should be disclosed to anyone, including the obligor company.

As soon as the hour set has arrived, the tenders should be opened, examined, and listed and a recapitulation made in the order of the prices at which bonds are offered. In the case of different issues with different interest rates and maturity dates, price should be computed on the basis of yield to maturity, the higher the yield the lower the price. Sufficient bonds should then be accepted at the lowest prices offered to exhaust the monies available. Mailing of notice of acceptance completes the contract.

A final method of operation is through selection of bonds for redemption through operation of the redemption provisions of the indenture. Bonds are usually redeemable at par for the purpose of the sinking fund, or at prices less than would be required in the case of an optional redemption. Selection of the particular bonds to be redeemed will be made as set forth in the indenture, and it is customary for such selection to be made by the trustee. In drafting such provisions it is desirable for the trustee to retain flexibility, and it is much better to have a provision for such selection made in such manner as the trustee shall deem equitable than to have the mechanics spelled out in detail. Once the particular bonds to be redeemed have been selected, the trustee arranges to mail an appropriate notice in the manner prescribed by the indenture.[12] Once the notice has been mailed, the designated bonds become due and payable on the date specified, and the necessary funds should be segregated by the trustee and held in a trust specifically allocated to their payment.

In the case of direct placements where all securities are held by institutional investors it is customary to provide that in lieu of application by lot, sinking fund monies proportionate to their holdings must be allocated among the owners. Care must be exercised both in drafting and administering the provision, the objective being for each holder to retain his proportional percentage of the debt obligations as nearly as may be possible. Normally, bonds must be retired in even multiples of $1,000, and no problem is presented where application of the sinking fund percentage to each separate holding would result in an even multiple of $1,000. This seldom happens, however, and it is necessary for the trustee to devise an appropriate formula for such operation. No particular formula is required so long as the same formula is applied consistently year after year and produces the desired allocation. Exhibit 6 describes a typical formula and illustrates the application thereof.

Bonds retired through the sinking fund are usually cancelled by the trustee and cannot be reissued or used by the obligor as a credit under any other indenture provision.

MAINTENANCE AND REPLACEMENT COVENANTS

As indicated previously, a maintenance and replacement covenant is sometimes used in lieu of, or in addition to, a sinking fund. This is more common in the case of a regulated company, such as an electric utility, which requires a more or less continuous supply of funds for capital purposes and for which a somewhat higher debt ratio is permissible. The fund established pursuant to such a covenant is more properly a renewal and replacement than a maintenance fund. Every corporation is expected to provide funds for normal maintenance of its properties, and these constitute expenses chargeable to its income account. The fund under consideration here is a capital fund and the expenditures therefrom are normally chargeable to fixed property accounts.

---

[12] If bonds are outstanding in bearer form, an appropriate notice must also be published.

There is no fixed formula by which the amount of such a fund is to be computed, and it will tend to vary with the type of company involved, the nature of its properties, and other considerations. In the case of regulated companies, the regulatory authority may require application of a particular formula, or it may otherwise be determined as part of the negotiations relating to the drafting of the indenture. Ordinarily, it should be closely related to the amount of the company's annual depreciation charges, and in any event should be designed to provide such amount as will enable the company to preserve the value of the property securing its outstanding bonds.

As an illustration, a more or less arbitrary rule of thumb was at one time applied to electric utility operating companies. It was developed that, as a general average, the investment of four dollars in fixed plant was required to produce one dollar of gross annual revenue. Also, as a general average, application to the entire property account of the amounts resulting from the application of required depreciation percentages to specified classes of property, indicated an annual average depreciation charge of 3¾ per cent. By use of these figures, a covenant to expend 15 per cent of annual gross revenues from operations for maintenance and replacement

EXHIBIT   6. ILLUSTRATION OF ALLOCATION FORMULA FOR
PRO-RATA REDEMPTION

Objective: To select bonds for redemption in even multiples of $1,000 from all holders in such manner that all holders retain same proportion of outstanding bonds as nearly as possible.

Procedure: Prepare chart on which is listed for each outstanding registered holder (if more than one bond is registered in same name determine if allocation is to be made separately for each bond or if holdings are to be considered in aggregate):

COLUMN A—The *original* principal amount.

COLUMN B—The *present* principal amount outstanding.

COLUMN C—The principal amount which *should be* outstanding after exact percentage allocation of all redemption payments including the present. This is determined by multi-

plying amounts in Column A by a percentage determined as follows:

$$\frac{\text{Sum of Column B} - \text{Current redemption payment}}{\text{Sum of Column A}}$$

COLUMN D—Exact *pro rata* allocation for each holding, determined by subtracting Column C from Column B.

COLUMN E—Adjusted to provide current *pro rata* redemption in terms of $1,000 and integral multiples for each holding.

Application of this formula may be illustrated by considering a $10,000,000 issue originally sold to ten holders. The indenture provides for an annual sinking fund computed on the basis of three per cent of the original amount for the first two years and four per cent for the third year. Allocation of the sinking fund payments for the first three years would be as follows:

First Year

BOND NUMBER	COLUMN A original P/A outstanding	COLUMN B present P/A outstanding	COLUMN C 97% of Col. A	COLUMN D Col. B minus Col. C	COLUMN E pro rata redemption
1	$3,500,000	$3,500,000	$3,395,000	$105,000	$105,000
2	1,800,000	1,800,000	1,746,000	54,000	54,000
3	1,250,000	1,250,000	1,212,500	37,500	38,000
4	950,000	950,000	921,500	28,500	29,000
5	878,000	878,000	851,660	26,340	26,000
6	720,000	720,000	698,400	21,600	22,000
7	540,000	540,000	523,800	16,200	16,000
8	175,000	175,000	169,750	5,250	5,000
9	140,000	140,000	135,800	4,200	4,000
10	47,000	47,000	45,590	1,410	1,000
	$10,000,000	$10,000,000	$9,700,000	$300,000	$300,000

Second Year

BOND NUMBER	COLUMN A	COLUMN B	COLUMN C 94% of Col. A	COLUMN D	COLUMN E
1	$3,500,000	$3,395,000	$3,290,000	$105,000	$105,000
2	1,800,000	1,746,000	1,692,000	54,000	54,000
3	1,250,000	1,212,000	1,175,000	37,000	37,000
4	950,000	921,000	893,000	28,000	28,000
5	878,000	852,000	825,320	26,680	27,000
6	720,000	698,000	676,800	21,200	21,000
7	540,000	524,000	507,600	16,400	16,000
8	175,000	170,000	164,500	5,500	6,000
9	140,000	136,000	131,600	4,400	4,000
10	47,000	46,000	44,180	1,820	2,000
	$10,000,000	$9,700,000	9,400,000	$300,000	$300,000

Third Year

BOND NUMBER	COLUMN A	COLUMN B	COLUMN C 90% of Col. A	COLUMN D	COLUMN E
1	$3,500,000	$3,290,000	$3,150,000	$140,000	$140,000
2	1,800,000	1,692,000	1,620,000	72,000	72,000
3	1,250,000	1,175,000	1,125,000	50,000	50,000
4	950,000	893,000	855,000	38,000	38,000
5	878,000	825,000	790,200	34,800	35,000
6	720,000	677,000	648,000	29,000	29,000
7	540,000	508,000	486,000	22,000	22,000
8	175,000	164,000	157,500	6,500	6,000
9	—[1]	—	—	—	—
10	47,000	44,000	42,300	1,700	2,000
11	105,000[2]	99,000[1]	94,500	4,500	[3]5,000
12	35,000[2]	33,000[1]	31,500	1,500	1,000
	$10,000,000	$9,400,000	$9,000,000	$400,000	$400,000

[1] Bond Number 9 for $132,000 (original $140,000) cancelled and new bonds 11 and 12 issued for $99,000 and $33,000, respectively.
[2] Seventy-five per cent and 25% of $140,000.
[3] Determined by lot.

purposes was frequently used in indentures of these companies. This percentage might be varied in particular cases where the character of a company's property differed substantially from the norm. More recent indentures have tended to pattern the covenant to fit the circumstances of the particular company rather than to follow a pre-established pattern, but the above illustrates the manner in which these percentages may be computed and the purpose of the provision.

The indenture will require annual filing with the trustee of a certificate in sufficient detail to show compliance with the covenant. All computations should be shown, and the trustee should check them carefully. To the extent possible, it should also check the data included against the financial statements and other data which it may receive.

All property acquired by the company and certified to the trustee in compliance with this covenant becomes funded property and cannot be used as a basis for the issuance of bonds or for other purposes. Accordingly, the trustee should receive all of the supplemental documents with respect to such property as it would receive were the property being used as a basis for the issuance of bonds. Such documents would include engineer's certificates as to value, an opinion of counsel as to the company's title to the property and as to the lien of the indenture thereon, and such instruments of specific conveyance as might be required.

As distinguished from the case of the issuance of bonds, property additions can be taken under this covenant at 100 per cent rather than at the bondable percentage of their value. On the other hand, if any of such property is subject to a prior lien, it is necessary to deduct an amount equivalent to the bondable property value of such prior lien. For example, if the bondable percentage of property additions under the indenture were 60 per cent, in such a computation 166⅔ per cent of any prior lien bonds would be deducted.

It is customary to combine the normal maintenance covenant with such a renewal and replacement covenant and to allow the obligor to take expenditures for normal repairs and maintenance as a credit. It is also necessary, as in the case of the issuance of bonds, to deduct the book value of property retirements from the gross property expenditures in order to determine the net credit to be allowed.

One of the difficult administrative problems is in dealing with property certificates under a number of different indenture provisions. While the value of a particular addition can be used only once, the value of the addition may be in excess of the amount certified for a particular purpose and the excess can be used for another purpose. Similarly, it is necessary that deduction for property retirements or prior liens be made only once. The certificates should be so drawn as to enable the trustee to check these facts.

Where during any particular year the obligor expends more than the required percentage for maintenance and replacement, it is normally allowed a credit for such excess against the requirement of subsequent years. This credit may be unlimited in that it can be taken at any time, or it may be required to be used within a specified time. If the latter is the case, a further word of caution is necessary. If, for example, the use of such a credit is limited to the three succeeding years and the company has excess expenditures for four successive years, the amount of the credit for the first of the four years is no longer available. This would seem to be obvious, except that the certificates may be so drawn as to indicate that in each year the company first uses the credit for the preceding year, and that the resulting larger credit for the current year is allocable to that year and not to both years. The result may be to carry forward indefinitely a substantial credit which should have lapsed.

If the computation indicates that the company has not expended the required percentage during the year, a deficit for the year is indicated. This deficit may be offset by the amount of any credit which the company was entitled to carry forward from previous years. To the extent not so offset, the obligor must deposit cash or bonds with the trustee. These may be subsequently withdrawn against certification of property additions or on the basis of a credit shown in a subsequent maintenance certificate. If the company desires, any bonds so deposited may be cancelled as a credit against the maintenance requirements. The bonds so cancelled have the same status as sinking fund bonds and cannot be reissued or used as a basis for any other action under the indenture.

EXHIBIT   7. SINKING FUND REQUIREMENTS CHECK SHEET
SINKING FUND REQUIREMENTS CHECK SHEET

1. Account: _____
2. Issue: _____
3. Sinking Fund Requirement: _____
4. Due Date: _____

A. RECEIPT OF BONDS FROM OBLIGOR
    1. *Instruct operations section to receive:*
        a. Principal amount;
        b. Coupons to be attached, if any;
        c. Bonds to be cancelled or held alive;
        d. If held alive, consider registration or disposition of future maturing coupons;
        e. If cancelled, their deposition.
B. APPLICATION OF CASH
    1. *Purchase of bonds in open market:*
        a. Instruct purchasing agent (bond department) on
            (1) Amount available;
            (2) Maximum price payable;
        b. Consider source of funds for interest and brokerage;
        c. Upon receipt of purchase orders instruct operations section:
            (1) To receive and pay bonds purchased,
            (2) On disposition of bonds.
    2. *Invitation for tenders:*
        a. Select date to close tenders (hour and day), dates of mailing of notice;
        b. Prepare notice;
        c. Clear form of notice and dates with obligor;
        d. Arrange for mailing to all registered holders, stock exchanges and clearing house banks and any co-agents;
        e. Prepare affidavit of mailing and send copy to obligor;
        f. Send memorandum to incoming mail division and to all reception desks;
        g. Consider source of funds to cover accrued interest;
        h. Receive and process tenders;
        i. Mail acceptance and rejection letters;
        j. Prepare report of tenders accepted for obligor and document file;
        k. Instruct operations section:
            (1) To receive and pay bonds accepted;
            (2) On disposition of bonds.
    3. *Call for redemption:*
        a. Determine principal amount of bonds to be called and select dates for drawing, mailing of notice, and redemption;
        b. If listed on Stock Exchange, send letter (at least 10 days prior to books closing) to Dept. of Stock List indicating amount of call and opening and closing dates for books with copy to appropriate Depository;
        c. If *pro rata* allocation required, secure lists of registered holders and make allocation in accordance with appropriate formula;
        d. If selection by lot required, instruct operations section to make drawing;
        e. Secure affidavit of drawing with lists of bond numbers;
        f. Prepare redemption notice and arrange for mailing to all registered

holders, stock exchanges and clearing house banks and any co-agents;

g. Compare proof of notice with list attached to affidavit;
h. Secure affidavit of mailing and send copy to obligor;
i. Consider source of funds to cover accrued interest and premium, if any;
j. If redemption date is interest date, pay registered interest separately;
k. Instruct operations section as to acceptance, payment, and disposition of called bonds;
l. Instruct co-paying agent, if any. Include report of stop payment orders on any called bonds;
m. Transfer funds to appropriate redemption account;
n. Prepare pending card to follow-up unpresented bonds after 1 month.

DATED____COMPLETED: ____CHECKED: ____APPROVED:____

7

Release and Substitution of Property

ANOTHER MAJOR SEGMENT of the indenture contract dealing with maintenance and preservation of the bondholders' security is the section dealing with the release and substitution of property. These provisions, of course, are not pertinent to the unsecured debenture or note agreement, but in almost every case where specific property is mortgaged to or pledged with the trustee, the indenture contains detailed provisions as to how the obligor may deal with its properties and prescribes conditions for the release and substitution of specific properties on which the indenture is a lien.

The necessity for and importance of these sections become clear when one considers that in the usual case the real security is the business of the obligor company as a going concern and not the aggregate of the individual parcels of property. It is now customary for mortgage indentures to continue for an indefinite period, and the needs of the mortgagor company will be likely to change considerably during the period. Also, many parts of the original property will become worn out and unfit for use in the company's business. The primary purpose of the release provisions is to enable the obligor to dispose of such obsolete and unproductive properties, free from the lien of the indenture, and to use the proceeds to acquire additional properties or improvements necessary or useful in its business operations. As it is desirable to provide as carefully as possible for almost every contingency, the release provisions cannot be limited to mere disposition of worn out or obsolete properties, and usually cover any property that the obligor may sell or otherwise dispose of.

114

Since the trustee's primary responsibilities revolve around the preservation of the bondholders' security, the duties discussed in this and the two preceding chapters might be regarded as the tripartite base on which most of the predefault administrative provisions of a secured indenture are founded. The sections dealing with the issuance of bonds limit the creation of additional debt to a prescribed percentage of the additional value added to the security, and are designed to insure that the requisite equity is maintained. The sinking fund and maintenance provisions have as their purpose the continuation of the predetermined minimum ratio of security value to debt through insuring the retirement of debt in proportion to the effect of depreciation and obsolescence factors on the obligor's properties. Finally, the release provisions enable the company to deal with its properties efficiently and expeditiously, provided that equivalent value is substituted for properties sold or otherwise disposed of. Once this basic concept is thoroughly understood, a proper foundation is laid for the intelligent consideration of applications or certificates filed under any of the various sections. While the entire indenture constitutes, and must be considered as, a single contract, it is of particular importance that these three major segments be complementary. In reviewing the terms of a proposed new mortgage indenture, the trustee should make sufficient analysis to insure itself that the various provisions are entirely consistent and designed to carry out the essential purposes outlined above.

From the viewpoint of both the obligor and the trustee, the release provisions are of the greatest importance, and some of the most intricate problems involved in indenture administration have to do with the release of property. It is simple enough to state the basic proposition that the trustee's duty is discharged if equivalent value is received for value surrendered, but how is "value" in such an instance to be determined? If a piece of property is sold as a result of arm's length bargaining, isn't the sale price fairly conclusive as to the "value" involved? But this means that we are dealing solely with intrinsic values. What happens to the concept that the important consideration is the maintaining of the value of the business as a going concern and not the intrinsic value of the individual pieces of property? On the "going concern" theory, is it ever proper for the trustee to accept less than the intrinsic value of the specific property being disposed of? In particular situations, should it insist on receiving a great deal more?

The problem is further complicated by the dual fiduciary responsibilities of the trustee. Preservation of the security is the most fundamental responsibility of the trustee, and to this end its fiduciary duty to the bondholders is absolute. On the other hand, prior to default, the obligor has the right within the terms of its contract to deal with its property in such manner as it deems to be in the best interest of all parties, and is in a much better position to make such a determination. The release provisions constitute a part of the contract between the obligor and the trustee, and if the necessary conditions precedent are fulfilled, the trustee is under a duty to assent to a requested release and may be liable if it refuses to do so.

This essential problem may be illustrated by considering a specific situation. Assume that two extensive railroad systems—Railroad A and Railroad B—serve exactly the same territory between two points on their lines approximately two hundred miles apart, and that for this distance their lines roughly parallel each other. The property of each is heavily mortgaged. As a result of detailed studies and with the approval of the Interstate Commerce Commission, the companies agree that Railroad A will grant to Railroad B the right in perpetuity to use its tracks between the points in question, and that the latter will abandon its trackage and right of way. The remaining single line is capable of handling all traffic and no revenue loss will be occasioned. Actually, a saving of several million dollars annually will result from reductions in property taxes, maintenance, and terminal expenses. Railroad B makes application to its mortgage trustee for release of its entire two hundred-mile line, the consideration being the mortgaging of the trackage right from Railroad A and the deposit of all proceeds of salvage, the latter to be used for the enlargement and improvement of certain facilities on the new joint line to facilitate the handling of the enlarged traffic. What should be the attitude of the mortgage trustee? Despite the economic desirability of effectuating the agreement, isn't the value of the trust estate being diminished? Does the trust estate benefit at all by the savings realized, unless they are set aside and used to reduce outstanding indebtedness? It is doubtful that the trustee could successfully impose this as a condition to the release, if it receives an engineer's certification to the effect that the value of the trackage rights is at least equal to the value of the right of way to be abandoned.

The Railroad A trustee also has a problem, although possibly not so great as that of the Railroad B trustee. The latter would have to insist that the rights granted be superior to all mortgages on the Railroad A property, although this would result in the imposition of a substantial encumbrance ranking ahead of the lien of the Railroad A mortgage, requiring a consent or release by the trustee thereof. Again, the consideration could only be the savings in expense which might or might not directly benefit the trust estate.

In administering the release provisions, the trustee of course must always insist upon receiving the certificates and other papers required, and must examine them to see that the proper statements and certifications are made. The question is the extent, if any, to which the trustee should examine the practical aspects and possible consequences of the proposed transaction and interpose its independent judgment. The matter is further complicated when the action requested is of an unusual nature, and there is uncertainty as to whether or not it is specifically authorized by the indenture provisions. The trustee is confronted with a difficult decision in these cases, even though the contemplated action appears to be clearly in the interest of the bondholders. If its assents to the proposed release without requisite authority and loss results, it may be liable for acting beyond the scope of its powers. On the other hand, if it refuses to execute a release and loss results, it may be liable both to security holders and to the obligor if in fact the transaction was within the scope of the indenture. All too frequently, time is of the essence and it is impossible in these situations to obtain a judicial construction of the indenture language.

The whole problem of releases has been the subject of considerable comment over the years, both in judicial decisions and by writers on the subject. Unfortunately, no consistent pattern has been established which might serve as a guide to the trustee. The cases considered have for the most part involved situations where substantial losses have resulted, and the trustees involved were subjected to severe criticism even though the facts indicated that the terms of the indenture had been followed strictly. In other cases where trustees have departed from indenture restrictions and logically might be subject to criticism, their actions have been upheld. A striking example of the latter situation is presented by the numerous cases involving the substitution of buses for municipal railway systems. Few of the railway system indentures provided for the release of lines of railway, and in fact, many contained an express prohibition against it. Most companies, however, would have faced serious financial trouble and possibly loss of franchises if a way had not been found to effect a change in the method of transportation. The courts almost without exception were able to find implied authority in the indenture sufficient to permit the transactions. One court held that bondholders acquired their obligations with implied knowledge of a possible change in methods of conducting business, and that this was implicit in the agreement. (Vid., Mayor, etc., of City of Baltimore v. United Railways and Electric Company of Baltimore City, 108 Md. 64, Atl. 436 [1908].) Another found the requisite authority in the provisions reserving to the company, prior to default, the right to possess, manage, and operate the mortgaged properties. (Vid., New York State Railways v. Security Trust Company of Rochester, 135 miscl., 456, 238 N.Y.S. 354 [1929].)

The extent to which a trustee may go in refusing to execute a release where, even though the necessary conditions precedent exist, it appears that the bondholders' security will be impaired, is problematic. Two cases on this point, both decided by the New York courts, will illustrate the problem.

The first case involved a collateral trust indenture where the collateral consisted largely of bonds secured by real estate mortgages. The indenture provided that such bonds could be accepted as collateral only when accompanied by appraisals showing that the unpaid balance was not in excess of 75 per cent of the value of the real estate. The indenture further provided that whenever the principal amount of bonds outstanding under the indenture was less than 83 1/3 percent of the par value of collateral pledged, excess collateral could be withdrawn until such percentage was reached. The case involved application for withdrawal of $8,000,000 excess collateral computed on this basis. The trustee refused to comply, arguing that, despite the fact that the collateral bonds were adequately secured at the time of deposit, depreciation in real estate values had wiped out the 25 per cent margin and that in many cases the value of the underlying real estate was less than the face of the bonds. The trustee's position was upheld by the court, which ruled that the release provisions were qualified by an implied intent that a 25 percent margin in security for all collateral be maintained.

(*Vid.*, Prudence Company, Inc. v. Central Hanover Bank and Trust Company, 261 N.Y. 420, 184 N.E. 687 [1933].)

The second case involved a mortgage indenture which contained a rather unusual provision permitting releases upon deposit with the trustee of a stated proportion of the consideration for which the property was sold, the percentage varying with the gross sales price of the property. On December 18, the obligor notified the trustee that it would default on the interest installment due on the succeeding January 1. On December 30 it applied for the release of certain property, tendering 20 percent of the sales price which was the required percentage under the applicable indenture clause. The trustee refused to release the property, but the courts upheld the company's suit for specific performance, holding that, since a default did not exist on the date of application, the trustee had no right to refuse. (*Vid.*, Indian River Islands Corporation v. Manufacturers Trust Company, *et al.*, 253 App. Div. 549, 2 N.Y.S. (2nd) 860 [1938].)

Under the Trust Indenture Act the trustee is afforded protection if it relies in good faith on certificates to see that they do conform to such provisions. In most situations, no problem will be encountered if the trustee follows this rule. No hard and fast rule can be established to guide the trustee in the unusual or special situation, however, and the requirement of good faith means that it cannot free itself from considering the practical aspects and potential consequences of the proposed transaction.

In considering the usual and customary provision of the indenture relating to these matters, the morgage indenture and the collateral indenture will be dealt with separately. While the essential purpose is the same in both, different problems are presented.

DEALING WITH PROPERTY UNDER MORTGAGE INDENTURES

Prior to default, the mortgagor corporation has the absolute right to possess, manage, and operate its properties free from restriction or interference, provided only that it complies with the covenants and provisions of the indenture. It is customary for this right to be specifically affirmed in general terms by the indenture. The first sections of the release article will then proceed to enumerate specific rights retained by the mortgagor in furtherance of this general affirmation.

The first such provision deals with the company's right to remove and dispose of property and equipment which has become obsolete or unserviceable, or is no longer useful in the company's business operations. This can be done without the necessity of release or other action by the trustee. The only condition is that the property so disposed of be replaced by other property of at least equal value or, to the extent of any deficiency, that cash be deposited with the trustee. Mechanically, the most feasible method of insuring compliance is to require the filing with the trustee of an annual certificate as to the aggregate value of property so retired, the value of property substituted, and the amount of the cash deficiency, if any.

A second section gives the obligor the right to relocate machines or equipment; to move any of the property from one location to another; to alter, remodel, or change the location of any building or structure; or to make any similar change or alteration so long as the aggregate value of the mortgaged property is not diminished. Since these rights do not affect the lien of the indenture, no accounting to the trustee is necessary.

Finally, the mortgagor is given the right to alter or amend any lease, contract, easement, license, franchise, or similar right, or to enter into any such agreements. This right is usually conditioned on a finding by the company's board of directors that the alteration or amendment will not prejudice the company's operations or the trust estate, or that it will be in the best interests of the company and its bondholders. Such other conditions may be imposed as may be appropriate to the circumstances of the particular company. For example, if the company is given the right to grant leases or other interests in its property, it is usually provided that these must be made expressly subject to the prior rights of the trustee as mortgagee.

The above reservation of rights in the company is a necessary and integral part of its right to possession and use of the property, and is to be exercised without reference to or action by the trustee. It is usually provided, however, that upon request by the company, the trustee will execute such release or other documents that may be necessary or desirable to confirm the company's action in any particular situation.

Since the trustee retains no control over such dealing with its security, it follows that these sections should be carefully examined by it to insure that the security cannot be prejudiced by any such action. Of equal importance, the restrictions and qualifications on the company's unilateral action under these sections should not be so broad as to prejudice the action which the company can take, with the concurrence of the trustee, under the general release provisions. In a recent situation, a provision prohibiting the granting of leases, except subject to the prior lien of the indenture, raised a serious question when a trustee was presented with an application for the release of a leasehold estate to enable the separate financing of substantial improvements to a particular property, in the absence of a clear right to execute such a release. It would have been simple to make the restriction applicable only to unilateral action by the company, carrying out the obvious intent of the parties.

While the sections permitting unilateral action by an obligor should be fairly restrictive, a great deal of flexibility is desirable as to the action which may be taken with the consent and concurrence of the trustee. As long as the essential character of the security is preserved, the company should be given the right to obtain the release of any property it considers desirable, upon the substitution of property of equivalent value, or upon an appropriate reduction in the amount of the secured indebtedness.

The conditions precedent to the company's right to secure a release of property and the documents required to substantiate compliance with such conditions are fairly uniform and, in general, must be included in the indenture pursuant to Section 314 of the Trust Indenture Act.

Many indentures provide that no property can be released unless the company has sold or contracted to sell the property in question. While this would appear to present no problem, a number of situations have arisen where this has proved to be too restrictive. Occasionally it may be desirable to effect a change in the terms of a lease, contract, easement, or other property right where no actual sale is involved and under circumstances requiring the consent or participation of the trustee. Any such general limitation or restriction should be questioned.

One of the basic documents to be required is a resolution of the company's board of directors reciting the essential facts surrounding the transaction, containing an adequate description of the property, and requesting execution of a release by the trustee. Also, while seldom specifically required, it is desirable to have the resolution specifically state that the company is not in default, and that the requested release will not impair the security of the indenture in contravention of the provisions thereof. These are required conditions and must be covered in other certificates. The basic purpose in requiring a resolution, in addition to seeing that requisite authority is given the company officers, is to insure that the transaction has been referred to and authorized by the senior responsible body of the corporation, and it is desirable to require affirmative consideration of all aspects of the transaction.

The value of the property to be released is determined by the certificate of an engineer, appraiser, or other expert. This certificate must also state affirmatively that the proposed release will not impair the security of the indenture. Under certain circumstances, where the value of the property to be released is in excess of a specified amount, this certificate must be made by an independent engineer, appraiser, or expert having no affiliation with the company. The certificate must recite in sufficient detail the scope of the examination and investigation which formed the basis of the opinion certified. Normally, the company is given the right to select the engineer or appraiser, but such selection should be made subject to the trustee's approval. In view of the importance of this certificate, the trustee should insist upon receiving an adequate statement of the expert's qualifications and should determine to its satisfaction that he is in fact qualified.

Two additional documents are always required—a certificate of designated officers of the company and an opinion of counsel, each of which must state that all conditions precedent to the requested release exist or have been performed, and must recite in sufficient detail the examination and investigation made by the signers to ascertain the necessary facts. In addition to such a general statement, it is customary to require the officers to certify affirmatively to all pertinent facts—that there is no default; that the property has been sold or that a release is necessary for the reasons set forth; that the release is desirable in the conduct of the company's business and will not impair the security of the indenture; and such other facts as may be appropriate to the particular situation.

Finally, a consideration for the release must be furnished. This should equal the greater of the fair value of the property released, or the consideration received by the company on the sale thereof. Such consideration is normally in the form of cash or other real or

personal property, but occasionally it may take the form of purchase money obligations secured by the property released. If the
latter, it should be limited to a fixed percentage (usually 66 2/3 per
cent) of the value of the property. It is also desirable to limit strictly
the aggregate amount of such obligations which may be held.
While they may constitute perfectly good security, they absorb the
working capital of the corporation which is not in the business of
investing in mortgages.

Any cash received is deposited with the trustee and may be
withdrawn by the company to reimburse itself for any additional
property acquired and subjected to the lien of the indenture, in an
amount equal to the lesser of the cost or the fair value of such
property to the company. Whenever any property is subjected to
the lien of the indenture, either as the basis for the release of other
property or for the withdrawal of cash, substantially the same documents must be filed as in the case of the issuance of bonds on the
basis of property additions. These must include an engineer's or
appraiser's certificate as to the fair value of such property to the
company; an opinion of counsel that all conditions precedent to the
withdrawal have been compiled with and that such property is
subject to the lien of the indenture; and an officers' certificate that
such property is useful and desirable in the conduct of the company's business and that all conditions precedent to the transaction
have been complied with. If counsel indicates that instruments of
conveyance are necessary or desirable to perfect the lien of the
indenture on such property, such instruments must be executed
and recorded and become supplements to the indenture.

Some confusion is frequently created in the mind of the inex-
perienced administrator by involved provisions, often included in
open end mortgages, which endeavor to classify properties used as a
basis for releases, and permit their re-use at a later date under other
provisions of the indenture. The reason for this becomes clear if the
distinction between funded and unfunded property is borne in
mind. "Funded" property is that which has been bonded or used as
a basis for credit under a sinking fund, maintenance, or similar
provision. "Unfunded" property, while subject to the lien of the
indenture, is excess property available for use by the company in
certifying compliance with the pertinent indenture sections. Property substituted for other property released should retain the lat-

ter's status, and when this is unfunded, the new property still remains available for use for other purposes, even though certified to the trustee as a basis for release of other unfunded property.

It is desirable also to include a provision which, while used infrequently, permits the trustee to apply any cash deposited to the purchase or redemption of bonds. In the normal situation, such application should be at the option of the obligor company.

Miscellaneous Provisions

In furtherance of the general purposes of the release clauses, and to provide for special situations or contingencies which may arise, it is customary to include a number of general sections in the release article, most of which become operative only on the happening of particular events.

Where it is contemplated that frequent sales of property will be made, it is desirable to include a provision permitting the company, without application to or release by the trustee, to consummate sales up to a specified aggregate amount each year. Preparation of individual release applications is time-consuming and expensive, and such a provision results in substantial savings in time and expense. The company is required to provide a single annual accounting to the trustee. While it is seldom required, it would be desirable to have a single release covering all such properties executed annually. The conveyance of property without a specific release of a mortgage lien will create a possible cloud on title which may require expensive proceedings to remove at a later date. Sometimes it is difficult to identify a particular parcel as one which was properly sold under such a general section, and the trustee is placed in an embarrassing position when it is requested, years later, to join in a confirmatory release.

There should always be included a statement to the effect that the purchaser of any property released by the trustee is protected and under no duty to inquire into the particular circumstances or the propriety of any such release. Where the trustee executes a release improperly or without the requisite authority, it is not clear what the effect on the title of the purchaser may be. Some cases have held that a release so executed is invalid, and the purchaser does not acquire good title. Courts have held, however, that where the indenture contains such a provision protecting the purchaser, the provision is controlling and the purchaser is protected even though the trustee's action was *ultra vires*. No one should question the desirability or equity of such a rule.

There should always be included provisions dealing with the disposition of property taken through the exercise of the power of eminent domain, or of any right of any government, bureau, or agency, or any public or quasi-public body to condemn or take possession or title to any property or interest therein. Usually, the award granted for any such taking will be paid to the trustee. It is desirable to include a greater degree of flexibility, however, and the procedure will be simplified if the company is given the right to compromise or settle its claim in such a situation. The practice now followed is to proceed under the general release section, but sometimes the conditions precedent are not completely satisfied, and since it is a special situation, not subject to the company's control, it is better to deal with it as such. An appropriate certificate as to the fairness of the proposed settlement would serve as a basis for the release of the property. This would enable the company to use the proceeds promptly in acquisition of substitute property and avoid the delay and expense of pursuing the condemnation route.

The normal release provisions are operative only on condition that no default exists under the indenture. Some thought should be given to the problem which will be presented should a default occur. It is customary to provide that the rights of the company under the release article may be exercised by a receiver or trustee appointed in receivership, bankruptcy, or reorganization proceedings. As a practical matter, such an official will operate under orders of the court having jurisdiction, which may direct the sale of particular property whether or not there is indenture authorization, but it is desirable nevertheless to provide for this contingency.

Of more significance is the situation which exists should no formal proceedings have been instituted. Here the trustee is required to exercise more discretion and judgment, and the release sections are usually made permissive. If in the judgment of the trustee the proposed transaction seems desirable, it is granted authority to execute a release but may refuse to do so. The trustee should receive the same certifications and documents as in the case of a predefault release and may require such additional evidence as seems indicated to enable it to reach an appropriate conclusion.

Finally, provisions should be inserted to deal with any special situation or special properties that may be significant in the case of the particular company involved. The nature of such provisions, if any, will depend on the special circumstances existing. Certain properties or classes of property may be of such significance in the financing arrangement as to warrant a prohibition against their disposal, or a provision that the proceeds can be applied only to retirement of the debt. Acquisition of particular classes of property with trust monies may be forbidden, or may be limited to a fixed aggregate amount or to a percentage of the indenture securities outstanding. There may be any number of variations, and the trustee should insure that it understands the purpose intended, and that the provisions inserted are designed properly to effectuate such purpose.

PROVISIONS AS TO PLEDGED COLLATERAL

The collateral trust indenture does not now occupy the importance in the field of corporate financing that it did during the period of the 1920's and 1930's. This was the era of the growth and influence of the large holding company systems, particularly in the public utility industry. The parent companies in these systems, and quite frequently the companies on the second and even third lines of the intercorporate structure, owned no physical operating properties at all, but merely held securities of subsidiary and affiliated companies in the system. Capital debt financing by these corporations was arranged through the collateral trust device, under which securities of affiliated companies constituted the sole security for the outstanding obligations. The rapid expansion of these systems and the numerous recapitalizations resulted in substantial pyramiding of the debt and frequent withdrawals and substitutions of collateral under the various indentures.

Viewed in retrospect, the criteria used in determining values left a great deal to be desired. In some cases, principal amount or par value alone was used; in others, an earnings test was applied; in still others, set up on an income servicing theory, "yield" alone was the determining factor. Even where market value was used, the tremendous inflation in security prices and the substantial write-up in property values that occurred as these companies were transferred, resulted in an unwarranted credit inflation and an unrealistic debt structure. Seldom was it necessary to establish any real intrinsic value in the collateral being pledged. Unfortunately, numerous instances occurred where valuable collateral was withdrawn on the substitution of securities that were essentially worthless. As a result, the losses eventually suffered by investors in a number of these issues were substantial, and trustees found themselves subjected to severe criticism for some of the transactions which had taken place, even though the record was clear that in almost every instance the express provisions of the respective indentures had been followed literally.

A number of events have occurred which have eliminated the relative significance of these arrangements. Of the greatest importance was the Public Utility Holding Company Act under which the giant systems have either disappeared or been substantially curtailed. In the process the old indentures were satisfied through the exchange of securities during the reorganization process. The capital structures of the companies have been simplified and valuation has been placed on a more realistic basis. Debt securities of the system are now usually issued by the subsidiary operating companies where operating properties rather than collateral constitute the security. Public financing by the parent holding company is normally done through equity, and where debt securities are issued, it is done on an unsecured basis.

The investment trust type of company was another form of collateral financing that was formerly of more importance than it is today. In some of these the same problems existed as in the case of the holding company financing, although the instances of loss to investors were insignificant and were due to economic factors rather than to unrealistic intrasystem security transactions. The independent judgment of the managers of the trusts was an important protective feature. Here again the growth in importance of the mutual shares has resulted in the decline in importance of this type of financing arrangement.

Where securities are held as part of the trust estate, requirements governing their release are now substantially the same as those relating to real property. Of particular importance is the requirement of certificates of value, both as to collateral being released and as to collateral being substituted for other property. These certificates must be made by experts who are required to set forth the criteria which form the basis of their appraisal and which can be subjected to objective scrutiny. In particular situations, these certificates must be furnished by independent appraisers.

Despite the decline in importance of the collateral trust indenture as such, the handling of collateral security is still a significant factor in many mortgage indentures. Numerous companies still conduct a portion of their business through subsidiary or affiliated companies, and to provide security on the complete business operation, it is necessary to create a combined mortgage and collateral trust indenture. The importance of the pledge of securities, however, is not their current market value but the granting of a collateral lien on the company's allied or subsidiary operations conducted through the companies whose securities are pledged. The pertinent indenture provisions should therefore be designed to carry out this essential purpose.

It is important that all securities of such affiliates or subsidiaries owned by the obligor company be included in the pledge. This need not necessarily cover open-book advances, although these too are frequently included through requirement for execution and pledging of an unsecured note. In the case of a real property mortgage, creation of a prior lien is effectively prevented by recording requirements. A collateral lien, however, can be impaired by the issuance of senior securities ranking ahead of those pledged. In the absence of a specific requirement for the pledging of any such securities, protection should be obtained in the form of negative covenants controlling the amount of such securities that can be issued.

Prior to default, no particular action is required of the trustee other than the custody of the securities pledged. The obligor company is entitled to all income thereon, and should be permitted to exercise all voting rights except as to matters which might affect the value of the collateral lien. Enforcement of the principal of any debt obligations so pledged is not important, and the trustee may properly be freed from any duty in this connection. Despite the lien nature of the pledge, however, any payments made on account of principal or received on retirement of equity securities should be received by the trustee. Such a requirement is roughly equivalent to the maintenance requirement relating to mortgaged property.

Adequate provisions should be included to facilitate any exchange, recapitalization, merger, or other type of intercompany transactions which may occur from time to time. These should authorize the trustee, upon receipt of appropriate resolutions and certificates establishing the desirability of the proposed arrangement, to execute such documents or give such consents as may be required.

By reason of the special purpose of this collateral pledge, normally no part of the securities of any particular company held (except on payment, exchange, or for a similar reason) should be released unless all the securities of the particular company involved are disposed of simultaneously.

As in the case of real property, any special situations should be dealt with specially, and appropriate authority should be included in the indenture for the trustee's guidance.

After default the trustee should have all rights of ownership with respect to pledged securities, including receipt and retention of income, right of sale or other disposition, and the right to exercise full voting control.

EXHIBIT 8. RELEASE CHECK SHEET

Indenture: _____

Date and document number containing last approval of counsel of similar transaction _____

Check all items when completed. If inapplicable, so indicate.

I. IF RELEASE OF PROPERTY OTHER THAN CASH:

☐ A. Obtain and review executed originals of following documents:

   1. Resolution of company board of directors containing request for release and description of property to be released.

   2. Officers' certificate as to compliance with all conditions precedent.

   3. Engineer's or appraiser's certificate as to fair value of property to be released.

   4. Opinion of counsel as to compliance with all conditions precedent.

   5. Other required documents, if any. List such documents herein.

_____

_____

_____

☐ B. Require independent engineer's or appraiser's certificate if fair value of all property released during calendar year (including current application) is 10 per cent or more of indenture securities outstanding, unless fair value of property in current application is less than $25,000 or less than one per cent of indenture securities outstanding.

☐ C. Check statements in certificates and opinion as to compliance with indenture provision corresponding to Section 314 (e) of Trust Indenture Act.

☐ D. Obtain deposit of cash equal to proceeds of sale or to fair value of property released, whichever is greater.

☐ E. Obtain approval of trustee's counsel. Required if no approval of substantially similar transaction on file; or if fair value of property released is one per cent of indenture securities outstanding, or $100,000; or if transaction involves unusual or special circumstances.

☐ F. Compare description of property in release instrument to that set forth in resolution and engineer's certificate.

☐ G. Execute and deliver instrument of release. If proceeds not deposited with application, deliver in trust.

☐ H. Prepare special report to bondholders if fair value of property released is 10 per cent or more of indenture securities outstanding.

II. IF WITHDRAWAL OF CASH OR RELEASE OF PROPERTY ON BASIS OF CERTIFICATION OF PROPERTY ADDITIONS OR DEPOSIT OF COLLATERAL:

☐ A. Obtain and check:
1. Resolution,
2. Engineer's or appraiser's certificate,
3. Officers' certificate,
4. Opinion of counsel,
5. Other required documents, if any. List such documents herein.

_____

_____

_____

☐ B. Required independent engineer's or appraiser's certificate if: (1) within six months prior to acquisition by obligor such property was used by a person other than the obligor in a business similar to that in which it has been or is to be used by

the obligor, or (2) if securities are being deposited, the fair value of such securities is 10 per cent or more of the indenture securities outstanding, unless the value of such property or securities is less than $25,000 or less than one per cent of the indenture securities outstanding.

☐ C. Obtain executed counterparts of supplemental indenture subjecting property to lien of indenture, unless opinion of counsel states property is subject to such lien without the necessity for any specific conveyance.

☐ D. If supplemental indenture is required, follow for receipt of properly recorded counterparts and further opinion of counsel as to sufficiency of such recording.

III. IF COLLATERAL IS DEPOSITED:
☐ A. Check negotiability.
☐ B. Ascertain whether income is to be collected, and determine its disposition.
☐ C. Consider nominee registration.
☐ D. Prepare requisite instructions re receipt and deposit.
☐ E. If collateral consists of purchase money obligations, check that such obligations and purchase money mortgage run to trustee, or that appropriate assignment is received.

Date _____   Prepared by _____   Checked by _____   Approved by _____

8

Indenture Covenants

IN ADDITION to provisions which relate specifically to the trust estate or to the debt and the rights of the parties with respect thereto, most indentures contain a number of covenants designed either to afford continuing information to the trustee and security holders about the company's affairs or to place restrictions on the activities of the obligor. The number and nature of the covenants included, result from negotiations between the obligor and the person or persons representing the prospective purchasers of the securities. The type of covenants which are included depends to a large extent on the nature of the business of the obligor, the term of the loan, the purpose for which it is being made, whether it is secured or unsecured, the extent and nature of other outstanding obligations, and other similar considerations.

The trustee, of course, has no responsibility as to what covenants are or are not included in a particular indenture, as this is essentially a part of the substantive contract between borrower and lender. Once the contract is executed, however, the trustee will have the primary duty of enforcing it, and therefore must be concerned with all provisions which are included. A more effective job can be done if there is a clear understanding, not only of what the language means, but also of the purpose it is intended to accomplish, and why the provision was included in a particular indenture. Unfortunately, some draftsmen have special provisions which they like and sometimes insert without regard to their relevance to the essential purpose of the contract. An astute trustee will examine these provisions closely, and make sure that their relevance and purpose are clearly understood by the parties to the contract. Once the

131

indenture is executed and delivered, it is difficult and expensive, sometimes even impossible, to have it modified. It is unfortunate when a particular covenant, designed to enhance the credit and protect the investor, actually threatens the security on which he is primarily relying, and places the obligor ·in a difficult situation. When faced with such a development, the trustee finds itself in an unenviable position that might have been avoided by the exercise of greater care in the initial review when the contract was still in draft form.

Of paramount importance, of course, is the cardinal rule applicable to all indenture language—that its meaning be clear and unambiguous. One of the most difficult jobs a trustee has is in the interpretation and application of a particular provision to a situation not in contemplation at the time it was drafted and which the covenant was not designed to resolve. No matter how sincere and honest corporate financial officers may be, they tend to interpret provisions in light of the particular problem with which they may be faced from time to time, and language tends to take on different shades of meaning as the circumstances of a particular company undergo change. Since many covenants require only unilateral action on the part of the obligor, it is possible for a default to occur unintentionally because of an incorrect or slightly distorted interpretation on the part of the company officials.

Of equal importance is the necessity that the covenant be so drafted that its violation is easily detected. Where the existence of particular facts or prohibited acts or situations is solely within the knowledge of the obligor, and not likely to be readily disclosed by the financial statements or other information furnished the trustee, an effort should be made to obtain periodic certification as to compliance with the covenant, either as part of a general certification or with adequate detail as to the facts indicating compliance or noncompliance with the specific provision.

In general, covenants should be related to, and designed to facilitate, the carrying out of the purposes of each particular loan contract. It is impossible to enumerate or recite all covenants that might be desirable in a particular case. The enumeration set forth below is intended to present only the more common covenants that are used. Many of those listed would not be applicable to particular indentures, but a thorough understanding of the uses and purposes of these should provide a basic background which should be adequate for indenture administrators in most situations.

Covenants may be classified in a number of ways, but possibly the simplest classification is to distinguish between *affirmative* covenants, which require specific action on the part of the obligor, either continuously or at specified periods, and *negative* covenants, which are prohibitive or restrictive in nature and require, not the taking of action, but the refraining from certain acts or things.

AFFIRMATIVE COVENANTS

As the name implies, an affirmative covenant requires some positive or definite action on the part of the obligor. It requires the taking of specific action or the performance of specific acts, either continuously, from time to time, or at specified times. A sinking fund covenant is, of course, of this type, although it is almost always covered in a separate section of the indenture and is not included in the enumeration below. Many affirmative covenants are pertinent only to mortgage indentures and relate to the mortgage security, while others are equally applicable whether the issue is secured or unsecured.

Some provisions are frequently included in the covenant section as such, although they are more in the nature of warranties. Typical of such provisions are the following:

(1) Covenant that the company has complied with all legal requirements and is duly authorized to execute and deliver the indenture and to issue the indenture securities, and that the indenture securities in the hands of the holders thereof will be valid and enforceable obligations.

(2) Covenant that the company is lawfully possessed of the mortgaged and pledged property and has good right and lawful authority to mortgage and pledge the same.

(3) Covenant that the company will warrant and defend the title to the property and the trustee's security interest therein against all claims and demands.

These provisions may be included as recitals in the indenture rather than, or in addition to, being included as specific covenants. It probably makes little difference where they appear, as the conditions recited go so obviously to the essence of the contract that a violation would provide a basis for immediately prematuring the debt and bringing the remedial provisions into play. Their inclusion as specific covenants provides a direct relationship with the default and remedial section, and is to be preferred for that reason. Whether included as covenants or recitals, or both, they serve as an estoppel against the corporation and prevent its questioning the validity of its acts, even though there may have been some technical failure to secure due and proper authorization of the indenture, the indenture securities, or the mortgage. Such estoppel would not be effective against third parties who obtained rights for value and in good faith. Its inclusion in the indenture, therefore, does not mean that the trustee and its counsel should be less diligent in assuring themselves as to the due and proper authorization of the indenture and the obligations issued thereunder.

Other types of affirmative covenants are applicable only to secured indentures and are usually to be found—in one form or another—in most mortgage indentures. Some of these may be included as parts of other covenants or undertaking, but are listed separately for clarity.

(4) Covenant to maintain and preserve the lien of the indenture.

(5) Covenant to give further assurances.

(6) Covenant to subject to the lien of the indenture, by supplement, if necessary, all property acquired after the date of the indenture and intended to be covered thereby.

All of these covenants are in the nature of undertakings to give further assurances, and provide a basis for a trustee's demand that additional documents be executed or things be done that will better insure maintenance of the security which the indenture purported to create, and the extension of the lien thereon to additionally acquired property if any question exists as to the effectiveness of an after-acquired property clause in any jurisdiction. For example, the further assurances covenant has been used as a basis for a request, in a non-qualified indenture, for an annual certificate of after-acquired property and an annual opinion as to the due recording and filing or the indenture and the necessity for any periodic re-recording or refiling.

(7) Covenant as to recording of the indenture and all supplements, and the furnishing of opinions of counsel, after each such recording, and annually, as to the due recording thereof and the necessity for any rerecording or refiling in order to preserve the lien thereof.

Section 314(b) of the Trust Indenture Act requires the inclusion of such a provision in all indentures qualified thereunder which include a mortgage or pledge of property. The matter of recording is of such obvious importance that this has become a more or less standard provision in all mortgage indentures whether or not qualified under the act. Because of the multiplicity of jurisdictions frequently involved, and the diversity of recording statutes, reliance must be placed on counsel who are familiar with the laws of the various states where the property is located.

(8) Covenants as to prior lien bonds.

Where prior lien bonds are outstanding, it is customary to include provisions with respect to such prior liens. These provisions are designed to prevent a default under the prior lien and to prevent its extension or refunding with other prior lien obligations. The indenture therefore will usually contain covenants that the obligor will comply with all provisions of prior lien indentures; that it will pay the obligations when due and will not consent to the extension of the maturity thereof (the indenture will usually contain provisions for the refunding thereunder of prior lien obligations); and that upon satisfaction of any prior lien indenture, it will cause the trustee thereunder to surrender to the trustee all specific property pledged with it. Where prior lien obligations are retired in part or acquired by the obligor, the indenture often provides that they will be held alive and pledged with the trustee. The theory of such a provision is that, to the extent of the obligations so held, the trustee will acquire rights *pari passu* with the other holders of such prior lien obligations. The validity of this theory is doubtful, however, except to the extent of value actually paid by the trustee for such obligations.

There are many other affirmative covenants equally applicable to secured or unsecured indentures, although their context or purpose may differ, depending on the nature of the company and the indenture. Some of the more common covenants of this type are set forth below.

(9) Covenant that the company will duly and punctually pay the principal of and interest and premium, if any, on all of the indenture securitites outstanding according to the terms thereof.

Since the obligations themselves contain an absolute promise to pay, inclusion of such a provision in the indenture might seem to be unnecessary and redundant. The obligation in the securities, however, runs directly to the holders thereof and not to the trustee. The indenture covenant runs to the trustee and enables it to enforce the obligation for the benefit of the security holders should there be a default in the payment of any installment of principal or interest.

(10) Closely related to the preceding covenant is a negative covenant or undertaking by the obligor that it will not, directly or indirectly, extend, or assent to the extension of, the time for payment of any coupon or claim for interest on any of the indenture securities.

The purpose of this undertaking is to prevent an accumulation of claims for interest that might rank on a parity with or prior to other indenture obligations, and it is frequently provided that should any claim for interest be so extended, it will be subordinate to the other indenture securities. It is necessary to except from this provision any extension pursuant to a plan proposed by the obligor to all indenture security holders.

(11) Covenant to maintain an office or agency where the bonds and interest coupons may be presented for payment and where notice and demands may be served on the company.

It is customary to provide that such an office or agency will be maintained in one or more specified cities, and that if the company should fail to keep or provide such office, presentation may be made and such notices and demands served at the principal office of the trustee. As a practical matter, the office of the trustee is usually designated as such an office or agency, and in any event demands and inquiries by security holders are customarily directed to the trustee.

(12) Covenant to pay all taxes, assessments, and other charges imposed upon the company's property, or upon the income or profits thereof, or upon the lien or interest of the trustee in respect of such property or such income.

It is usually provided that the obligor may delay payment of any such claim so long as it is, in good faith, contesting the validity thereof by appropriate legal proceedings. The purpose of such a covenant is to prevent the creation of any lien or claim which might be given preference by operation of law to the indenture securities.

(13) Covenant to maintain its corporate existence and maintain, preserve, and renew all rights, powers, privileges, and franchises owned by it.

The purpose of this undertaking is obvious. Since the loan is made on the credit of the corporation as a "going concern," all rights essential to its continuing as such must be preserved. This covenant is usually made subject to the merger clause and occasionally to the release and other provisions of the indenture.

(14) Covenant to maintain, preserve, and keep its properties in good repair, working order, and condition.
(15) Covenant to set aside from earnings each year proper reserves for renewals and replacements, obsolescence, depletion, exhaustion, and depreciation.

These are customary covenants in most indentures, whether secured or unsecured, and relate further to the importance of the "going concern" concept of the business and to maintenance of the security for the debt. In some types of mortgage indentures—particularly those of regulated companies, such as public utilities and railroads—the covenants are combined and enlarged into an elaborate maintenance covenant as outlined and discussed in Chapter 6.

(16) Covenant to maintain insurance.

Some indentures require maintenance of specific types of insurance; for example, in some businesses, public liability insurance may be of great importance, and failure to provide it in proper amounts might result in a severe loss to the company and prejudice to the security holders' claims. Needs and requirements tend to change over the years, however, and as a general rule it is unwise to try to be too specific. The customary and more desirable form is to provide that insurance of such kinds and amounts will be maintained as is customary in the industry, or as is customarily maintained by other companies operating similar properties. So long as the covenant requires maintenance of adequate insurance, it is desirable to permit as much flexibility as possible. The obligor should be permitted to select the insurance companies, to participate in an insurance pool or, if desired, to provide its own system of self-insurance. Where properties are widely scattered with no great percentage of the total value concentrated at one point, the latter may be a very desirable arrangement. Other innovations may also be appropriate in particular cases, such as inclusion of a deductible clause of a substantial amount to avoid a multiplicity of small claims and correspondingly heavier premium charges. In any system of self-insurance, the trustee should insist that the indenture contain requirements for appropriate certification to it of the adequacy of such a system and the reserves maintained.

In many of the older type of indentures, the insurance policies were required to be deposited with the trustee. The modern practice is to provide instead for a periodic certificate to be furnished, usually on an annual basis. This certificate should set forth proper details as to the kinds and amounts of insurance and the names of the companies, and contain a statement as to the adequacy of the insurance. While such a detailed statement is not as essential in an unsecured indenture, it is frequently provided for, or the trustee is given the right to request it. If the certificate indicates that policies expire before the next certificate is to be furnished, an appropriate tickler should be set up and a follow-up made to see that the insurance is renewed.

Where the indenture constitutes a lien on the company's properties the trustee should be named in the policies as an assured, so that any proceeds of insurance will be received by it. It is usually provided that any such proceeds up to a specified amount may be turned over immediately to the obligor, but amounts in excess thereof should be retained by the trustee until receipt of appropriate evidence that the property has been restored or replaced.

(17) If an important part of the company's property consists of leaseholds or ground rent estates, it is advisable to include a covenant that the company will perform all covenants and obligations as lessee, and will see that the lessor observes all its covenants and obligations in the leases; also, that it will renew the terms of any leases which expire prior to the maturity date of the indenture obligations.

(18) Covenant to continue to engage in a particular business, or in the business in which the company is presently engaged.

This is an example of the type of covenant which should be examined carefully and used only if particular circumstances would seem to make it appropriate. If the indenture is to run for a long period of time, there is danger in such an undertaking, as any harness maker could verify. In a majority of indentures, it is obviously unnecessary. It might be appropriate to a situation where the loan is of relatively short duration and the principal security is a special inventory or special purpose machinery and equipment suitable only for a particular business.

(19) Covenant to keep true books of record and account.

(20) Covenant to file with the trustee balance sheets, income and surplus statements, and other pertinent financial statements.

(21) Covenant to furnish copies of all reports forwarded to stockholders or filed with the Securities and Exchange Commission, and such other information as may be prescribed from time to time by regulations of such commission.

(22) Covenant to permit a representative of the trustee at all reasonable times, upon request, to inspect the books and properties of the company.

(23) Covenant to furnish such other data and information pertaining to the affairs of the company as the trustee may reasonably request.

These covenants all relate to the keeping of proper financial and accounting records and the filing with the trustee of periodic reports relative to the company's financial affairs. Section 314 (a) of the Trust Indenture Act requires each qualified indenture to contain a covenant requiring the obligor to file with the trustee, copies of the reports required to be filed with the Securities and Exchange Commission pursuant to Sections 13 or 15(d) of the Securities Exchange Act of 1934. These sections require the filing of periodic financial reports and supplementary reports to keep current various data filed with the original registration statement. This has become a fairly common covenant in all indentures of industrial and utility companies. In addition, copies of the annual audited statements certified by independent public accountants are customarily required to be filed within a specified period after the close of the company's fiscal year. Interim statements may also be required in particular cases, and it is usually sufficient to have these certified by one of the company's financial officers. In a situation where the condition of the business may be subject to rapid change and where the maintenance of certain ratios or a minimum amount of working capital is important, a more frequent check on the company's condition than is provided by the annual audited statements may be desirable.

The extent to which the trustee should make a detailed examination and analysis of the financial statements is not prescribed. Some corporate trust departments follow the practice of having all such statements reviewed by outside accountants. This seems extreme and, except in a most unusual situation, should not be necessary. Finance is a bank's business, and a trust company that purports to act as a corporate trustee should have personel sufficiently qualified to make whatever analysis would seem to be indicated. The trustee is charged with any facts that would be disclosed by a reasonable examination, and the minimum required would seem to be a sufficient check to see that no violation of any indenture provision is disclosed. Any unfavorable trend or situation that might warrant a more careful follow-up should be noted. The nature of the business, the financial standing of the obligor, the purpose of the loan, specific responsibilities of the trustee, and other similar considerations will serve as a guide to the degree of care and attention that should be devoted to the examination beyond the limits indicated.

(24) Covenant to furnish to the trustee annually a certificate signed by designated officials of the company stating that

a review of the activities of the company during the preceding year has been made under their supervision to determine compliance by the company with all conditions and covenants of the indenture, and that to the best of their knowledge the company has kept, observed, and performed all such covenants and conditions, or, if there has been a failure to so comply, specifying the full details thereof.

This is a most important covenant and every effort should be made to see that some provision along these lines is included in each indenture. Not only does it give the trustee appropriate evidence on which it is entitled to rely, but more importantly, it also assures that responsible officials of the obligor company will familiarize themselves with the indenture covenants and will review the activities of the company in light of its covenants and undertakings.

It is also desirable to have the independent accountants who audit the company's books include in their certificate, or in a special certificate addressed to the trustee, a similar statement. When such a provision is included in the indenture, however, it is advisable to check with such accountants before the language is finalized to make sure that the scope of their examination is sufficient to permit their making such a certification. In this connection, it is good practice to have a draft of the proposed certificate prepared and reviewed by the accountants to avoid difficulty at a later date.

NEGATIVE COVENANTS

The distinction between negative and affirmative covenants is not so much in the form of phraseology used, as almost any covenant can be expressed in the positive as well as the negative. The distinction lies rather in the fact that the so-called "negative" covenants, as a general rule, place restrictions on the activities of the obligor for the purpose of protecting the interests of the investor or lender. While certain of these covenants are common to both bond and debenture agreements, the negative type of covenant is most commonly associated with the debenture indenture, or unsecured financing. Their essential purpose is to insure, to the extent possible, that the investor for whose benefit they are made will remain in essentially the same relative position (as to other creditors) as exists at the time of the extension of credit. Their use has been severely criticized from time to time, particularly in an early report of the

Securities and Exchange Commission. The argument was made that these covenants tended to lead the investor into a sense of false security, and were of only limited value because of the ease with which they could be violated and the lack of any effective legal remedy to prevent such violation. These conclusions stemmed from a number of early court decisions which seemed to indicate that security holders did lack an effective remedy. Two will suffice for illustration. In 1932 Paramount-Publix Corporation had outstanding an issue of debentures under an indenture which provided that, so long as the debentures should be outstanding, the company would not create any lien on any assets directly owned by it. The company needed additional cash and was also faced with the maturity of large bank loans. Its banks agreed to renew the loans and provide the additional cash if all the loans were secured. The company had on hand a large supply of unfinished negatives. A subsidiary company was created and these assets transferred to it. Notes of the subsidiary in payment of these assets were pledged with the banks. In suits brought by individual security holders, the courts refused to enjoin the transfer to the subsidiary (Vid., Relmar Holding Company v. Paramount-Publix Corporation, 147 miscl., 824, 263 N.Y.S. 776 [1932], affirmed 237 App. Div. 870, 261 N.Y.S. 959 [1933].), or set it aside after it had been effected. (Vid., Ernst et al. v. Film Production Corporation, 148 miscl., 62, 264 N.Y.S 227 [1933].) These decisions may have been influenced by the technical fact that the suits were brought by the security holders and not the trustee, and that no demand on the trustee for action, as prescribed in the indenture, had been made.

The other case involved Insull Utilities Investments, Inc., which had outstanding a large issue of debentures under an indenture which provided that the company would not mortgage or pledge any of its property without securing the debentures pro rata, except for loans in the ordinary course of business with maturities not exceeding one year. In 1931 the company borrowed $17,000,000 from banks, secured by the pledge of various stocks. The loans were for less than one year but were renewed. Debenture holders sued to have the pledge set aside or to be ratably secured thereby. The court dismissed the suit, holding that the negative pledge clause referred only to long term funded debt and would not prevent bank loans, even though not in the ordinary course of business. (Vid., Kelly v. Central Hanover Bank and Trust Company, et al., 11 Fed. Supp.

497 [S.D.N.Y. 1935].) On appeal from this decision, however, the U. S. Circuit Court indicated that the holders might be able to succeed in their suit if they could establish: (a) that the loans were not in the ordinary course of business and (b) that the lending banks had knowledge of the negative pledge clause. (*Vid.*, Kelly v. Central Hanover Bank and Trust Company, *et al.*, 85 Fed. (2d) 61 [C.C.A. (2d) 1936].) In line with this dictum, the courts in New York have indicated that if the trustee bank itself, in its individual capacity, advances money to an obligor in violation of such a clause, the holders might be able to set a pledge aside, and that this would be so if the total term of the loan, including renewals, ran for more than a year, even though each note was for a shorter period.

The results in the two cases cited appear to have followed from a basic ineffectiveness of the clauses themselves. The problem in the Paramount-Publix case is now generally resolved by including the principal obligor and all its subsidiaries within the scope of the restrictive provisions, and prohibiting transfer of substantial properties from the company or a restricted subsidiary to an unrestricted subsidiary (i.e., one to which the covenant does not apply) or other company. Quite frequently, also, covenants against the incurring of additional debt extend to current as well as funded debt, or place very specific conditions and limitations on either or both.

The statement that no effective remedy exists against the violation of these clauses is also subject to question. Theoretically, in an appropriate case, an action for specific performance or for injunctive relief should be possible, although it is likely that these remedies will offer little protection in the average case because the trustee will probably not know of the violation until the transfer or pledge of assets or the obtaining of a prohibited loan or advance is an accomplished fact. To have such a transaction set aside would require proof not only of the violation but also of knowledge on the part of the pledgee or transferee. There is one remedy, however, that can be most effective. This is the right to declare a default under the indenture and premature the indenture obligations. While this may not result in placing the security holders in as good a position as formerly, and therefore cannot be said to constitute full protection, it does stand as a potent weapon which should deter all but the most callous. Faced with such a threat, the company is more likely to endeavor to resolve a difficult situation through frank disclosure and negotiation rather than through intentional violation of a restrictive covenant.

In many cases, an unsecured obligation under a carefully drawn indenture will provide as much protection and security to the investor as will a mortgage bond. The principal considerations in either case are the credit of the obligor as a going concern and the caliber of its management. In some cases the unsecured credit of the borrower is so good that few restrictions or covenants are necessary. Where the investors are obtaining a senior creditor position, all that is reasonably required are provisions in the agreement that under normal conditions will assure the retention of such a position. It is impossible to protect against every possible contingency, and an effort to do so by placing too restrictive conditions on the continued operation of the business is as likely to prejudice as improve the security holders' position.

Since it is impossible to foresee every contingency that is likely to arise over the extended period that the obligations are to be outstanding, it is desirable to provide for some degree of flexibility. This is a difficult problem. Where the notes or debentures are purchased directly by informed institutional investors, such a situation can be resolved by an agreement among such holders to amend the indenture or to modify or waive a particular provision either permanently or during a temporary period of stress. A different problem is presented where an issue is sold publicly. The first principle to be observed is to include only such restrictive covenants as under reasonably foreseeable conditions are not likely to cause undue hardship or seriously impede the normal conduct of the company's business. If the credit is not good enough under those conditions, it is best avoided. It is also desirable to include a provision permitting modification of the indenture by the holders of a specified percentage of the indenture securities. The customary percentage used is 66 2/3 per cent. While it is almost impossible to contact all holders of a publicly held issue, consent of a reasonable percentage can normally be obtained if the modification proposed is reasonable and desirable and if adequate foresight and preparation are exercised.

The trustee is frequently asked to consent to a temporary waiver or modification of a particular provision, or at least to consent to take no action for some period of time after a breach. Under the circumstances in which it is presented, the proposed action by the obligor usually appears reasonable and, frequently, highly desirable from the viewpoint of the security holders. While a good argument can be made for granting such discretionary powers to a trustee, under the usual indenture it has no such power and no authority or right to give any such consent or waiver.

Once a breach has occurred and matured into a default under the indenture, the trustee's conduct is subject to the prudent man's standard of judgment. It is unfortunate that few judicial precedents exist for the trustee's guidance in such situations, as the trustee may quite logically be inclined to take immediate action under the remedial provisions to avoid subjecting itself to substantial potential liability. In a great number of cases, the exercise of patience and a reasonable degree of judgment and discretion would enable the situation to be worked out without subjecting the company and the security holders to the substantial expense and loss from a reorganization proceeding. To avoid this, some indentures provide that a default will not occur for breach of an indenture covenant of this type unless and until the trustee has received notice thereof from a specified percentage of the security holders. This type of provision is generally undesirable as tending to restrict the trustee's right to take action to too great an extent. A more desirable provision, and one that is common in modern indentures, is to permit a majority of the security holders to waive a default or direct the trustee's course of conduct in the event that a default occurs.

As in the case of affirmative covenants, the types of negative clauses are many and varied. It is desirable, therefore, to pattern the restrictive provisions inserted to fit the circumstances of each particular case rather than to endeavor to apply a set pattern or formula to each and every situation. The provisions discussed below are some of the more common covenants used, and are set forth to illustrate the types of clauses under discussion and the purposes they are designed to accomplish. It is important to bear in mind that where the company conducts part of its operations through subsidiaries, or may subsequently do so, the covenants should be so phrased as to apply to subsidiaries as well as to the obligor itself.

(1) Covenants relating to the maintenance of working capital.

Covenants of this type relate to maintenance of working capital (sometimes called "Net Current Assets" and representing excess of current assets over current liabilities) at a certain minimum level. The covenant takes different forms. Sometimes the company is required to maintain working capital of a certain stated amount; sometimes the current ratio (current assets to current liabilities) cannot fall below a prescribed minimum; frequently the covenant requires maintenance of working capital as a stated percentage of funded debt; occasionally there will be a combination of several requirements of this type. It is common practice to combine this requirement with other negative covenants; for example, the company may be permitted to borrow additional funds as long as the net working capital is maintained at the required percentage of total funded debt.

This type of covenant is of particular importance and is almost always found where the principal purpose of the credit being arranged is for working capital, such as expansion of inventory. Regardless of the proposed use of funds, if the nature of the business is such as to require a large amount of working capital, this is one of the factors that should be followed closely in examining the company's statements, and it is desirable to provide some basis for action if there is indication that the company's position may be deteriorating.

(2) Covenant against creation of additional debt.

This is a fairly common covenant that is found in most debenture agreements. Since the obligations to be issued are unsecured, it is obvious that continued unrestricted borrowing might seriously prejudice the security holders' position or impair the equity on the basis of which they undertook to extend credit.

The basic prohibition is against creation of additional funded debt (usually defined as that having maturity in excess of one year at the time incurred), but it is sometimes extended to include current debt or current borrowings above a stated amount.

There are normally a number of permitted exceptions to this restriction which can be expressed in any number of ways. Always exempt from its operation are the incurring of liabilities (other than for borrowed money) in the ordinary course of business, accrual of taxes, claims for labor, and other similar accruals that are an essential part of the orderly operation of the business.

As indicated above, the restriction is frequently made ineffective as long as certain ratios are maintained. The ratios most frequently so used are working capital to total debt and net tangible assets to debt. The latter requirement is frequently expressed in another way; namely, aggregate debt is limited to a certain percentage of the total capitalization of the company. These requirements are usually combined with an earnings requirement. An example of this would be a provision that the average earnings during the past five years, and for each of the two preceding years, available for interest, must have been at least five times the total interest requirements on all funded debt, including that proposed to be issued.

Finally, the only limitation of debt may be merely a total dollar limitation and this may be expressed either with or without the exclusion of liabilities incurred in the ordinary course of business.

(3) Covenant against sale and leaseback.

An increasingly popular form of financing arrangement in recent years has been the sale and leaseback. Under this type of deal, a company which owns substantial real estate, such as an office building, warehouses, retail stores, etc., arranges for the sale of such property to one or more investors and takes back a noncancellable lease for a specified term at a rental aggregating the purchase price plus an amount equivalent to the going rate of interest on the unamortized purchase price. This not only provides a convenient method of raising funds but also enables the company to keep its capital invested in its primary business purpose rather than in the ownership and operation of real estate.

The covenant is designed to prohibit or limit such arrangements during the term of the loan. The limitation may be expressed in any number of ways, such as a dollar limitation on the gross value of property so transferred; a limitation on the aggregate annual rentals equal to a percentage of net earnings for a prescribed period; or as in the case of the preceding covenant, the limitation may be expressed in terms of maintenance of certain ratios of working capital or net tangible assets to debt, where the aggregate of all leaseback sales is added to debt.

The purpose of the covenant is twofold. The first consideration is substantially the same as the restriction against debt. Rentals under the leases become fixed obligations, and a limitation on the incur-

ring of such obligations is usually important. A second consideration is related to the "negative pledge" clause and involves a prohibition against sale of productive facilities to which recourse might
be had in event of a default. Thus, in some cases, sale of an office
building, or similar holding, may be permitted while sale of fac-
tories, warehouses, or other essential productive property is restricted.

(4) Covenant against execution of lease of real property or
equipment.

(5) Covenant against rental or lease of personal property
sold by the company or acquired by an investor for rental or
lease to the company.

These covenants are similar in nature and serve the same purpose
as the restriction on sale and leaseback arrangements. Here again
the prohibition may be absolute or may be expressed in terms of
certain limitations or exceptions. Such limitations may be expressed in terms of a maximum dollar amount of annual rentals, or
aggregate rentals as a percentage of net earnings; or such leases may
be permitted if the term thereof (including renewals) does not
exceed a stated period (usually not more than five years).

(6) Covenant against creation of prior liens (negative
pledge clause).

This restriction is designed to prohibit the creation of claims or
obligations paramount to those of the indenture securities so as to
insure maintenance of the same priority position of the holders
thereof as exists at the time of extension of credit. This essential
purpose may be accomplished in either of two ways, and the covenant is frequently expressed either in terms of an absolute restriction against creation of liens on company property, or by permitting their creation only on condition that the indenture obligations are equally secured at the same time.

In order to permit the orderly conduct of the company's business,
certain logical exceptions to the restriction are usually permitted.
These include: (a) liens for taxes not yet due; (b) liens existing on
property at the time of its acquisition by the company or purchase
money mortgages created in connection with the acquisition of

additional property. These liens may be limited to a certain percentage of the value of such property, and it is usually expressly provided that they cannot extend to any other property of the company. It is also customary to include a maximum dollar limitation on the aggregate of all such liens; (c) renewals or extensions of liens referred to in (b), provided they are not increased and do not extend to other property; (d) liens incurred in the ordinary course of business not involving the borrowing of money; and (e) deposits of money or property to secure performance of a contract or obligation, such as deposits required by workmen's compensation laws, under government contracts, required in connection with self-insurance arrangements, and the like.

This covenant is frequently referred to as a "negative pledge" clause, which is actually a misnomer. The clause does not create a pledge on any assets nor does it give an equitable lien on any property which may be thereafter pledged or transferred in violation of the covenant.

(7) Covenant against loans, advances, and guarantees.

(8) Covenant against pledge or discount of receivables, or their sale at less than par.

(9) Covenant against mortgage of patents, copyrights, or similar property.

(10) Covenant against ownership of securities, except stock or indebtedness of subsidiaries or obligations of the United States.

These covenants fall into the same general category as the preceding one, and are intended to prevent the encumbering, dissipation, or use of company assets except in the orderly conduct of its business. The covenant against loans, advances, and guarantees usually includes an exemption of intrasystem transactions if a portion of the company's business is conducted through subsidiaries, and the restrictive covenants in the indenture apply to both company and subsidiaries. Transactions in the ordinary course of business may also be excepted if guaranties are normally granted as a part of the conduct of the business.

(11) Covenant restricting payment of dividends or purchase or retirement of stock.

Equity capital or the stockholders' investment in a business is made up not only of the stated capital and surplus which they have paid into the business as consideration for the issuance of their shares, but also of the amount of the earned surplus which represents the aggregate of the earnings which have been retained by the company for use in the business. Generally speaking, earned surplus is subject to no restrictions and could be paid out or distributed to stockholders at any time as dividends. Such distribution could be in cash or in property.

One of the principal concerns of an investor in extending credit is the amount of this stockholders' equity, particularly in relation to the amount of debt that will be outstanding. Since debt represents a priority claim against the assets of the company, any excessive distribution to stockholders may be regarded as in the nature of a preferential distribution to a subordinate claimant.

It is therefore quite common in all indentures, whether secured or unsecured, to include a provision that will prevent any unwarranted distribution. This is usually done by placing a substantial portion of the unrestricted earned surplus in a restricted category for the duration of the loan. A portion of such surplus is usually left in an unrestricted category available for dividends, the amount being a matter for negotiation, but quite frequently it represents a sum approximately equal to one year's dividends on the stock. In working out the other terms of the credit, the amount so unrestricted is usually disregarded by the investor and, to the extent it is thereafter retained, it provides an additional cushion to bolster the credit extended.

The covenant usually provides that no dividends will be distributed to stockholders or any funds of the corporation applied to the purchase, redemption, or other retirement of shares of stock in excess of the sum of (a) the amount of the earned surplus left in an unrestricted category, (b) net earnings of the company after a stated date (usually the end of the next preceding fiscal year), and (c) the amount received by the company as proceeds of sale of additional shares of stock.

Payment of dividends or other distributions to stockholders is always made contingent on there being no default under the agreement and, quite frequently, on the existence of certain minimum ratios at the time of declaration.

(12) Covenants relating to subsidiaries, the most common being: (a) against the sale of stock or debt of a subsidiary; (b) against the issue of stock of a subsidiary except to the parent company or to another subsidiary; (c) against permitting a subsidiary to issue preferred stock except to the company or to another subsidiary.

As indicated above, where subsidiary companies are important to a system operation, all general restrictive covenants such as those against additional debt, against creation of liens, etc. are made applicable alike to parent company and subsidiaries. Since the companies are viewed as an entity for the purpose of the credit, intrasystem transactions are customarily excluded from operation of these restrictions. It is therefore necessary to add other restrictions to prevent the weakening of the entity by reducing the system percentage ownership of any subsidiary company.

The first of the covenants prohibits disposal of the investment in a subsidiary. In order to permit flexibility, the restrictive provision usually states that no stock or indebtedness of a subsidiary may be sold except as an entirety, and then only if: (1) the operations conducted by such subsidiary do not represent a significant part of system operations; (2) in the judgment of the obligor's board of directors, retention of the investment therein is no longer necessary for system operations; (3) the sale is for a cash consideration representing the full value of the system investment in such subsidiary; and (4) such subsidiary owns no stock or indebtedness of another subsidiary.

In the case of subsidiary companies which are less than 100 per cent owned by the system, covenant (b) above is usually qualified to prohibit any issuance of stock that would result in a decrease in the pro rata interest of the system.

The reason for prohibition of a public issue of preferred stock of a subsidiary follows the same theory as the prohibition against prior liens. As far as the obligor itself is concerned, the indenture securities have priority over any preferred stock issue. Stock of a subsidiary company, however, is an asset of the obligor, and permitting the issuance of another class of stock having priority would be equivalent to subjecting the property represented by such asset to a prior claim.

(13) Covenant against merger of the obligor or sale or lease of all or substantially all of its assets.

The indenture usually contains a separate section dealing with mergers, consolidations, and so on. It is included here because it is, in effect, a restrictive covenant. There is usually no absolute prohibition against mergers or consolidations or sale of company assets, but such activities are permitted only under certain conditions which should be carefully and explicitly stated. The following conditions are usually included:

(a) Either the obligor must be the surviving corporation, or the obligations under the indenture must be expressly assumed in writing (usually by supplemental indenture) by the survivor;

(b) There must be no default under the indenture and no default can exist after completion of the merger;

(c) If any other debt will become a lien on any properties of the obligor upon completion of the merger, the indenture securities must be secured by a mortgage or other lien on the obligor's properties prior to the merger;

(d) If the surviving corporation will have secured debt outstanding in excess of a given amount (whether or not the obligor's property will become subject to such lien), the indenture securities must be first secured by a lien on the obligor's properties;

(e) If the indenture requires the maintenance of certain specified ratios (such as minimum working capital, working capital to debt, net tangible assets to debt, etc.), it is usually provided that these ratios must exist in the prescribed minimum amount immediately following the merger.

In reviewing a draft of a proposed indenture contract, all the provisions thereof should be read together as in the aggregate constituting a single entity. This is particularly true of all the covenants of the indenture. In order to administer a contract properly, the trustee must understand it. This means not only making sense out of the language of each provision considered separately, but understanding the meaning and purpose of the whole indenture as a single contract. The investor is willing to extend credit on certain terms and conditions which the borrower is willing to meet. The indenture contract should spell out those terms and conditions completely and unambiguously, and all the provisions thereof should fit together as a pattern. Once the concept of the entire contract is understood thoroughly, each separate covenant will take on its proper meaning, and the job of administration will be rendered much easier.

9

Servicing Debt Securities—Agency Functions

CORPORATE TRUST officers must be concerned not only with protecting the security of the indenture and administering its provisions, but they must also provide facilities for the performing of the many responsible and detailed duties involved in the handling of the indenture securities themselves, from the time of their issuance until they are finally retired and disposed of. In the larger institutions which handle a substantial volume of corporate trust business, these "operating" functions are usually performed by a separate staff in charge of an officer experienced in operating procedures and techniques. In the smaller banks, however, which constitute a majority, a single officer may be responsible for both indenture administration and security servicing activities. Even in the large institutions, an administrative officer cannot discharge the functions properly unless there is an understanding of the basic problems which are involved in servicing the indenture securities.

These functions are separate and distinct from the specific duties of the trustee, although of necessity the responsibilities overlap at many points. However, they are performed by the bank in an agency capacity, and separate appointing documents and instructions should be received. Since the relationship involved is essentially that of an agency, it may be terminated by the obligor at any time without a change in the basic trustee relationship.

Similarly, while the bank designated as corporate trustee is usually appointed principal agent of the corporation to service the indenture securities, and in most instances such designation facilitates handling the many problems involved, the obligor may, and sometimes does, designate other banks to act in one or more agency capacities. A particular company might desire to have all of its securities serviced by one bank. If such a bank were acting as corporate trustee for a secured bond issue, it would be disqualified from acting as such under an unsecured debenture indenture. Nevertheless, such a bank could be appointed the agent to service the debentures with another bank acting as corporate trustee.

New York City is the principal financial center in the country, and most purchasers of securities like to have facilities provided in New York for the servicing thereof. Since many millions of bonds are held in the custody of New York banks and brokers, a great deal of expense is avoided if shipment to other areas of the country is made unnecessary. Accordingly, many indentures require the obligor to designate an office or agency in New York City where demands or notices may be served and where the indenture securities may be presented for payment, registration, exchange, and so on. Where a local bank outside New York City is named trustee, it is quite common to designate such a bank as the principal agent to service the indenture securities with a New York bank (usually a correspondent of the trustee) named as co-agent to perform all requisite agency functions, including an appointment as authenticating agent for the trustee to authenticate securities to be issued on registration of transfer, exchange or partial redemption. Occasionally, a co-agent is named in one or more cities in addition to New York. The activities of all the agents must be closely coordinated, and appropriate controls should be maintained by the trustee and principal agent, with the other agents reporting and accounting to it.

Procedures will tend to vary widely, depending on volume handled, local practices and, in some cases, requirements of specific laws and regulations. Since we are concerned primarily with the trustee's responsibility, no effort will be made to discuss procedures in detail, except to the extent with which the administrative officer should be familiar. The more important services which have to be performed are those of bond registrar; interest paying agent; principal paying agent; exchange agent; conversion agent; accounting and destruction agent.

APPOINTING DOCUMENTS

The only documents normally required to support an agency appointment are: (1) a resolution of the company's board of directors; (2) a copy of the indenture or supplemental indenture creating the issue; (3) incumbency certificates; (4) a specimen of each authorized denomination of the bond or debenture; and (5) such supplemental instructions from the company as may be required to set forth the specific duties and responsibilities of the agent. Where the agent is also the trustee, most of these documents will have been received by the trustee and duplication is unnecessary.

Where the agent is designated by name in the indenture itself a general resolution approving the indenture is all that is required, although it is a desirable practice to have the resolutions sufficiently broad to cover each agency appointment specifically. No special form is required, but it is suggested that the text of the resolution follow the indenture language as closely as possible to indicate that this is the specific appointment which the company covenanted to make. It is also recommended that the resolution contain general language designating the company officials (by title) who are authorized to issue instructions to the agent. While it is not necessary to name the agents in the securities themselves, it will facilitate subsequent processing if the bond contains the name of the bank to which it should be presented for payment, transfer, and so on.

The incumbency certificates should include specimen signatures of the officers of the company, particularly those who signed any of the bonds or debentures. If facsimile signatures are used, the specimen bond will suffice for this purpose, but the agent should still have the signatures of the officers authorized to instruct it. If the agent is someone other than the trustee, it should also have specimens of the signatures of all officers of the trustee who authenticated the bonds. This information is desirable for subsequent verification of the bonds.

Finally, the agent should obtain such detailed instructions from an authorized official of the company as are necessary to enable it to carry out its duties expeditiously. This would include such things as: source of funds to pay principal and interest; disposition to be made of cancelled securities; statements and reports to be rendered, and so on. As a practical matter, since the agent will wish to fit this agency into a customary pattern, and will usually know more than the principal about what should be done, it is customary for the agent to outline to the principal the procedure it intends to follow and to request the confirmation and approval of the latter.

BOND REGISTRAR

The registrar appointment is of great importance in the modern fully registered corporate issue, and there are many reasons why the trustee should be designated as principal registrar to maintain the record of registered holders and of transfers. The list of holders is essential for other purposes, such as selection of bonds for partial redemption and mailing of notices. Both time and expense are saved if the trustee is made responsible for maintaining this record. All interest payments will be by check and it is important that this be done by the bank which maintains the record of holders. The paying agency appointment for such issues now relates primarily to the making of principal payments. In the event the trustee is not located in New York City, it will be necessary in most cases to provide facilities for transfer of registered bonds in New York. In particular cases it may be desirable to provide such facilities in one or more other financial centers. In any place where registration facilities are required that is not the location of the trustee, the registrar or co-registrar should also be given the necessary authority to "authenticate" the obligations. This is an agency function and the granting of this authority constitutes an appointment in addition to the registrar function. This was done only rarely until several years ago, and presented no particular problem because of the relative infrequency of bond transfers. Where a new bond had to be issued, however, it was necessary for the New York registrar (if the trustee was located elsewhere) to obtain the trustee's authentication of the new pieces prior to delivery. This has been the primary reason for delay in consummating transfers and exchanges in many cases.

While a number of unlisted stock issues have no New York City transfer facilities, the situation is different in the case of bonds because of the accrued interest factor and the fact that the average bond transaction involves a substantially greater dollar value. Dealers therefore run a greater risk of loss through delays in processing transfers of debt obligations. With the tremendous increase in the volume of registered bonds, it is apparent that, in those situations where the trustee is not located in New York City, facilities must be provided to accommodate the New York security market. The procedure which has been found most desirable is the appointment of the New York registrar as an agent of the trustee to authenticate the bonds to be issued on registration of transfer. Such agent enters into an agreement with the trustee indemnifying it with respect to exercise of such authority by the agent.

Authentication on original issuance should be only by the trustee, as should the authentication of bonds in replacement of mutilated, lost, stolen or destroyed bonds. These transactions involve creation of additional indebtedness with respect to which the trustee has special fiduciary responsibilities. However, authentication of securities on transfer, exchange or partial redemption does not involve the same degree of responsibility, and where desirable to facilitate consummation of transactions promptly or to avoid unnecessary expense to holders, may properly be done by a responsible institution other than the trustee under appropriate safeguards.

Many existing mortgage indentures are intended as permanent financing media, and some question may exist as to whether an authenticating agent can be appointed for additional series of bonds to be issued under these indentures by reason of certain language in the original indentures. This is an example of the type of inflexibility which should be avoided in drafting indentures. In such indentures, every effort should be made to find a legal resolution since it is obvious that the rights of holders of existing obligations will not be affected. If these legal questions cannot be resolved, simplified procedures for obtaining consent of the requisite percentage of holders should be considered.

A fully registered bond means that both the principal and interest are registered in the holder's name. From the standpoint of such holders, there are a number of advantages to registration. Negotiability is restricted and in the case of theft or loss, the expense of replacement is reduced, and the risk of total loss of investment almost eliminated. Interest is paid by check, and the chore of detaching and collecting interest coupons every six months is eliminated. In the event the bond is called, or the trustee or issuer wish to communicate with the holder, a notice or letter can be mailed directly to such registered holder. The principal disadvantage is that the bond cannot be disposed of by delivery to a purchaser, but must be surrendered to the registrar to effect the registration of transfer.

To effect a transfer, the bond must be accompanied by a form of assignment which has been executed by the transferor, assigning such holder's interest in the bond in blank or to a specified transferee. The registrar will require that the holder's signature to the assignment be guaranteed. A New York registrar will require that such guaranty be by a member firm of the New York or American stock exchange or other acceptable regional stock exchange, by a New York commercial bank, or a commercial bank having a New York correspondent.

Registration as to both principal and interest requires that a new bond or bonds be prepared and issued on every transaction, such being usually issuable in any denomination that is a multiple of $1,000. If the registrar has been appointed as authenticating agent, it will authenticate the new certificates, under advice to the trustee that it has cancelled (obligor's signature only) an equal principal amount of bonds, including in the certification the serial numbers of the certificates issued and cancelled and will ship the cancelled bonds to the trustee. If the registrar is not an authenticating agent, both the old and new certificates must be delivered to the trustee, which will cancel its authentication certificate on the old bonds and authenticate the new ones to be delivered. Information as to the particular transaction, including name, address and taxpayer identification number of both the transferor and the transferee, and the bond numbers cancelled and issued, and the principal amount must be inputed to the registrar's bondholder record file. A transfer or journal sheet will normally be prepared reflecting each day's activity for the particular issue. Although most major bond registrar banks maintain the permanent record as part of their computerized record-keeping procedures, it is desirable to produce daily "hard copy" of such transactions, either for research purposes if such is not otherwise readily available, or to forward it to the obligor. Where more than one registrar is involved, only the principal registrar will maintain individual registration records of the names of the holders. All co-registrars must therefore furnish the information (usually a copy of their transfer sheets) to the principal registrar.

Almost all state and municipal debt securities currently issued are in bearer form, but provide for the registration thereof at the holder's option. Most corporate obligations sold prior to 1965 were similarly issued. Such registration privilege may be as to principal only, or as to both principal and interest. In the case of corporate issues, the privilege however, had to be set forth specifically in the indenture.

Registration as to principal only means the principal of the bond is registered in the holder's name. The bearer interest coupons remain attached, and are used for collection of the semi-annual interest in exactly the same manner as if no registration had occurred. Registration of such bonds is also accomplished by presenting the bond to the registrar accompanied by an executed assignment, with the signature guaranteed in the same manner as a fully registered bond. The registrar will enter the date and name of the registered holder on the special registration panel on the back of the bond, and such registration will be authenticated by the signature of an authorized officer of the registrar opposite the name of the holder. A special transfer sheet will usually be prepared by the registrar showing the bond number and a transfer from "bearer" to the name of the holder. This transfer is posted to a special record file (or ledger sheet) under the name and address of the holder, which will show the date, number and principal amount of the bond registered as to principal in that holder's name. Any subsequent registration as to the principal of bonds of the same issue in that holder's name will also be posted to the particular record file by showing a debit to the transferor and a credit to the transferee.

A release of a bond registered as to principal to bearer is accomplished in the same manner as a transfer, except that the word "bearer" instead of the name of a transferee is entered in the registration box. Full negotiability by delivery is then restored. An assignment in blank by the former registered holder is required to effect such "deregistration".

No posting to the trustee's ledger Record of Bonds Issued is required in the case of registration as to principal only, or transfers of such bonds, as no change occurs in the serial number or amount of bonds outstanding.

PAYMENT OF INTEREST

The first obligation of the agent is to make certain that requisite funds are obtained prior to each interest payment date. A few banks follow the practice of billing their principals for all interest payments due. This is an expensive and unnecessary step and has become the exception. The obligation of the issuer to provide the necessary funds is an absolute one, and their officials are capable—without reminder—of making funds available on time and in the proper amount. Where deposit with the paying agent is by check, it should be in sufficient time to enable the agent to complete collection of the check and have available funds on the payment date.

Under qualified indentures, all funds deposited for payment of interest must be held in trust, whether or not they are held by the trustee. If the agent is a bank other than the trustee, it must—at the time of accepting its appointment—execute a letter of undertaking to the trustee to hold in trust for the benefit of the security holders all sums deposited with it for the payment of principal or interest on the securities, and to give prompt notice to the trustee of default by the obligor in the making of any such payment.

The responsibility of the paying agent is further complicated by the necessity of complying with the relevant provisions of the Internal Revenue Code and with the regulations of particular taxing jurisdictions. All payments of registered interest on corporate bond issues in excess of $10. must be reported to the federal government. Many pre-1933 issues contained a covenant by the obligor assuming all federal income taxes on the interest obligations. This is no longer permitted, and the necessity of processing government ownership certificate forms for these issues have almost completely disappeared. Should this be revived, either through a tax withholding requirement or otherwise, the work of the paying agent would be increased substantially. It is also necessary to withhold the requisite income taxes on all payments to non-resident aliens, and to process and file with the federal government the appropriate income tax forms. Of increasingly more significance are the requirements of particular state tax laws. For example, any corporation incorporated in Pennsylvania or with a treasurer's office in that state is subject to the Pennsylvania Corporate Loans Tax. Unless the tax is assumed by the corporation, it must be withheld from all payments to Pennsylvania residents. The corporation is entitled to a credit with respect to payments to all non-Pennsylvania residents, but proof of such payments must be supplied. The agent must, therefore, obtain evidence of the residence of each holder to whom payment is made, so that the necessary proof to support the corporate return may be supplied. In the case of bearer bonds, this is accomplished through the use of a memorandum certificate of ownership. (See Exhibit 11.)

Payment of Registered Interest

Interest is usually payable semi-annually, although infrequently provision is made for payment at different intervals. Such interest will be due and payable on fixed dates; all accruals of such interest being for the prescribed periods. A transfer of the obligation normally transfers the right to any interest accrued, the purchaser paying this amount as part of the purchase price. The traditional method was the closing of the transfer books for a brief period immediately preceding the date of payment. This did not create any problems when normal trading was in bearer obligations. With the advent of the all registered corporate issue, objection was raised by many dealers to the suspension of transfer privileges for an entire issue thus making it more burdensome in accepting such obligations in settlement of contracts. It was, therefore, necessary to devise a procedure to overcome this objection and provide for the continuance of orderly trading. The procedure which has been universally accepted is a modification of the contract between obligor and holder to provide for a record date prior to the end of the accrual period for determination of holders entitled to the payment.[13] As a result, the transfer books need not be closed at all during this period.

Since the basic obligation calls for payment of interest on the interest payment date, and the full six months interest does not become payable as a debt until such date, the obligation to pay on such date to holders of record as of a preceding date must be set forth clearly and unambiguously in the indenture and on the face of the bond.

The recommended uniform record date for interest payable on the first day of a calendar month is the close of business on the 15th day of the calendar month preceding the date of payment. If interest is payable on the 15th, the record date should be the close of business on the last day of the calendar month next preceding. In the event of a failure to pay on the due date, the established record

---

[13] See note 7 *supra.*

date is of no effect and the transfer of the bond will transfer all rights of the holder for the defaulted interest to the transferee. This should be set forth clearly in the indenture and provision should also be made for determination of the persons entitled to payment of such defaulted interest. It is recommended that, upon receipt of notification of intention to pay the defaulted interest on a certain date (including arrangements satisfactory to the trustee for the deposit of the funds), the trustee establish a special record date which should be not more than fifteen nor less than ten days prior to the proposed payment date, and not less than ten days after receipt of the notice of proposed payment. Notification of the proposed payment and of the special record date should be mailed to the bondholders by the trustee not less than ten days prior to such special record date.

Interest so payable to the "record date" holders of fully registered bonds is made by check issued and mailed to them, as shown by the registration records. If the interest disbursing agent is other than the registrar, the latter will prepare a certified list of registered holders, as of the record date, with the total holdings of each, and deliver it to the disbursing agent. These checks are usually mailed on the business day preceding the interest due date to insure that in most cases the check will be received by the holder on the date the interest is due.

The total amount to be disbursed should be proved to the registered bond control record of the trustee to insure that the registrar's bondholder records are in proof with the trustee's control. Each transaction involving a change in the outstanding principal amount of registered bonds should be posted to the trustee's Record of Bonds Issued ledger, and the requisite control may be provided by use of such ledger record. Where, however, an issue is outstanding in both bearer and registered form, it is necessary to maintain a subsidiary ledger control of the outstanding fully registered bonds (see Exhibit 13). This practice facilitates a quick proof of registered interest disbursements, certifications of registered bonds outstanding and other transactions relating to such bonds. A record is maintained by posting from a daily journal prepared by the appropriate operations personnel covering all registration activity for each day. This journal records the total principal amount of fully registered obligations cancelled or discharged or issued during the day for each separate issue on which there was activity. The totals are then posted to the registered bonds outstanding control ledger for each such issue.

Payment of Bearer Interest

As most corporate debt obligations issued prior to 1965, and almost all state and municipal obligations are issued and outstanding in bearer form, it is necessary to examine in some detail the means whereby interest is collected by the holders thereof. This is accomplished by attachment to each such obligation of a sheet of bearer coupons, one for each interest payment date to, and including, the date of maturity of the principal obligation. Until they become payable, these coupons are an essential part of the bond itself and together with it constitute a single obligation. Once they have matured and become payable, however, they constitute separate and distinct obligations and may be transferred by delivery separate from the bond itself. Payment to bearer, even though other than the holder of the bond, will discharge the debt represented thereby.

As noted before interest is usually payable semi-annually, although infrequently provision is made for payment at different intervals. On a $20,000,000. twenty-five year bond issue consisting of all bearer bonds of $5,000. denomination which remain outstanding to maturity without interim sinking fund or redemption payments, 200,000 separate interest obligations will have to be processed. It follows that the function of the coupon paying agent is one of the more important to be performed in servicing the obligations of state and municipalities, the older corporate bond issues, and the so-called Eurodollar issues.

As the coupon, when due, will become a separate obligation, it must incorporate a separate and distinct promise to pay. Where the bond is subject to prior redemption, all coupons maturing after the first possible redemption date should have this promise qualified by language such as: "Unless the bond hereinafter mentioned shall have been called for previous redemption and payment of the redemption price thereof duly provided. . . ." Each coupon will contain the name of the issuer, the date on which it will become due, the specific amount due thereon, the place of payment, and a statement that it represents interest for a specified period on the bond designated by serial number. The coupon will be validated by the signature (usually facsimile) of the treasurer or other authorized official of the issuer. To facilitate identification and processing, the coupons attached to each bond should be numbered in consecutive order, the first maturing coupon being Number 1, the second, Number 2, and so on. All coupons maturing on the same date from bonds of the same issue will bear the same coupon number.

The holder of a bond may detach the coupons and forward them directly to the paying agent and receive a check in payment. As this check must also be processed, this method of collection will delay receipt of usable funds by the holder, and it is not the method most frequently used. From the viewpoint of the agent, it is the most expensive way in which payment has to be made. The normal collection procedure follows the same pattern as is used in processing checks, except that credit usually is not passed to the depositor's account until collection is actually made. Each bank provides special envelopes for its depositors in which coupons may be enclosed and deposited for collection. The holder writes his or her name and address on the envelope, together with a description of the bond, the denomination of the coupon, and the total face amount of coupons deposited. The bank of deposit will then forward the envelope, together with all envelopes received from other depositors, to its correspondent bank in the city of collection. The latter will accept it as a deposit from the forwarding bank, and will assign a collection number to the total deposit, which may represent many coupon envelopes for many different issues. After proving each collection, this bank then sorts the envelopes by issues and paying agents and presents the coupons to the respective paying agents. Most of this processing takes place prior to the maturity date, and the paying agent will accept coupons for processing about a week before the actual due date. On the due date the paying agent will make payment to the presenting bank for all coupons presented, up to and including such date. On the same date each bank through which the coupon has been processed will pass the pre-established credit to its depositor.

Where default has been made in payment, or where a particular coupon is mutilated or is otherwise irregular, it must be returned through the same channels used in its collection and each depositor's account must be charged back for the amount of the item.

An innovation which has been developed by the New York banks and followed in only one or two other cities, is to provide for collection of all coupons through a clearing house. Each morning all collecting banks transport all their collection items to the clearing house, where they are delivered to the paying banks. For the total deposits and receipts, a net credit or debit is made to the bank's account at the Federal Reserve Bank. The aggregate of return items which have to be charged back is handled in the same manner. This arrangement facilitates the collection process and reduces to a minimum the number of checks which have to be prepared and issued by the agents. Together with the preliminary work performed by the banks in their capacity as collecting agent, it has also minimized the costs to issuers for servicing of their coupons.

The paying agent must examine each separate coupon presented to see that it is a valid obligation; that it is a matured obligation and one which the agent is authorized to pay; that the bond from which it was detached has not been previously called for redemption; that the coupon has not been cancelled; that it is not otherwise mutilated; and that no stop order is on file with respect to the particular coupon. Each separate collection must also be proved as to amount. If everything is found to be in order, the coupons are cancelled by perforation. The total of all coupons for each issue received each day is proved to the total collections received and the appropriate account charged for the total payments. If payment is refused for any reason, the coupon is returned uncancelled to the presenting bank (or to the presenter if not a collecting bank) and, if an aggregate credit has been made, against an appropriate charge back. All coupons must be processed and either paid or returned on the same day they are presented to the agent.

Most coupons are payable on the first or fifteenth day of the month, and the few days immediately preceding and following these dates are days of heavy volume. During the remaining days of the month, the work processed during these periods is audited and verified by personnel other than those who handled the payment. In this operation the coupons are broken down by maturity date, and the total coupons paid for a designated period (usually monthly) are proved to the total charges made during the period to the coupon account.

Some banks still follow an expensive practice of maintaining a separate cash account for each interest maturity. Since it is necessary in any event for the coupons to be segregated by coupon number (or maturity date), it is much easier to maintain the appropriate breakdown by subsidiary record. Where a single obligor has a number of separate issues of securities outstanding, it is entirely appropriate to maintain a single cash account for all issues and to provide the necessary breakdown by issue and maturity by subsidiary records.

Where a great volume of coupon payments is handled, the responsibility of the administrative officer is to furnish operations personnel with essential instructions and information in as concise and clearly understandable manner as possible. Any information which will facilitate ready verification of the validity of the obligation is helpful. Exhibit 9 shows the form of a typical coupon paying card used by coupon payers, and Exhibit 10, a form of card used by the verification clerk. The forms vary by reason of the different functions performed by each. For example, most stop payments are checked only in the verification process. Each clerk has a copy of the appropriate card for all issues for which he or she is responsible. Responsibility for accuracy of the instructions is that of the account administrator.

It is obvious that a great deal can be done at the time the issue is being prepared to facilitate subsequent efficiency in the paying operation. Appropriate selection of colors for each issue is an obvious aid. It has been found also that it is simpler to use a number designation for each separate issue of an obligor than a full descriptive statement of the issue. For example, let us assume that the Capital City School District has ten separate issues of bonds outstanding. A designation of CC1 to CC10 is given to each of the issues. With the co-operation of the obligor, these numerical designations can be imprinted on each separate coupon obligation. The work of the paying clerks in segregating these obligations by issues is considerably simplified, as the necessary breakdown can be accomplished by reference to the appropriate designation on the coupon, thus eliminating the necessity of reading the full descriptive text. This procedure is of particular benefit in the case of state and municipal issues where a number of different issues (for various purposes) may be put out on the same day, at the same rate, and with identical maturity dates.

A corporate issuer is required under qualified indentures to maintain a list of all information coming into its possession as to names and addresses of its security holders. This information must be filed with the trustee semi-annually. If this information is derived from the collection of interest coupons, the agents must maintain it in current form for filing with the trustee. The information is derived from ownership certificates filed with the coupons or from the envelopes in which the coupons are received.

Where two or more banks act as paying agents for a particular issue, arrangements must be made for appropriate co-ordination of the work of all the agents. The normal procedure is for one bank (usually the trustee) to be designated the principal agent, and for all funds to be deposited with that bank. If the other agents are correspondents of the principal agent, authority is given for charging the account of the principal agent for payments by the co-agents, and the principal agent is responsible to the issuer with respect to all payments made. Once the coupons have been paid, verified, and cancelled, and appropriate charge made to the coupon

EXHIBIT 9.   COUPON PAYING ISTRUCTION CARD

| ISSUE | Capital City School Building Bonds 6 1/2% Dated July 1, 1971 | TAX STATUS | No Tax (Municipal) |
| | | CERTIFICATE | None Required |

| DESIGNATE | C - 2 | CHARGE | Capital City School District interest account. |

AMOUNTS & COLORS $162.50 Light Brown - $5,000. Denomination

PAYING STOPS	SPECIAL INSTRUCTIONS
1/1/73 SCA - 147	Cancel future coupons as received. Refer stops to group head.
7/1/74 - 579	Coupon Identification No. CC 10

CPN. NO.	DUE	AUTH	REMARKS	CPN. NO.	DUE	AUTH	REMARKS
1	1/1/72	PH	All paid				
2	7/1/72	PH	" "				
3	1/1/73	PH	" "				
4	7/1/73	PH	" "				
5	1/1/74	PH	" "				
6	7/1/74	PH	" "				
7	1/1/75						
8	7/1/75						
9	1/1/76						

D-22-A

paying account, the work of the paying agent is concluded. The problem of making appropriate disposition of the cancelled coupons still remains, and it will be discussed later in this chapter in connection with accounting and destruction procedures.

PAYMENT OF PRINCIPAL

Theoretically, the same principles which govern payment of coupons should apply to payment of the bonds themselves. The procedures followed, however, are usually quite different. In the case of bonds, the amount involved in the handling of each item is many times greater, and consequently the risk is substantial. Coupons are handled on a volume basis; bonds on an individual basis. While the trustee is responsible for proper accounting for both

EXHIBIT 10. COUPON VERIFICATION INSTRUCTION CARD

CREMATION

ISSUE	Capital City School Building Bonds 6 1/2% Dated 7/1/71
CHARGE	Capital City School District interest account.
TAX STATUS	No tax (Municipal)
CERTIFICATES	None required.
DESIGNATION	C - 2
NUMBER OF HIGHEST BOND ISSUED	2000
SPECIAL INSTRUCTIONS	Refer all stops to group head. Remove coupons from shells and segregate by coupon number. Prepare monthly recap.

LOSS NOTICES

INDIVIDUAL COUPONS		ALL COUPONS
DUE	NUMBER	NUMBER
1/1/73		147
7/1/74	579	

CPN. NO.	DUE	REMARKS	CPN. NO.	DUE	REMARKS
1	1/1/72	All paid			
2	7/1/72	" "			
3	1/1/73	" "			
4	7/1/73	" "			
5	1/1/74	" "			
6	7/1/74	" "			
7	1/1/75				
8	7/1/75				
9	1/1/76				

D1334

EXHIBIT 11. MEMORANDUM CERTIFICATE OF OWNERSHIP

Memorandum Certificate of Ownership ·
for
ABC Power & Light Co.
4% bonds due March 1, 1984

Correspondent_____

Collection No. _____ Date _____

I certify that to the best of my
knowledge and belief the information entered hereon is correct.

_____
(Signature of owner, trustee, or
agent)

_____
(Address of trustee or agent)

_____

Owner of bonds from which accompanying
interest coupons were detached:

Name &
Address   _____

            _____

            _____

            _____

Principal amount of
     bonds owned $ _____
Date interest was due _____ Date pd. _____
     Amount of interest $ _____
NOTE: *If name and address of bond holder is
not known to final collecting agent, please
show, in space to left, name and address of
correspondent and collection number if any.*

bonds and coupons, the latter are usually accounted for by total amount by maturity date, while accounting for principal obligations is done individually, by serial number.

The bond payment clerks work from instructions prepared by the account administrator. Although in the case of coupons one set of instructions is normally sufficient for all maturities, it is usually desirable to prepare a separate set of instructions for each separate principal payment. These instructions should contain all essential information so that the paying clerks do not have to refer to the indenture or other source material. In the case of a redemption payment, the amount of the premium payable must be shown as well as the specific serial numbers of the particular bonds called.

Since payment for principal obligations is made by check, the identity of the individual presenter can be preserved.[14] During a heavy maturity period, each day's work will represent a large dollar volume, and one of the more important factors in any procedure is maintenance of proper controls. In a large volume operation, it is

[14] Commencing in the fall of 1973, a matured municipal bond clearing system was implemented by members of the New York Clearing House, following procedures similar to the daily clearing of coupons.

desirable to have a control maintained separate and apart from the clerks making the actual payment. The control clerk prepares a control ticket for each item presented, on which is listed the name of the presenter, a description of the issue, the aggregate face amount of the bonds, and the serial numbers thereof. One copy of the ticket is retained by the clerk for follow-up purposes, and the remaining copies accompany the bonds to the payment desk. The paying clerk examines the bonds to determine their validity, that they are in good order with no mutilations, and that no stop payment order is on file with respect to any particular bond, and makes such other checks as may be indicated for a particular issue. The amount of the payment is computed and entered on the control ticket. The item is then checked by a second clerk, and a check is prepared on which the number of the control ticket is entered. The bonds are subsequently cancelled and the check returned through the control clerk for delivery or mailing to the presenter. The control clerk is responsible for seeing that a check is delivered for each control ticket processed. As a separate audit, another clerk proves the total bonds cancelled for the day to the total funds disbursed. A copy of the control ticket accompanies each block of cancelled bonds, and the original, with the number of the check issued entered thereon, is filed for record purposes.

Where part of the bond issue is called prior to its stated maturity, the paying clerks must check the particular serial numbers of the bonds presented to insure that they appear on the list of called bonds.

Care must be exercised that payment is made only to the registered holder or that an appropriate assignment is received. Where payment is made to the registered holder, no assignment is necessary. Registered bonds must also be delivered to the bond registrar for proper discharge from the registration records.

In the case of a partial call, most registered bonds of large denomination are called in part only. The holder of such an obligation is given a new bond for the unredeemed portion. A special transfer sheet is prepared for the registrar showing reduction in the amount of such registered bonds.

Because all bonds are controlled on the trustee's Record of Bonds Issued, a special cancellation ticket must be prepared, reducing the trustee's control of outstanding bonds. Since for purposes of the indenture bonds cease to be outstanding on the redemption date

EXHIBIT 12. BOND REDEMPTION CONTROL TICKET FOR
   WINDOW DELIVERY

CUSIP NO. 837649]28	PRESENTOR NO. 099999	**WB** 65875

SECURITIES RECEIVED	DATE
ISSUE ABC Manufacturing Corporation	10/1/74
8 1/2% Sinking Fund Debentures	AMOUNT $3,000

DUE 4/1/95   S.C.A.

PRESENTOR

JORGE CARIL & CO.

RECEIVED FROM BANKERS TRUST COMPANY CORPORATE TRUST OPERATIONS THE ABOVE DESCRIBED SECURITIES OR THEIR EQUIV-ALENT VALUE

☐ REG1   ☐ FOREIGN SECURITIES

☐ REG2   ☐ CPN PAY

☐ CONVERSION   ☐ SECURITIES DISP.

☒ REDEMPTION   ☐

RECEIPT COPY

	PREP.	1st Ck	2nd CK	D.E.
DATE _____ MESSENGER'S SIGNATURE _____	G.P.			
THIS RECEIPT MUST HAVE COMPANY OR BANK STAMP AND MUST BE SIGNED IN INK BEFORE SECURITIES WILL BE DELIVERED. THE OWNER OR OWNERS OF SECURITIES DELIVERED BY THIS RECEIPT AGREE WITH BANKERS TRUST CO. THAT SUCH SECURITIES MAY BE DELIVERED TO BEARER HEREOF WITHOUT IDENTIFICATION.		STOP	STOP	PER PRO

1815 (5-73)

---

*Exhibit 12 is prepared in quaduplicate. The copies illustrated go
to the presenter and to the redemption processing group respectively. Another copy accompanies the securities and is used to de-*

when the required funds are deposited in trust, the recommended
procedure is for the entire principal amount called to be debited
from the trustee ledger on the redemption date. A control is set up
on a separate redemption sheet which is then posted for each day's
total redemptions. The balance on this redemption control sheet
should always prove to the funds in the redemption account.

EXCHANGE AGENT

The function of the exchange agent is similar to that of a
registrar in that it involves the exchange of bonds of an issue for
other bonds of the same issue. In actual practice, a separate exchange agent is usually not appointed, the registrar assuming this
function. The indenture governs the privilege and terms of inter-
changeability of bonds, and it desirable to provide as great flexibility as possible.

One form of exchange is that of fully registered bonds for the
coupon bearer type, or the reverse, for issues where such bearer
bonds are authorized. Upon receipt of bearer bonds with a request
for issuance of an equivalent amount in fully registered form, the

CUSIP NO. 837649128	PRESENTOR NO. 099999	**WB** 65875
SECURITIES RECEIVED		DATE
ISSUE ABC Manufacturing Corporation		10/1/74
		AMOUNT
8 1/2% Sinking Fund Debentures		$3,000.
DUE 4/1/95	S.C.A.	

PRESENTOR

JORGE CARIL & CO.

A/C DESIGNATION   A-4

PRINCIPAL $3,000.
PREMIUM   120
INTEREST   0
TOTAL $3,120
CHECK NO.   CT3295762
CREDIT A/C

REG 1	FOREIGN SECURITIES
REG 2	CPN PAY
CONVERSION	SECURITIES DISP.
X REDEMPTION	

	PREP.	1st Ck	2nd CK	D.E.
	G.P.	E.Y.	J.C.	E.B.
		STOP	STOP	PER PRO
		E.Y.	J.C.	J.S.

PROCESSING GROUP COPY

1815 (5-73)

control the item when the redemption check is delivered. The fourth copy goes to the security control (audit) group.

former will be cancelled and a registered bond or bonds prepared, with the transaction information inputed to the bondholder records file. The cancelled bearer bonds and the registered piece will be delivered to the trustee with a request for authentication of the latter. (If the registrar-exchange agent has been appointed as authenticating agent, it will authenticate the registered bond, under advice to the trustee that it has cancelled an equal principal amount of bearer bonds, including in the certification the specific serial numbers of the bonds issued and cancelled). On a reverse transaction, involving the issuance of bearer for fully registered bonds, the cancelled registered piece is delivered to the trustee after discharge, and the appropriate number of bearer bonds are requisitioned. After detaching all coupons for which interest has been paid, the trustee (or the authenticating agent) will authenticate and deliver the requisite amount of previously unissued bearer obligations. A number of companies follow the practice of having the trustee "hold alive" any bearer bonds which have been surrendered for exchange, on the theory that on an exchange back to bearer form, a supply of certificates will be available. Although this does reduce somewhat the cost to the company in the initial printing of bonds, it adds substantial liability to the trustee, who must safely control the authenticated bearer bonds pending their possible reuse and is not a recommended practice.

EXHIBIT 13. REGISTERED BONDS OUTSTANDING CONTROL LEDGER SHEET

SHEET NO. 1

COMPANY ABC Manufacturing Corporation   INTEREST DATES January and July 1

DESCRIPTION OF BONDS First Mortgage Sinking Fund Bonds due 7/1/85

RATE 5 1/2%   RECORD DATE

TRUSTEE Bankers Trust Company   BOOKS CLOSE December 21 and June 20

PAYING AGENT Bankers Trust Company

SPECIAL INSTRUCTIONS: List of holders to treasurer of company as of record dates.

DATE	CANCELLED	ISSUED	BALANCE
July 1, 1960		12,450,000.00	12,450,000.00
Sept. 20, 1960	150,000.00		12,300,000.00
Feb. 9, 1961	25,000.00		12,275,000.00
July 3, 1961	1,000,000.00		11,275,000.00
July 2, 1962	1,000,000.00		10,275,000.00
March 12, 1963		95,000.00	10,370,000.00
May 23, 1963		5,000.00	10,375,000.00
July 1, 1964	1,000,000.00		9,375,000.00

For purpose of proper control, it is much more desirable that all bonds received for exchange be cancelled and that no bonds bearing the same serial number ever be reissued for any purpose. Where there is likelihood for frequent requests for exchange, a supply of unissued bearer bonds should be lodged with the trustee for this purpose.

Where both coupon and registered bonds are authorized, special provisions must be made for the interchange of the two forms between the record and payment dates. The coupon for the interest payable on the payment date should be detached from the bearer bonds before their presentation for exchange, or delivery in exchange of, an equal amount of registered obligations.

The function of the interdenominational exchange agent is very important in fully registered issues to permit bondholders to "split" or "consolidate" the number of pieces they hold. In the case of securities issued in connection with a subscription offer to stockholders, denominations of $500, $100 and even $50 may be authorized. Frequently these denominations are freely interchangeable, although the more common provision is to permit consolidation into bonds of $1,000 denomination or multiple thereof, but no split of $1,000 bonds into smaller denominations. The reason for this limitation is the cost of servicing small denomination bonds.

CONVERSION AGENT

The use of the convertible type of debt security has been very popular during the past fifteen years. In the case of a corporation whose business is expanding, it provides a means of raising equity capital, usually at considerably less cost than direct equity financing. During a period of rising stock prices, the conversion privilege is a valuable one, and many convertible debentures will sell at substantial premiums in excess of the price they would command as straight debt securities. The usual security into which such an obligation is made convertible is the common stock of the issuing company.

The indenture controls the terms and conditions on which the privilege may be exercised, and these terms and conditions should also be set forth in the debenture itself in reasonable detail. The debenture may be made convertible into a fixed number of shares of stock, but the more usual provision is to fix a dollar price at which shares of stock may be purchased by use of the principal of the debenture. This price is subject to adjustment to reflect any change in the ratio of number of shares outstanding (other than through conversion of other debentures of the same issue). It is also customary to provide for an arbitrary increase in the conversion price at stated intervals during the life of the debenture, to encourage conversions during the earliest period. A common practice is to set the initial conversion price at a figure somewhat higher than the current market price of the common stock. This provides the advantage of the company's having a less expensive debt security for a period of time, but one which it will likely never be called on to pay, except through the issuance of common stock at a price higher than could be obtained by an immediate issue of such stock. To achieve the same purpose it is sometimes provided that the conversion privilege cannot be exercised until a stated time has elapsed after issuance of the debentures.

Upon the issuance of convertible debentures, the company must authorize and reserve for issuance the maximum number of common shares which could be issued on conversion of the entire debenture issue. Such authorization involves all the steps which would have to be taken were a number of shares being concurrently issued publicly, including the necessary registration under the Securities Act of 1933 and the listing of such additional shares on any securities exchange on which the stock is listed. The trustee should make certain that all proper steps have been taken.

The function of the conversion agent is to receive any debentures surrendered for conversion, compute the number of shares issuable, requisition such shares from the company's transfer agent and, upon their receipt, cancel the debentures and deliver the shares to the presenter.

Often a fractional interest will be involved, which may be handled in a number of ways. A common practice is to pay the value of the fractional interest in cash. This is sometimes done on the basis of the conversion price, on the theory that the obligor is paying the unconverted portion of the debt at par. The usual practice is to use the current market price of the stock to give the holder the equivalent value of the fractional interest. The indenture should set forth clearly the particular method to be followed.

Exercise of the conversion right is a privilege of the holder of the debenture, who has the option of deciding when to exercise the privilege. Conversion can frequently be forced by the company, however, by its calling the outstanding debenture issue for redemption. This will place a termination date on the conversion privilege and, if conversion is favorable, result in conversion of substantially the entire issue. If the conversion privilege is not favorable, there is seldom reason for a redemption call.

It is desirable to have the conversion privilege continue to the maturity or redemption date of the debentures. Some issues provide for an earlier termination date of convertibility, and invariably substantial losses are sustained by security holders who receive no actual notice or misunderstand the provisions of their security. There is usually no good reason for such earlier termination, since it is to the advantage of neither the company nor its security holders and should be avoided. The trustee should be diligent in endeavoring to change any such arbitrary provision. Where it does exist, the trustee should insist that every effort be made to inform security holders of their rights to minimize their losses.

A further problem to which attention should be paid is the matter of accrued interest to the conversion date. The problem may be handled in a number of ways. Occasionally an adjustment is made as between accrual of interest and accrual of dividends. This is an exceptional provision and is feasible only where the company has a fixed dividend policy with fixed dividend payment dates. The more usual provision is to state that no adjustment for accrued interest or dividends will be made. It is up to the holder to time the conversion in such a way as to be of the greatest advantage.

A convertible issue presents special problems where a record date is involved if a debenture is presented for conversion after a record date and prior to the interest payment date. Rather than suspend the conversion privilege during this period, the person converting should be required, as a condition to conversion, to deposit funds equal to the amount of interest which would otherwise be payable on the interest payment date on the debenture or portion thereof to be converted. These funds will then be used to offset the payment which is made to the person in whose name the debenture was registered on the record date. This practice is especially desirable in a situation where the record holder has sold a debenture after the record date to an individual who converts prior to the interest payment date. As part of the sale, the seller normally delivers a check for the full interest due to the purchaser, conditional on the payment of interest by the obligor, with the expectation that the seller will receive this amount back on the interest payment date. The purchaser having received this check, deposits equivalent funds at the time of conversion.

The necessity for requiring such deposit can be illustrated by a hypothetical situation in which, after a record date, dealer A buys twenty-five $1,000 debentures from twenty-five individuals and exchanges them for five $5,000 debentures. Dealer A then sells the $25,000 principal amount to various other dealers, of whom dealer B receiving $5,000 principal amount decides to convert before the interest payment date. As the result, the obligor is not required to deposit funds for payment of interest on that $5,000 principal amount. Since the twenty-five individual holders of record are entitled to receive their interest on the payment date, the amount equivalent to interest payable on $5,000 debentures must be obtained from dealer B at the time the debenture is presented for conversion.

In the event that the obligor defaults in the payment of interest on the payment date, the funds so deposited would be repaid to the person effecting the conversion. The provisions in the indenture establishing this condition to conversion must, however, be qualified to the extent that such deposit need not be made if the obligation converted has been called for redemption on a date prior to the payment date. Since no obligation exists for payment of interest on an interest payment date on bonds called for prior redemption, there would be no record date for such payment. One question which may arise is the possibility of receipt from a debentureholder of a check which cannot be collected before mailing of the interest checks has to be made. Should such check prove uncollectible a loss may result. This can be resolved by withholding delivery of the new securities for a sufficient period to allow for collection. Probably no special indenture language is required, but this problem should be borne in mind.

It should be noted that most convertible debenture issues provide for a sinking fund. It is both customary and proper to provide that the obligor will receive credit against its sinking fund requirements for all debentures converted into stock of the company.

SUBSCRIPTION AGENT

One of the collateral and important functions frequently performed is that of subscription agent in connection with the issuance of convertible debentures. In states where stockholders have pre-emptive rights, any issuance of stock or securities convertible into stock must first be offered to existing stockholders. Even where no pre-emptive right exists, such offering to existing stockholders is frequently the most feasible way of completing a successful offering.

The offering is made through the issuance of subscription warrants to existing stockholders. After the amount of the total offering has been determined, an appropriate ratio to existing shares is determined, and each shareholder is given the right to subscribe to a pro-rata portion of the new offering. These rights are often valuable, the measure of value being the difference between the offering price and the market value of the debentures. Warrants are usually issued by the company's stock transfer agent, and evidence the right to subscribe to a specified principal amount of debentures. The offer is normally underwritten; the underwriters agreeing to purchase all debentures not subscribed for through the exercise of warrants. As a result of the underwriting agreement, the life of the warrants is customarily limited to a period of two or three weeks from their date of issue.

The function of the subscription agent is twofold. First, it accepts and processes subscriptions to the debentures. This involves receipt of warrants with checks in payment of the subscribed debentures. When issuable, the debentures are requisitioned from the trustee and delivered to the subscribers.

The second function concerns the purchase and sale of rights. A stockholder who is unwilling to subscribe to the debentures is still entitled to the value of the rights as represented by the warrant. Others may wish to exercise only a portion of their warrant and sell the balance of the rights, while some may wish to acquire a larger interest than their warrant entitles them to, and therefore need to acquire additional rights. By reason of the large number of small holders, trading of such rights through normal brokerage channels might be very expensive. For the convenience of such holders, the subscription agent is permitted to purchase and sell rights. It offsets purchase and sale orders for each day's activity, and either purchases or sells the net position in the open market. The average price received on all transactions for the day is used to determine the price at which all purchases and sales will be computed. A small commission charge is imposed on the holders for this service.

ACCOUNTING AND DESTRUCTION

The purpose of every bond or debenture indenture is to secure payment of the obligations issued thereunder. Proper accounting for all such obligations is one of the important functions of the trustee. Provision must also be made for proper disposition of all obligations cancelled because of payment, exchange, or conversion or for other reasons. These functions are usually performed by the trustee, but since a separate fee is charged for their performance, and since they may be performed by the operating staff, they are included among the agency functions.

Accounting for Interest Obligations

A fully registered bond represents the obligation for both principal and interest. When such a bond is surrendered and cancelled, the trustee is entitled to assume that all amounts due with respect thereto have been paid or otherwise discharged. It is desirable, however, for the trustee to maintain a more current account as to interest payments. Where it acts as registrar and interest disbursing agent, its own records will provide requisite evidence of payment of all amounts due for registered interest. Where the company or another agent disburses registered interest, the trustee should establish an appropriate procedure for ascertaining that all registered interest payments have been made. One way of doing this is for it to receive all paid interest checks for examination. It may also receive and rely on a certification by the disbursing agent as to payments made. Whatever the form of the evidence received, it should be sufficient to establish the fact of payment.

Accounting for coupon interest is a different matter. The coupons represent separate and distinct obligations, and satisfactory evidence of their payment or cancellation should be received. A great deal of progress has been made over the years in simplifying the procedure of accounting for interest coupons. In the early days of corporate bond issues, a very elaborate procedure was followed. Large coupon ledgers were prepared which included a separate page for each bond that was issued. As the coupons were paid they were carefully pasted in the appropriate page on this ledger sheet, with the date of payment entered. This provided a complete record but the expense involved was substantial. In most corporate issues this practice has been obsolete for many years, although it is still followed by a number of municipalities.

A major step forward was achieved when issuers permitted trustees to dispose of cancelled coupons by completely destroying them (usually by cremation). A cremation certificate was prepared as evidence of such destruction. At first, cremation was witnessed by both company officials and the trustee; later, the trustee was permitted to perform this task alone. An elaborate exhibit was attached to the destruction certificate which described the coupons in detail. This included a description of the issue, the maturity date and amount of the coupon, and the bond serial numbers. This costly procedure necessitated that all coupons paid be sorted in numerical order so that they could be listed on the appropriate schedules.

In the late 1940's, a number of trustees began to question the necessity for such an elaborate procedure. Investigation revealed that these detailed schedules were seldom if ever referred to. Such detail, therefore, was unnecessary for proper accounting. As a result of these studies a major change in the accounting and destruction procedure was initiated. All accounting is now made by total number of coupons and total dollar amount for each coupon maturity date. The necessity for sorting and listing of coupons by bond serial number has been eliminated.

To insure proper accounting control, a subsidiary destruction ledger is maintained by the trustee. For each interest maturity date, the total interest due is entered. Credits against this amount are made for total registered interest disbursed, and for total value of coupons of that maturity shown by each destruction certificate. The resulting balance, if any, shows the amount of coupons outstanding and unpaid.

Where the coupon paying agent is other than the trustee, the cancelled coupons are usually shipped to the trustee, which verifies the amount and prepares them for destruction along with coupons paid by the trustee or received from other agents.

In the early 1960's an innovation to this procedure was introduced. Where paying agents other than the trustee pay a substantial percentage of the coupons, their subsequent shipment to and audit by the trustee involves an expensive and time-consuming arrangement. The trustee and the company may authorize the paying agents to complete disposition of the cancelled coupons by satisfactorily destroying them. The certificate of such agent may be relied on by the trustee as evidence of such destruction.

Accounting for Principal Obligations

Each bond cancelled for any reason must be included in an appropriate accounting. The destruction certificates covering principal obligations are similar to those covering coupons, except that the serial numbers of the bonds are shown on the certificate or the supporting schedule. The reason for cancellation is always shown, to conform to the entry in the trustee's records.

Registered bonds are handled in a different manner than are coupon bearer bonds. Where cancellation was made because of transfer or for any reason requiring assignment of the bond, destruction is usually deferred for a reasonable period of time, usually one year, and a microfilm record is made of the bond and the assignment prior to destruction. Where assignment is received separate from the bond, it is usually microfilmed with the bond and destroyed with it together with any documentation supporting a "legal" transfer (e.g. one involving a corporation or a decedent). It is important that the laws of each particular jurisdiction be examined carefully in establishing cancelled security retention and destruction periods.

LOST, STOLEN AND DESTROYED SECURITIES

Securities are sometimes stolen, or more frequently, they are lost or misplaced by the holders. The holder will then notify the trustee and request that a stop order be placed against the particular bond or coupon. Care should be used in acknowledging any such request, as the trustee may be placed in a position where it cannot comply. Registered bonds which have been endorsed, and bearer bonds and coupons are fully negotiable, and as such are valid obligations in the hands of a bona fide purchaser.[15] The trustee

---

[15] Defined in Article 8 of the Uniform Commercial Code as "a purchaser for value in good faith and without notice of any adverse claim. . . ."

receiving a stop order should promptly note its records and communicate the information to all agents. Holders sometimes fail to notify the trustee that a lost security has been found, particularly in the case of coupons. Neither the trustee nor any agent should take it upon themselves to remove such stop, even if a long period of time has elapsed, unless (1) the missing security has been surrendered to the trustee and is cancelled by it or (2) prior to the issuance of a replacement (or payment, as later discussed), the holder who requested the stop order notifies the trustee and requests that it be removed.

Where a stop order has been filed with the issuer (or trustee or agent) and the security is thereafter presented, the issuer or agent is permitted to discharge its responsibility as to such adverse claim [16] in any reasonable manner. It is recommended that the procedure outlined in the Code always be followed.[17] It should be noted that notice to the adverse claimant must always be by registered or certified mail, and that the person presenting the security must be named. Such notice must also grant the option of a court order or the filing of a sufficient indemnity bond.

Most indentures provide for replacement of securities which have been lost, stolen or destroyed upon the furnishing of satisfactory evidence of such loss, theft or destruction and the furnishing of satisfactory indemnity. Such indemnity is usually a bond executed by the holder and an indemnity company, satisfactory to the obligor issuer and the trustee. Some outstanding security issues have no provision for issuance of replacements, including a number of municipalities and other public and quasi-public issues, as well as some old corporate indentures which do not make any provision for replacement of stolen bonds.

Under the Code, the issuer (and the trustee) must issue a new security in place of the original if the owner (1) so requests before the issuer has notice that the security has been acquired by a bona fide purchaser; (2) files with the issuer a sufficient indemnity bond; and (3) satisfies any other reasonable requirements imposed by the issuer.

---

[16] A claim by someone not in possession of the security. It includes a claim that a transfer was or would be wrongful, or that a particular person is the owner or has an interest in the security.

[17] Uniform Commercial Code 8-403.

There are two conditions which will preclude the owner from demanding a replacement security. These are a failure to notify the issuer within a reasonable time after the owner has notice, and registration of transfer of the original security before the issuer receives notice. If the original when presented was properly endorsed, the issuer is protected under this rule, and may refuse the demand for a replacement.

If, after the issue of a replacement security, a bona fide purchaser presents the original for registration of transfer or payment, the issuer must register the transfer unless registration would result in overissuance, in which case the issuer must either purchase and deliver a like security if reasonably available, or if not, pay the amount such purchaser paid for the security with interest from the date of demand. The issuer may recover the replacement security from the purchaser to whom it was issued (or anyone taking from such person except another bona fide purchaser) in addition to any rights it may have under the indemnity bond.

Many indentures will permit the obligor company to avoid the complications of issuing a replacement security by paying the lost bond or coupon if it has, or is about to, become due, and if the other conditions related to replacement are complied with. In the case of a convertible debenture, the indenture should specify that the right to convert is not destroyed by paying instead of issuing a new debenture.

MISCELLANEOUS FUNCTIONS

Certain other functions may be required to be performed by the trustee or the company's agents, depending upon the terms of a particular issue. The more significant of such subsidiary functions are outlined below.

Validation of Bonds and Coupons

Where a bond is mutilated for any reason, the readiest solution is to cancel it and issue a new bond in replacement. Where mutilation relates only to a single coupon, however, it is sometimes simpler to validate such coupon. This may be accomplished by having an official of the company sign a statement on the back of the coupon to the effect that it is a valid obligation. If this procedure is not feasible, the trustee itself may validate the coupon. The language used should be substantially as follows: "This coupon belongs to Bond No. _____ and is a valid obligation of the obligor." The bond itself should always be examined to ascertain that it is in fact a valid obligation.

Exchanges under Reorganization or Recapitalization Plans

An important function is involved in consummating a reorganization or recapitalization plan. The agent is in effect acting for the reorganization managers or the court and is usually appointed by court order. The work involves receipt and cancellation of all claims recognized in the reorganization proceedings and delivery of the cash and securities authorized in respect thereof.

Because of the complexity and diversity of such plans and arrangements, no effort will be made to describe the procedure in detail. In considering acceptance of any such appointment, the agent should insure that the plan has been validly confirmed by appropriate court order; that the claims and distribution schedule are clear; that proper direction and instructions as to its functions have been received and approved by the court; that a definite termination date for the exchange is set; and, most importantly, that the compensation to be paid for its services is sufficient to cover the expense and detail of the work involved.

Agent for Securities Not Issued under an Indenture

The most important securities of this type are those issued by states and municipalities. Generally the same type of services are required as in the case of corporate obligations, with however, a much greater emphasis at present on the paying agency function. The procedures followed are similiar except that the cancelled securities are either shipped to the finance officer of the state or municipality, or the agent itself performs the accounting and destruction service customarily performed by the trustee in the case of corporate obligations.

In connection with direct placement financing of corporations, long term notes are sometimes issued under purchase agreements not requiring the service of a trustee under an indenture. A bank is frequently appointed agent of the obligor company to service such a note issue, however. It maintains a record of the note holders, makes interest payments, determines allocation of periodic sinking fund installments, acts as exchange agent, and in general performs all the ministerial details which the company itself would otherwise be required to perform.

10

Payment and Redemption of Bonds

WHILE THE "perpetual debenture" without a fixed maturity has been used with success in the United Kingdom and certain of the Commonwealth countries, this practice has never developed in the United States. Such obligations are frequently regarded as more in the nature of stock than debt, and certainly they have many of the aspects of permanent equity capital. Almost without exception, debt obligations issued in this country under indentures have a fixed maturity. This, of course, is an essential condition to the negotiability of the securities.

The fixed obligation in the bonds and the corresponding indenture covenants to pay the principal and interest as they become due, are the most important undertakings of the obligor. On or before the fixed maturity of the debt, funds must be provided to make payment thereof, although this is not always easy. We have heretofore discussed the use of the sinking fund device whereby a portion of the debt is retired each year over its life, thereby eliminating, or substantially reducing, the problem presented at final maturity. Another common device which is used in issues of states and municipalities is to provide for serial maturities, with a portion of the debt actually falling due by its terms each year. This practice is seldom used in issues of business corporations because of marketing problems.

It is unusual for a corporation to be able to pay off a large fixed principal maturity out of available cash. Even where a sinking fund covenant has been included, there is often a substantial amount of obligations to be taken care of at final maturity. The corporate financial officer must therefore plan the cash flow sufficiently in advance of the maturity date to assure that funds will be on hand to pay the obligations at that time. Some form of refunding which involves the issuance of other bonds to provide the cash to pay off the maturing issue is usually necessary. As pointed out in Chapter 5, among the purposes for which additional bonds are customarily authorized to be issued under open-end indentures is the refunding of prior lien bonds or other series of bonds outstanding under the indenture.

Where the obligor enjoys a good credit rating, and where adequate thought has gone into the drafting of the contracts involved in the company's financial undertakings, no serious difficulty is presented by an approaching debt maturity. An important question of timing and cost may be involved, however. If a company is faced with the necessity of meeting a maturity during a period of relatively high interest rates, its annual fixed charges may be substantially increased. From the company's point of view, therefore, it is desirable that a considerable degree of flexibility be reserved in the indenture to facilitate its dealing with its debt obligations.

To provide such flexibility, the redemption provisions of the indenture are important. These provisions are usually set up in a separate article of the indenture and constitute the reservation by the obligor of the privilege of prepaying its securities, or designated portions thereof, at its option, prior to their stated maturity. For the exercise of this privilege the obligor pays a price, in the form of a redemption premium, in addition to the principal and accrued interest to the date of prepayment. The right of redemption prior to maturity is an important right and the terms on which it may be exercised, including the amount of premium which must be paid, are important elements in the original negotiations. It is fairly common, however, to set the initial redemption premium at an amount equivalent to one year's interest on the securities. This premium is then scaled down, in substantially equal amounts, throughout the life of the issue, with no premium being payable during the last year.

Since this is a substantive provision which affects the rights of the holders of securities, the redemption privilege must be set forth in the text of the securities themselves as well as in the indenture. The language should be in sufficient detail to put the holder on notice as to the essential terms and conditions on which his obligation may be called for prepayment.

During periods of relatively high interest rates, investors like to protect themselves against the possibility that the obligations they purchase will be refunded as soon as a change in market conditions makes it advantageous for the issuers so to do. In 1955, for example, when there was a rapid change in market conditions and a substantial decline in interest rates, many issues were called during the first year of their life (some within the first six months). Many investors suffered substantial losses because of their having sold other issues to purchase these obligations which were then redeemed, necessitating reinvestment at much lower yields.

The protection against such a possibility takes the form of a noncallable or nonrefundable provision in the bond and indenture. A noncallable provision means merely an absence of the right of the obligor to redeem its securities (except for sinking fund purposes) for a stated period of time. A nonrefundable provision permits redemption but specifies that this cannot be done with other funds borrowed at a rate of interest less than that borne by the indenture securities. These restrictions are usually limited to a specified period of time following the date of issue—commonly five or ten years.

A noncallable provision is easily administered. A nonrefundable provision may present difficulties, however. The trustee should insist that there be included in the indenture a provision for its receipt of a certificate from appropriate officials of the company that a proposed redemption does not violate the restriction, and it should be authorized to rely conclusively on such a certificate.

MECHANICAL PROVISIONS

The terms and conditions on which the securities may be called for prepayment should be carefully spelled out in the indenture. While it is the company which theoretically exercises the right, as a practical matter the trustee will usually be called upon to carry out all details. Therefore, these provisions should receive its careful attention as it reviews the prospective contract. Under an open-end indenture, providing for different series of bonds, the redemption terms (other than the amount of premium payable) are usually set forth in the original indenture and are made applicable to all series of bonds, including those to be issued in the future. As an alternative, the terms of the original indenture may be made applicable only to the initial series of bonds, the terms and conditions for subsequent series being included in the supplemental indenture creating each such series. While not as frequently used, the latter practice is recommended as providing the greater degree of flexibility.

The first condition to which attention should be directed is the nature and extent of the right. Subject to any provisions as to nonrefundability, this right should be as broadly based as possible. The right should be reserved to redeem all, or any part, of the indenture securities at any time or from time to time. Occasionally, a partial redemption is restricted to a minimum principal amount, and such a restriction is proper both from the point of view of the obligor and the investor. Some indentures restrict the redemption to an interest date, although such a provision should be avoided unless the particular circumstances make it necessary.

The redemption premiums should be set forth explicitly. They are customarily expressed as a percentage of the principal amount. If a formula for a declining percentage is to be used, it should be worked out in advance and the actual prices (by dates) set forth in the indenture and in the bonds. This formula avoids any possibility of error or misunderstanding at a later date. When there is a sinking fund, the redemption premium for sinking fund redemption will normally be less than that for an optional retirement or, frequently, bonds may be callable for sinking fund purposes at par, without premium. If there are other circumstances under which the sinking fund redemption price rather than the optional price will be applicable, these should be carefully and specifically enumerated.

Notice of redemption must be given to the holders of the securities. The indenture must specify not only the method of giving notice but also the period of time prior to the redemption date when such notice must be given. A minimum of thirty days notice is ordinarily required, and it is also common for a maximum period to be specified. A usual provision is to require the first notice to be given not less than thirty, nor more than sixty, days prior to the date designated for the redemption.

The indenture should specify the information to be included in the notice. Such information would include a full description of the issue; the date of redemption; the price payable; the place or places of payment to which the called securities should be presented; if less than the entire issue is called, the total principal amount called, and that a new bond will be issued for the unredeemed portion; and any other information which may be pertinent to the particular situation.

It is important that the notice state that on the designated redemption date, the called securities (or portions thereof) shall become due and payable, and that on and after such date all interest thereon will cease to accrue and the holders shall cease to be entitled to the benefits of the indenture, their rights being limited to receipt of the redemption price in the hands of the trustee, or paying agent, upon presentation of their securities for cancellation.

In the case of a partial call of a fully registered bond issue, use of the traditional form of notice listing all the bond numbers and applicable principal amounts called for redemption can be avoided by using a letter form of notice incorporating the required details of redemption. This notice should be accompanied by a special form addressed to each holder affected by the call setting forth the principal amount of holdings selected for redemption and the bond against which the selection was allocated, and which is to be presented for payment. Copies of this form can also be used for follow up and posting operations. Such notice should be given by mail to the registered holders at their addresses as indicated in the bond register. The notice need only be sent to the holders of bonds which have been selected for redemption. Notice by registered or certified mail should never be required. No requirement should be set forth in the indenture for any publication of the notice, as such is expensive and unnecessary where all bonds are registered. However, where an issue is actively traded, it is very desirable to have a list of the numbers of the called bonds made available to any exchange on which the securities are listed, to the standard financial services, such as Moody's and Standard and Poor's, and to the dealers for checking on the numbers of bonds delivered in settlement of trades.

Where securities are outstanding in bearer form, notice is given by publication in an authorized newspaper. What constitutes an "authorized newspaper" should be carefully defined in the indenture. Since a number of papers are not published on Saturdays, Sundays or legal holidays, this fact should be borne in mind if it is planned to use any such periodical. It is desirable to provide for a number of publications so that the information will be disseminated as widely as possible. Only the first of these notices need be within the prescribed time limits, and considerable flexibility as to subsequent publication is desirable. Neither should publication be restricted to the same day of the week.

In addition to publication of the required notice, which should also indicate the specific serial numbers of the bonds to be redeemed and the coupons which must be attached to them, a copy should be sent to each registered holder of called bonds. While it is usually provided that if proper publication is made, mailing is not a required condition, the trustee should be most careful to see that such mailing is effected, and at the same time as the initial publication. While not required, it is also recommended that a copy of the notice be mailed to each holder whose name has been filed with the trustee for the purpose of receiving reports (see Chapter 13, *infra*). It is also suggested that copies be sent to any exchange on which the securities are listed and to the standard financial services.

If the redemption is for the sinking fund, or is achieved by use of special funds constituting a part of the trust estate, the particular notice should be mailed (or published) under the name of trustee (or sinking fund agent, if other than the trustee). If redemption is pursuant to an optional right reserved in the obligor, it should be mailed (or published) under the name of the company, even though it was actually prepared and disseminated by the trustee.

Provision should be made for deposit with the trustee of the funds required to effect the redemption. It is not necessary that this be done prior to the selection and mailing (or publication) of notice, although it should be made on or before the date of payment and in the full amount. Such a deposit should be made in trust, and the funds held in a special account specifically allocated to payment of the securities to be redeemed.

If such deposit is made with a paying agent other than the trustee, it should be placed in a special trust account in the name of the trustee and should be under its control and not that of the company. An appropriate undertaking letter to this effect should also be obtained from the paying agent unless such an undertaking is included in a general letter at the time of execution of the indenture. If not so deposited, or if the company acts as its own paying agent and retains the redemption funds under its control, the called bonds should not be discharged from the trustee's records until they are actually received and cancelled by it.

Where, by reason of a refunding or for other reasons, funds

necessary to effect the redemption are deposited prior to the date of the mailing (or first publication) of notice, a prior payment offer is sometimes made. This is an offer to pay the full redemption price upon presentation of bonds at any time after mailing (or publication) of notice even if presentation is prior to the redemption date. The making of such an offer is an accepted, although seldom used, practice, but it should be made at the discretion of the company. The trustee should not undertake, by agreement with anyone other than the company, to effect such a prior payment, even though the funds may be in its possession.

From the viewpoint of practical handling of redemptions, two provisions are desirable for the trustee: where registered securities are involved, no endorsement or assignment should be required if payment is to be made to the registered holder. Where redemptions is on an interest payment date—the interest check should be mailed to the registered holders as of the record date in the normal manner; in the case of the bearer securities the holders should be instructed to detach and present separately the interest coupon maturing on that date, otherwise a great deal of confusion may arise in subsequent accountings.

PARTIAL REDEMPTIONS

Where fewer than all of the bonds of an issue are to be redeemed, provision must be made for selection of the particular bonds. This should be done by the trustee, and the method followed is the same as in the case of selection of bonds for redemption by a sinking fund. As noted in Chapter 6, it is very desirable that the indenture give to the trustee the utmost flexibility in determining the particular method to be used. Rather than setting forth in detail the particular procedures to be employed, indenture draftsmen should leave this entirely to the trustee's discretion. The only requirement should be that the method adopted be fair and equitable to all holders. In this way the trustee is enabled to keep up with current practices rather than be bound by possibly antiquated procedures.

The traditional method of selection has been by bond number, with a basic unit of $1,000; bonds of larger denominations being assigned as many unit numbers as there are multiples of $1,000. Where all or a substantial portion of an issue is outstanding in registered form, this can become a cumbersome and expensive procedure, particularly if there has been substantial transfer activity. Other methods of selection are equally fair and may prove much more easily administered, depending on the circumstances of the particular case. In the case of an all registered issue it is frequently easier to make the selection by holder (either pro-rata, or by lot in terms of the number of "units" of the holding) and then allocate the portions selected against a particular bond or bonds. The significance of this method is that the selection is of a portion (or all) of a holding as of a particular date, and not of any one specific bond by serial number. Accordingly, the validity of the call is not affected if the particular "allocation" is made against an incorrect serial number.

Frequently the holdings of a single registered holder are represented by more than one bond. Where it is clear that a single beneficial holding is involved, it is desirable that the portion of the holding affected by a call be allocated against a single bond. This practice is now fairly common. In the case of bank nominees or brokers, where there is a reasonable presumption that different pieces represent different beneficial holdings, the preferred practice is to treat each separate bond as a separate holding. Here again a more uniform practice would seem desirable. It is suggested that for the purpose of any selection (1) each separate bond in the name of a nominee or broker be considered a separate holding; (2) the total holdings of all other registered holders be considered a single beneficial holding; and (3) any holder have the right to direct the trustee that the holdings be considered an entity or that separate bonds be regarded as separate beneficial holdings, such direction to be effective for all selections until rescinded.

The necessity for closing of the bond register during the selection period is obvious and there is no way in which changes in the holders or numbers of outstanding registered bonds can be permitted. The indenture should provide that the privilege of transfer or exchange of bonds may be suspended for a period of fifteen days preceding the mailing of notice of redemption of a part of an issue. It is incumbent upon the trustee, however, to use its best efforts to keep the suspension to a minimum period of time, especially in an active bond issue, so that registration of transfers as a result of trading will not be unduly disrupted. Where the parties desire, an interim receipt could be issued for a bond presented for registration of transfer or in exchange during the period the bond register is closed. In such event, however, the registrar should place a legend on the receipt to the effect that the bond register is closed for purpose of partial selection of bonds for redemption at a designated price on a designated date; that the bond presented for registration of transfer or exchange is subject to selection for redemption in whole or in part; and that in the event of such selection, new bond(s) registered as indicated on the receipt for the uncalled portion will be delivered in exchange for the receipt together with a redemption ticket redeemable on the redemption date, for the called portion of such bond.

Once the selection has been completed, and a list of the bond numbers prepared and proved, an appropriate affidavit should be prepared by the trustee and filed as part of its records. (This would be attached to the affidavit of mailing of the redemption notice to the registered holders by the trustee.) In the case of bearer bond issues, the list of numbers arranged numerically by denomination will be included as part of the redemption notice as published and mailed. Appropriate affidavits of such publication and mailing should also be obtained by the trustee.

Once the selection has been made and the notice mailed (or first published), the bonds selected become due and payable on the date designated. On such date they cease to be outstanding for any purpose of the indenture (except to receive payment) and should be removed from the classification of outstanding bonds by appropriate entry in the trustee's records. It is desirable to control them in a subsidiary redemption ledger, with appropriate entry being made as the bonds are actually surrendered and paid.

It is possible that some of the bonds will not be presented promptly. Care should be taken on the next record date for payment of interest that appropriate stop payments are noted on the registrar's records. In the case of bearer bonds, the stop payment should be noted against the coupons appurtenant to all such bonds which remain outstanding. This will not only prevent the making of an unauthorized payment, but will facilitate notice to such holders who have not surrendered their called bonds.

After the selection has been completed and the bond register reopened, any bond not affected by the call may of course be transferred, exchanged, or otherwise dealt with. Where a portion of a bond has been selected for redemption and such bond is presented for transfer or exchange prior to the redemption date, it is perfectly proper to effect the requested transaction with respect to the uncalled portion of the bond. The original bond, now representing only the called portion, should be retained by the trustee (or forwarded by the registrar to the trustee or paying agent) for payment on the redemption date. It has been suggested that provision be made for transfer of called bonds between the date of selection and the redemption date. It is difficult to understand why this should be desired, since the status of the obligation has now been changed. It represents only the right to receive payment of the redemption price on the redemption date and can no longer be used in settlement of a contract to deliver a "bond" of the issue.

If the entire issue has been called for redemption, it may be desirable to continue the transfer activity and permit the trading of "called" bonds. In such a situation, any bonds delivered should be overstamped with an appropriate legend as to the redemption.

CONVERTIBLE SECURITIES

Where debt securities are issued which by their terms may be converted, at the option of the holder, into other types of securities of the issuer, the trustee should see that this privilege is protected. The common practice where any such securities are called for redemption is to continue the conversion privilege to and including the redemption date. The trustee should urge that such a provision be included. Some issues provide that a conversion privilege will terminate several days before the redemption date. No matter how carefully it is spelled out in the notice, many holders invariably miss the cutoff date and consequently sustain substantial loss.

In preparing the redemption notice, it is recommended that the conversion privilege, if of value, be stated separately so that the holder's attention is drawn to it. It is inevitable that some holders will lose their privilege through misunderstanding or carelessness, but every effort should be made to keep such loss at a minimum.

Funds held in the redemption account for payment of securities converted are usually returned free to the obligor. This is proper, since payment for the securities has been made by the issuance of stock. The trustee should make certain that this is explicitly covered in the indenture.

11

Satisfaction and Defeasance

AN IMPORTANT PART of every mortgage indenture is the defeasance clause, which sets forth the conditions on which the mortgagor is entitled to a satisfaction of the mortgage and to receive the property free from the mortgage lien. The indenture is executed to secure payment of principal and interest on the obligations issued and insure performance by the obligor of all the covenants and undertakings contained in the indenture. When this has been done, its purpose has been fulfilled.

In the usual case the indenture covenants are included as additional security provisions to guarantee performance of the basic covenant; namely, to pay the indenture obligations as they become due. Accordingly, if all such obligations have been paid, or satisfactory provision made therefor, the obligor is entitled to a satisfaction even though a default may have occurred or may at the time exist under a particular security covenant.

The obligor must have discharged, or provided for the discharge of, all its obligations to the security holders, however. For example, if the securities contain a convertible provision, an option to purchase stock, or any other condition or provision which constituted an additional consideration for purchase of the securities by the holders thereof, it is not sufficient merely to provide for payment of principal and interest on the indenture securities. All other conditions must be performed or their performance provided for before the obligor is entitled to a formal satisfaction and discharge of the indenture.

The obligor must also have discharged all obligations owing to the trustee and other agents. These include payment of all dis-

197

bursements, repayment of all advances (with interest if properly chargeable), and payment of all fees and other compensation due, including reasonable fees for execution of a satisfaction and any other duties required to be performed subsequently.

If the trustee executes and delivers a satisfaction improperly, it will be liable for legal damages to anyone injured by its action. On the other hand, if it improperly withholds a satisfaction, it may be liable to the obligor. The trustee must therefore exercise due care in all matters relating to the satisfaction and discharge of the indenture.

It would be impractical and unfair to require actual payment of all the outstanding bonds before the mortgagor could obtain a satisfaction. Over a long period of time, some bonds become misplaced and lost, or holders are slow in presenting them for payment. Occasionally, a small percentage of the obligations are never presented, and in cases several years may elapse before all the obligations are actually retired. On the other hand, the bondholders are entitled to their security until they receive payment for their bonds and it is important that such payment be secured for them before the mortgage is satisfied.

The usual provision is to require deposit with the trustee (in trust) of funds sufficient to pay all principal and interest on the bonds to maturity date, or to the redemption date, if the bonds have been called, and for the indenture to provide that, upon such deposit, the obligor shall become entitled to a satisfaction of the indenture. Where any facts must be established or any conditions precedent performed, the indenture should provide that the trustee will be protected if it accepts and relies in good faith on an officers' certificate and opinion of counsel as to the existence of such facts or the performance of such conditions.

It is not essential that all steps be taken to effect the redemption before a satisfaction can be given. This fact may be important if the redemption funds are being provided through refunding under another indenture. In order that the obligor give a proper lien under the new indenture, which is essential to enable it to secure the necessary funds, it must at the same time be able to secure a legal discharge of the former lien. It is sufficient if the requisite funds are deposited with the trustee together with irrevocable instructions to perform all acts necessary to effect the redemption.

For the trustee to determine what funds are required, an appropriate accounting may have to be prepared. This may take any form so long as it is reasonably detailed and accurate, and includes all obligations which have become due under the indenture and the provision made for their discharge. If the appropriate records have been accurately maintained throughout the life of the issue (especially if bearer obligations are involved), the analysis for a final maturity (or redemption) will present no problem; if not done or if the records are out of proof, then a major task may be involved.

Exhibits 14 and 15 set forth a typical accounting analysis for a mixed (*i.e.* bearer and registered) issue. However, these cover only a single series of bonds. If more than one series has been issued under the indenture, an analysis should be made for each series.

The analysis of principal requires accounting for the total principal amount authenticated by the trustee at any time under any provision of the indenture. Since bonds will have been issued because of registration, exchange, or replacement or for other purposes, the aggregate of obligations to be accounted for will usually exceed the amount outstanding at any time under the indenture. Offsetting principal obligations so authenticated will be the aggregate of all such obligations which have been cancelled by the trustee. In a usual case, all such cancellations will be evidenced by executed destruction certificates in the trustee's possession. To the extent that the total bonds cancelled are not evidenced by destruction certificates or cancelled bonds in the trustee's possession, the trustee should satisfy itself that proper disposition has been made of the cancelled obligations. If the trustee's records do not disclose cancellation of such obligations, it should insist on surrender thereof so that proper disposition may be insured. Subtracting the principal amount of obligations cancelled from the aggregate authenticated will give the principal remaining to be accounted for. This may be offset by funds on deposit with the trustee, by monies to be deposited, or by satisfactory indemnity bonds on file.

In preparing any interest accounting, the principal amount of obligations outstanding on each interest payment date should be ascertained and the interest calculated for each such date. The amount of registered interest paid, the aggregate amount of coupons cancelled, and the coupons paid against bond of indemnity for each period should be shown separately. The sum of these subtracted from the interest due leaves the balance due for each interest date represented by outstanding unpresented coupons. The

Exhibit 14. Final Principal Accounting Statement

COMPANY: Global Electric Company
INDENTURE: Dated as of November 1, 1963
ISSUE: 6% Twenty - Year S/F Debentures due November 1, 1983
PURPOSE: Redemption of all outstanding debentures as of November 1,
              1971 and satisfaction of indenture

Principal amount issued under Indenture	$ 60,000,000.
Principal amount retired	20,975,000.
Principal amount outstanding	$ 39,025,000.

CASH ACCOUNTS	*Principal*	*Premium*
Cash held in Sinking Fund A/C		
#G-7	$ 25,000.	0.
Cash to be deposited in Redemption A/C		
#G-8	39,000,000.	0.
	$ 39,025,000.	

TOTAL PRINCIPAL AMOUNT OF SECURITIES AUTHENTICATED AND ISSUED	$117,950,000.

TOTAL PRINCIPAL AMOUNT OF SECURITIES
AUTHENTICATED, ISSUED AND CANCELLED

A/C Conversion	0.
A/C Correction, Split and Transfer	$ 36,500,000.
A/C Exchange of coupon securities for fully registered	18,500.000.
A/C Exchange of fully registered securities for coupon	2,150,000.
A/C Mutilation	15,000.
A/C Ressuance of uncalled portion	750,000.
A/C Retirement for Sinking Fund	20,975,000.
A/C Temporary securities exchanged for permanent	0.
Total principal amount authenticated, issued and cancelled	$ 78,890,000.

DISPOSITION OF CANCELLED SECURITIES

Principal amount of securities cancelled and destroyed per destruction certificates on file	$ 45,672,000.
Principal amount of securities cancelled and awaiting destruction	33,218,000.
Total principal amount cancelled or destroyed	$ 78,890,000.

Principal amount of securities authenticated and issued covered by Bonds of Indemnity	$ 35,000.

aggregate of these amounts should represent the funds on deposit with the trustee or paying agent.

If the trustee is not the agent for paying registered interest, arrangements should be made for surrender to it of the cancelled checks representing such interest shortly after each interest period. These checks should be examined and proved to the total of the registered interest due, and appropriate record should be made for use on the subsequent accounting. In lieu of actual receipt and examination of such cancelled checks, the trustee may accept an appropriate certificate of a responsible disbursing agent.

Coupons paid are customarily destroyed by the trustee, and the destruction certificates provide the evidence necessary to support this phase of the accounting. Where there are paying agents other than the trustee, the latter should arrange to have all interest obligations surrendered to it periodically for verification and destruction. In lieu of such surrender, the trustee may accept a destruction certificate from a reliable agent, although good practice should prohibit acceptance of such a certificate of the obligor company without independent verification.

Most indentures permit replacement of lost, stolen, or destroyed obligations, or their payment, in lieu of replacement, upon furnishing of evidence of such loss, theft, or destruction and provision for satisfactory indemnity. Such replacement securities, however, constitute additional contractual obligations entitled to the security of the indenture. In connection with a final accounting, it is customary to give credit for all obligations covered by a satisfactory bond of indemnity, if an original counterpart is on file with the trustee and if the latter is named as an obligee. This is a matter for the trustee's discretion, however. If the security afforded by such bonds of indemnity is not in all respects satisfactory, the trustee is entitled to insist on the furnishing of adequate security or to the deposit of funds to cover such obligations.

The trustee is entitled to, and should insist on, deposit with it of all funds due for all outstanding obligations before it executes a satisfaction. If funds to meet matured and unpresented obligations are on deposit with other agents, arrangements should be made for their transfer to the trustee. This is true even though deposit with such other agent is in trust. The fact that a statute of limitations may have run against particular interest obligations is immaterial

EXHIBIT 15. FINAL INTEREST ACCOUNTING STATEMENT

Final Interest Accounting Statement

Company: Global Electric Company
Issue: 6% Twenty-Year Debentures due November 1, 1983

INTEREST DATE	TOTAL INTEREST DUE	REGISTERED INTEREST PAID	COUPON DESTRUCTION CERTIFICATES ON FILE		COUPONS PAID AGAINST BOND OF INDEMNITY	CANCELLED COUPONS ON HAND	BALANCE OUTSTANDING
			A/C payment	A/C surrender by company			
5/1/64	$1,800,000	$540,000	$1,252,200	$7,800	0	$ 0	$ 0
11/1/64	1,800,000	740,000	1,046,710	13,200	0	60	30
5/1/65	1,710,000	713,000	996,880	0	$30	30	90
11/1/65	1,710,000	713,000	991,030	5,760	30	30	150
5/1/66	1,620,000	686,000	933,820	0	0	0	150
11/1/66	1,620,000	686,000	933,670	0	30	90	210
5/1/67	1,530,000	659,000	870,670	0	30	60	240
11/1/67	1,530,000	662,900	866,860	0	30	0	240
5/1/68	1,440,000	645,720	780,360	13,500	0	150	270
11/1/68	1,440,000	645,720	775,830	18,000	0	210	240
5/1/69	1,350,000	718,510	624,950	6,000	0	210	330
11/1/69	1,350,000	818,510	515,980	15,000	0	210	300
5/1/70	1,260,000	888,990	0	0	0	370,530	480
11/1/70	1,260,000	888,990	0	0	0	370,380	630
5/1/71	1,170,000	961,930	0	0	0	206,900	1,170
Totals:	$22,590,000	$10,968,270	$10,588,960	$79,260	$120	$ 948,860	$4,530

Form of accounting for interest obligations.
The balance outstanding represents matured coupons unpresented and should equal funds in the
hands of the paying agent. If held by an agent
other than the trustee, such funds shoud be paid
over to the trustee prior to satisfaction.

unless the indenture contains a specific provision that no further claim may be asserted with respect thereto.

In the exceptional cases where deposit with the trustee is not feasible, either because the latter is not an authorized depositary or for other reasons, the despositary should be satisfactory to and approved by the trustee, and the deposit should be under the exclusive control of the trustee. In such a case the trustee will not be liable if reasonable care was used in the selection of the depositary, even though the funds may be subsequently lost through failure of the depositary.

The issuer's obligation contained in its bonds runs directly to the holders thereof. Where requisite funds for their payment are deposited with the trustee, however, it has been held that this is equivalent to payment to the holders, and the issuer is not liable if the trustee misapplies the funds or becomes bankrupt. This is true, however, only from and after the date on which funds in the hands of the trustee become available to the bondholders upon surrender of their bonds.

When all requisite accountings have been prepared and checked and the trustee has satisfied itself that it has funds in its possession to pay all obligations shown to be still outstanding; when it has received an officers' certificate and an opinion of counsel as to compliance by the obligor company with all conditions precedent; and when it has received from the obligor company irrevocable instructions to complete all conditions requisite to redemption of the securities not previously completed, it is then in a position to execute and deliver a satisfaction and discharge of the indenture.

The instruments of satisfaction will usually be prepared by counsel for the obligor, but they should be checked carefully by the trustee.

In the case of a debenture agreement or unsecured indenture, execution of a formal instrument of satisfaction is not absolutely necessary, since no property has to be reconveyed. It is good practice, however, to acknowledge formally the compliance by the obligor with its obligations, and this is almost always observed. Complete and final accountings should be prepared in any event, as in the case of a mortgage indenture.

Under a mortgage indenture, the instrument of satisfaction constitutes a reconveyance of all the trustee's interest in the mortgaged property. It must therefore be in a form which can be recorded in

EXHIBIT 16. GUIDE FOR USE IN CONNECTION WITH
            SATISFACTION OF INDENTURE, MATURITY OR
            COMPLETE REDEMPTION OF OBLIGATIONS

Obligor _____

Indenture _____

Issues to be
paid or redeemed _____

_____

Maturity or redemption date _____ Trustee's counsel _____

Check each item as completed. If inapplicable, or pending, so indicate.

I. PRIOR TO CLOSING
_____A. Instruct control clerk to prepare an accounting for out-
       standing bonds and coupons.
_____B. Ascertain that funds are on hand for payment of any
       matured and unpresented obligations. If any of such funds
       are on deposit with other agents, arrange for their transfer
       to trustee at or prior to closing.
_____C. Consider satisfaction fee (including fees for final pay-
       ments) and review status of unpaid fees and disbursements
       with billing group.
_____D. Review pending file and dispose of any open items.
_____E. Determine action to be taken with respect to any demands
       or notices of other indenture trustees or claimants served
       upon trustee claiming a lien upon collateral or other prop-
       erty subject to above indenture at time of satisfaction.

_____F. Review and prepare, if necessary, drafts of supporting documents, including notice of redemption and form of satisfaction. Get approval from our counsel and obligor.

_____G. If notice of redemption required to be published, prepare instructions to advertising agents as to dates of publication, newspapers, affidavits of publication, number of prints required, etc.

_____H. Copies of notice mailed to:
   1. Obligor
   2. Registered holders
   3. Names received from obligor, other paying agents, or on two-year list, if bearer issue.
   4. Stock exchanges
   5. Any co-agents or co-trustees
   6. Financial services
   7. Copies of notice furnished to operations for bond windows and Clearing House Banks.

_____I. Affidavit of mailing prepared and sent to obligor.

_____J. Affidavit of publication received and sent to obligor.

_____K. Determine disposition to be made of:
   1. Cash on hand
   2. Collateral held
   3. Insurance policies on file
   4. Unissued obligations
   5. Cancelled obligations
   6. Supplies of executed and/or conformed copies of indenture, etc.
   7. Recorded counterparts of indenture and other instruments.
   8. Stamped original of indenture

_____L. Reserve conference room for closing.

_____M. Consider necessity for obtaining county clerk's certificates on notarial acknowledgment on satisfaction.

_____N. Verify with obligor amount of funds to be deposited at closing and arrange for proper receipt and disposition.

II. AT CLOSING

_____A. Obtain requisite funds to cover redemption or maturity of bonds.

_____B. Receive requisite supporting papers.

_____C. Execute and deliver satisfaction.

_____D. Make disposition of items referred to under I, K.

III. AFTER CLOSING

_____A. Consider obtaining written opinion of counsel.

_____B. Prepare, delete or note following office records:

1. Memorandum for officers' daily bulletin
2. Memorandum to relations index if all corporate trust relations are terminated.
3. Officers' account summary cards
4. State of incorporation and mortgage files
5. Parent-subsidiary files
6. Obligor's information return file
7. Authorities file
8. Trustee and other appropriate instruction sheets
9. Individual trustee file
10. Tickler cards and register sheet
11. Bank credit file
12. Cash and/or security accounts
13. Note conflict check records
14. Pend to check with operations division as to unpresented bonds after 3 months.

_____C. Notify all stock exchanges on which securities being retired are listed.

_____D. Ascertain provisions of indenture relating to return of undisbursed funds to Obligor after a definite period of time. Prepare appropriate tickler notice.

_____E. Documents closing papers.

_____F. oprepare documents for disposition in accordance with appropriate standing instructions.

Dated: _____   Prepared: _____ Checked: _____ Approved: _____

the necessary jurisdictions to discharge the lien of the indenture of record. Care should be used to see that the instrument is in the form of a release or quitclaim deed and that no warranties are included. It is good practice to have included in the instrument an affirmative statement to the effect that the instrument is executed without covenant or warranty, express or implied, and without recourse against the trustee in any event. The instrument should always run to the obligor and never to a third party.

Arrangements should be made for return to the obligor of pledged collateral or other items of property physically in the possession of the trustee. In this connection, the trustee should make sure that there is no junior lienor entitled to possession of such property. If such lien exists, arrangements should be made to surrender the property to the trustee of the junior lien against proper receipts. This may include the right to proceeds of any released property, insurance proceeds, or similar funds in the hands of the trustee.

It is desirable to provide in every indenture for return to the obligor company of all unclaimed funds deposited to pay the indenture obligations after a specified number of years have elapsed following satisfaction of the indenture. The most common period used is six years. The specific period is not material as long as some period is included. If no such provision is included, the trustee may be required to retain a small balance on its books permanently, as it is unlikely that each and every obligation will be presented to it. On the other hand, securities have been discovered and surrendered for payment as long as sixty years after their stated maturity.

In the absence of appropriate indenture authority, the trustee runs a risk in returning any unclaimed funds to the company, no matter how many years may have elapsed, as the latter has no legal right to such return. Similarly, the obligor is not entitled to have such funds invested for its benefit; and if such an investment is made, the trustee may be liable if loss results.

In recent years, a number of states have further complicated the problems of corporate financial officers by the enactment of sundry escheat or abandoned property laws. The general purport of these statutes is to require the transfer to the state of all funds held unclaimed for a stated period of time. Since theoretically a state can seize only property belonging to its residents, a difficult problem is presented where funds are held for the payment of bearer securities.

This is particularly true where no provision is made for subsequent payment to a rightful claimant and outright confiscation is involved.

The indenture provisions relating to disposition of unclaimed moneys should be drafted in relation to any applicable escheat or abandoned property law. Where an appropriate indenture provision is lacking, the trustee is presented with a difficult decision when called upon to execute a satisfaction. For example, let us assume that during the life of a particular issue the obligor has paid over several thousands of dollars pursuant to an escheat law requiring transfer of all interest moneys held unclaimed for six years. The issue matures and the obligor tenders, to the trustee, funds to pay the principal and all unclaimed interest due within the preceding six years, and demands execution of an instrument of satisfaction. Should the trustee comply or should it insist upon deposit of an amount equivalent to the funds previously escheated? This is not an easy decision, but unless the escheat law was sufficient to discharge the trustee's obligation with respect to such unclaimed interest, it may act at its peril if it executes a satisfaction without adequately securing such unpaid interest, the coupons for which may be subsequently presented to it. Under such circumstances, the trustee would be well advised to secure at least an appropriate indemnity from the obligor.

One final problem remains. Now that the indenture has been satisfied and appropriate provision made for payment of all outstanding obligations, what disposition should be made of the mountain of documents and papers which the trustee has accumulated during the life of the indenture? Obviously the answer will depend to some extent on any laws or regulations which exist in the jurisdiction of the trustee relating to the disposition of fiduciary records. Most corporate trustees tend to follow a very conservative practice, and to hold on to papers and documents for many years beyond the time when they can serve any conceivable purpose. This is an expensive folly and it is urged that each trust company give consideration to establishing a reasonable schedule for the systematic disposition of obsolete records.

Certain records accumulated by a corporate trustee should be retained permanently. These would include: one original executed counterpart of the indenture and of the instrument of satisfaction; a copy of its final accounting with respect to all indenture securities;

copies of all destruction certificates; originals of all bonds of indemnity or assumptions of liability of others with respect to any indenture securities or other obligations; and any document relating to an obligation or undertaking beyond the maturity of the indenture securities or essential to establishing the basic historical continuity of the trusteeship, such as an assumption agreement by a successor obligor.

Most other data can be disposed of within a reasonable time after termination of the appointment, or after the running of applicable statutes of limitation.

Once the indenture has been satisfied, the recorded counterparts of the indenture and all supplements are no longer of any value to the trustee. They may be returned to the obligor corporation if it desires them. Otherwise they should be destroyed.

The original counterparts of indentures executed prior to 1966 bear cancelled federal documentary stamps evidencing payment of the original issue tax and should be dealt with carefully. Since this evidences payment of an obligation by the obligor, it may be returned to the obligor if the latter wishes. A receipt should be obtained which should recite the principal amount of cancelled tax obligations affixed. If the obligor does not wish to have this document returned, which is usually the case, it may be destroyed by the trustee. The destruction certificate should include a statement as to the face amount of such tax stamps so destroyed.

12

Default and Remedial Provisions

ADMINISTRATION OF indentures after default provides the greatest test of the corporate trust officer's skill. Most indentures can and do provide that prior to default the trustee shall be charged with performance of only such duties as are specifically set forth in the indenture. The instrument itself serves as the guide for the action to be taken on each problem that arises.

It is impossible to prescribe an exact course of conduct to be followed in the event of a default. The indenture is essentially a security instrument, and the primary objective of the trustee, both before and after default, should be to protect the security position of the indenture security holders. If liquidation or reorganization should become necessary, the trustee should see that the security holders realize in full, or to the greatest extent possible, on their claims.

The rights and powers of the trustee after default are derived from the authority granted by the indenture, or are such as may be properly inferred from the authority expressly granted. Before discussing the general principles of default indenture administration, it might be well to consider the default and remedial provisions customarily included in trust indentures.

EVENTS OF DEFAULT

The events which will constitute a default and give rise to the remedial provisions must be set forth clearly in the indenture. Although there is occasional variance by reason of particular circumstances existing in a given case, the provisions in general are fairly uniform and consist of the following:

210

(1) Default in the payment of the principal of any of the indenture securities when the same become due, whether at maturity, by call, by declaration, or otherwise. Because of the serious nature of this type of default, no period of grace is provided, as it is unlikely to happen by inadvertence. Also, prompt action on the part of the trustee may be indicated and it should not be hampered by having to wait for the running of a period of grace.

(2) Default in the payment of any installment of interest on any of the indenture securities when the same becomes due. Most indentures provide a period of grace, usually thirty to sixty days, within which the obligor may cure such a default. The remedies provided in the indenture are stayed until this period of grace has expired.

(3) If the indenture provides for any sinking fund or purchase fund, or similar payments to be made to the trustee, failure to make any such payments will constitute an event of default. It is desirable to allow a period of grace for the curing of such default and this is customarily, although not always, included.

(4) If there are prior lien bonds outstanding, or other obligations which constitute a lien prior to the lien of the indenture securities on the trust estate or some part thereof, a covenant to pay such prior liens and comply with all provisions of the indenture securing the same should be included in the indenture. Failure to discharge such prior lien obligations when due should be made a default under the indenture after a period of grace. There is a sound reason for this. Although failure to discharge the prior lien will normally constitute a default under the prior lien obligation, the holder thereof may take no action to enforce the obligation. Unless this also constituted an event of default under the indenture securing junior obligations, the holders of the latter might be unable to take steps to protect their equity in the property until it had been substantially dissipated.

(5) The filing of an involuntary proceeding in bankruptcy against the obligor and the entry of a decree adjudging the obligor a bankrupt, or the approval of a petition for the reorganization of the obligor, will constitute a default unless the order is discharged or stayed within a specific period of time. Likewise, an order of the court appointing a trustee or receiver of the obligor, or a substantial part of its property not discharged or stayed within the specified period of grace, will constitute a default. The period of grace is

provided in the case of involuntary petitions to give the obligor an opportunity to have the proceedings dismissed if in fact the petition was improperly filed.

Accordingly, the filing of a voluntary petition in bankruptcy or for reorganization, or an assignment for the benefit of creditors, or a voluntary petition under any insolvency act should be made an event of default without the running of any period of grace.

(6) Finally, the breach of any covenant or the failure of the obligor to perform any condition provided for in the indenture will in turn lead to a default. It is customarily provided that an event of default shall not occur for this reason until the expiration of a stated period of time after the trustee or a specified percentage of the indenture security holders shall have notified the obligor in writing of the breach of the covenant or condition.

While both notice and a period of grace should be provided for in the event of a breach of most indenture covenants, circumstances may exist when either or both may be unwise. For example, in the case of certain negative covenants, such as those against the incurring of indebtedness, the creation of prior liens, the transfer of properties, or a declaration of dividends, time may be of the essence and the trustee should have the right to move promptly if such action seems warranted.

REMEDIAL PROVISIONS

The indenture contains various remedial provisions to which, theoretically, recourse may be had once an event of default has occurred. To the average security holder the powers of enforcement granted the trustee system seem entirely adequate, and he is therefore at a loss to understand why in many situations he winds up with less than he bargained for. Unfortunately, remedial action normally requires judicial proceedings of some kind, and the remedies included are those with which courts and lawyers are familiar. Where the intrinsic value of the security is sufficient, these remedies might be adequate. In the case of the usual corporate obligor, however, they are often inadequate, unenforceable, or impractical.

The remedies found most frequently in secured indentures are:

(1) The right to accelerate maturity of the indenture securities, and to declare all principal due.

(2) The right of the trustee to recover judgment in its own name and as trustee of an express trust.

(3) The right to sue in equity or at law for specific performance of any covenant or agreement, or to enforce any rights of the trustee and security holders, or for the enforcement of any appropriate equitable or legal remedy.

(4) The right of entry on and possession of the mortgaged property by receivers, agents, or otherwise, such possession to continue until all defaults are cured.

(5) The right to sell the trust estate at public auction, with or without entry.

(6) In the case of a collateral indenture, the exercise of full rights of ownership with respect to any collateral held.

(7) The right to the appointment of a receiver of the mortgaged property and to foreclose thereon by appropriate judicial action.

(8) The right to file proofs of claim on behalf of all the security holders in any judicial proceedings.

In the case of an unsecured indenture, the same remedies will usually be included, except for numbers (4), (5), (6), and (7) above, which relate to specific action for realizing on the indenture security. The unsecured indenture customarily contains a general provision permitting the trustee to have a receiver of the obligor's property appointed and to bring suit to foreclose on such property to satisfy its judgment for the amounts owing on the indenture securities. The advantage of the mortgage indenture is that the lien on the properties is already established.

In aid of the trustee's powers of enforcement, the remedial sections usually contain three covenants on the part of the obligor:

(1) In the event of a default in payment of principal or interest (whether at maturity, on redemption, or by declaration), to pay to the trustee promptly all amounts then due and owing. Since it is obvious that if the obligor could do this no default would have occurred, the provision may appear meaningless. It is intended as an aid to the trustee's obtaining a prompt judgment on the basis of which it may proceed to the enforcement of other remedies;

(2) Upon the commencement of any action, suit or proceeding by the trustee, to waive the issuance and service of process and to enter its voluntary appearance in such action, suit or proceeding, and to

consent to the entry of judgment in favor of the trustee for all amounts owing under the indenture;

(3) So far as it lawfully and effectively may, to waive and relinquish the benefit and advantage of any and all valuation, stay, appraisement, extension, or redemption laws then existing or thereafter enacted.

RIGHTS AND DUTIES OF TRUSTEE
ON DEFAULT

Nature of the Trustee's Responsibility

Prior to enactment of the Trust Indenture Act, most indentures provided that the trustee was under no duty to take action to enforce the remedial provisions of the indenture until it had received an official demand by a specified percentage of the indenture security holders, together with whatever indemnity might be required to protect it against expense and liability. This provision was accompanied by broad exculpatory clauses which relieved the trustee of liability except for acts amounting to willful misconduct or gross negligence.

Despite the great amount of criticism which was directed against these provisions, there was a sound and logical basis for their existence. Initially, as has been noted, the trustee was a mere stakeholder, and its function was limited to that of holding the specific security for the benefit of the bondholders. Despite the grant of broad rights and powers to the trustee, this concept did not disappear entirely. While the trustee was given the right to proceed on its own to enforce the remedial provisions, in practice it was regarded more as the instrumentality of the security holders in exercising the right. Accordingly, the customary procedure whenever a default occurred or seemed imminent was for the trustee: (1) to confer with the obligor to ascertain the essential facts and, if possible, to work out some tentative program or course of action; (2) to take such action, with the co-operation of the obligor, if possible, as might be necessary to preserve the status quo insofar as was possible; (3) to communicate the essential facts to the indenture security holders and, if indicated, to assist in the organization of a committee to represent the security holders; and (4) to work with the security holders and their committee and to take such action in the enforcement of the indenture remedial provisions as might be decided upon by the trustee and the committee. Whenever possible, an effort was made to work out a compromise solution without recourse to the drastic indenture remedies.

This process, of course, was time consuming. The indenture provisions referred to above were included as a protection to the trustee to enable it to delay pursuit of the indenture remedies until opportunity was afforded for consultation with the security holders as to its action.

While the procedure outlined above was the one most frequently followed, at times the trustee initiated action without awaiting direction of the security holders. It is possible, though by no means certain, that had this been done more often, some of the serious consequences which resulted might have been ameliorated. In any event, the security holders were regarded as having the inherent right to decide for themselves whether their interests would be served best by compromise or strict enforcement of the indenture remedies.

The position of the trustee has been rendered more difficult by incorporation in all qualified indentures, and in most other indentures since 1940, of certain provisions required by the Trust Indenture Act. Although no specific course of action is prescribed, the act has established a new standard for trustees after default. This is contained in Section 315 (c), which requires the inclusion in each qualified indenture of a provision that the indenture trustee shall exercise, in case of default, such of the rights and powers vested in it by the indenture, and shall use the same degree of care and skill in their exercise as a prudent man would exercise or use under similar circumstances in the conduct of his own affairs.

It is questionable whether the change of rules brought about by the forced inclusion of this provision and elimination of the provisions protecting the trustee has materially improved the situation. Unfortunately it is true that a trustee sometimes took unfair advantage of the immunity clauses, although this was the exception rather than the rule. There is a real danger that under the new language, a trustee, to protect itself from a charge of negligence, may initiate precipitate action to the detriment of all parties in interest.

The "prudent man" standard is not a novel concept. It exists in the law of numerous states as the fiduciary standard for executors, administrators, or *inter-vivos* trustees. Precedent is a significant factor in determining compliance in a particular case and, in relation to the various types of "personal" trusts, precedent is not too difficult to establish. By reason of the generally high level of economic activity from 1940 to 1972, there were few defaults under qualified indentures. As a result, the indenture act provisions have not been fully tested and adjudicated. With the increase in the number of defaults during the past two years, and as a result of the filing in bankruptcy by the Penn Central Transportation Company in 1970 (which involved approximately seventy-three bond issues exceeding one billion dollars of funded debt), it can be expected that there will be an acceleration of the development of legal principles related to the trustee's role in this area. At present, almost all of the "precedents" which exist for the conduct of indenture trustees are those of pre-Trust Indenture Act days. These should not be relied upon in the future since it must be assumed that the primary reason for changing the rules was dissatisfaction with such precedents.

Of more importance is the fact that the trustee still has only limited powers. It is axiomatic that imposition of responsibility should be accompanied by the grant of sufficient power and authority to discharge it properly. Yet what has occurred has been the establishment of a new standard of conduct for indenture trustees without any change in its limited authority. The prudent man in managing his own affairs can take *any* action which seems to be indicated by the circumstances. The same is generally true with reference to the classes of fiduciaries to which the rule has been applied heretofore. As applied to indenture trustees, it will be noted that the trustee is limited to the exercise of the rights and powers vested in it by the indenture. A review of the customary remedial provisions set forth earlier in this chapter will indicate clearly that they contemplate action to be taken only on the most serious type of default. What course of action should the trustee follow when prudence dictates remedies or procedures not included within the rights and powers vested in it by the indenture?

This question will arise many times, and for purposes of illustration, let us consider two possible "defaults." The first involves default in a covenant to maintain working capital in a specified amount. The obligor's financial condition remains basically sound, but because of circumstances beyond its control, its working capital falls below the minimum required. No judicial action will remedy the situation. What should the trustee do?

The second situation involves a sinking fund default. Due to depressed business conditions the obligor is unable to meet its large principal payments. It appears, however, that a rearrangement of the maturity schedule through deferment of a portion of the current installments will resolve the difficulty. Can the trustee properly co-operate in securing the necessary adjustment, especially when it may require a substantial period of time to secure the requisite consents?

The answer to these and other questions must await the course of future court decisions. In the meantime, indenture trustees should consider the following possibilities:

(1) Since the limitation of liability to performance of duties specifically set forth in the indenture is, by the terms of the indenture, related to pre-default activities, courts may very well find implied discretionary powers to perform acts or take action not specifically embraced within the indenture language.

(2) Despite this possibility, the taking of any action for which express authority is not included within the indenture may subject the trustee to the highest degree of care.

(3) The right of the trustee to rely conclusively on certificates or opinions conforming to indenture requirements is limited to certificates with respect to pre-default activities. After a default occurs, such certificates and opinions may not constitute adequate protection if an independent investigation would have disclosed a different state of facts.

(4) In appropriate situations, full advantage should be taken of the indenture provisions permitting amendment of the indenture with the consent of a requisite percentage of security holders. The two hypothetical cases cited above would seem appropriate situations for recourse to this provision. Since this would seem the prudent course, the trustee should be fully protected in co-operating with the obligor in presenting a proposal to the security holders and requesting their consent. Care must be exercised to see that no material adverse change in the situation occurs during the interim.

(5) Where the default is merely technical, or seemingly temporary, or in the judgment of the trustee is capable of being cured or

resolved through appropriate negotiation or adjustment with the obligor, the trustee undoubtedly has sufficient authority to take the necessary action without reference to the security holders or without recourse to the remedial sections. This authority is necessarily implicit in other provisions of the indenture.

(6) Upon the occurrence of a serious default, the trustee is under an affirmative duty to take appropriate action. It is doubtful that the changes imposed by the Trust Indenture Act were intended to alter the basic concept of the trustee's responsibility. Accordingly, if the trustee acts reasonably and in a manner calculated to preserve the status quo until it has an opportunity to consult with the indenture security holders, this should be sufficient in the normal situation. The circumstances of each case, however, will determine the degree of care and course of action which should be followed. No prescribed course of action for every situation is possible.

Notice of Default

One of the first problems with which the trustee is confronted is whether or not to notify the indenture security holders of the occurrence of a default. In qualified indentures the trustee is now under a duty to give security holders prompt notice of all defaults known to it. Such notice must be given within ninety days after the occurrence of the default. This giving of notice is mandatory with respect to any default in the payment of the principal of, or interest on, any security, or in the payment of any sinking fund or purchase fund installment. The trustee is protected in withholding notice of other defaults as long as its board of directors, executive committee, or trust committee determine in good faith that the withholding of notice is in the interest of the indenture security holders.

Under most indentures prior to the Trust Indenture Act, the trustee was under no express duty to notify the security holders of a default. While such a general notice was sometimes given, it was the exception rather than the rule. Where action by security holders seemed indicated, the trustee frequently contacted institutional and other holders of substantial amounts of securities known to it and also consulted with any security holders who made inquiry. General circularization of security holders was usually deferred until it was determined that committee organization was desirable, and then notice was given by committee representatives rather than by the trustee. In other situations where some arrangement or adjustment appeared feasible, the trustee would work out an appropriate proposal with the obligor, which would then be submitted to security holders by the latter.

The absence of a specific indenture requirement, however, did not always serve as full protection to the trustee in withholding notice. In one case, an indenture contained a covenant that the obligor would not consolidate or merge with another corporation. With the knowledge of the trustee, the company merged into another corporation and the latter continued to pay interest. Subsequently, bankruptcy ensued. The court held that the trustee was guilty of gross negligence and bad faith in failing to give notice of the default despite the fact that the indenture provided that the trustee need take no notice of a default unless notified by a specified percentage of the bondholders. (*Vid.*, Seelig, *et al.*, v. First National Bank of Chicago, 20 Fed. Supp. 61, D.C. N.D. Ill. [1936].) Another court held that a trustee, in a suit brought against it by bondholders, was under a duty to explain why it had permitted a default for several years without taking action to notify the bondholders or protect their interests. (*Vid.*, Boylston v. Senate Apartment Building Corporation, 11 N.E. (2d) 636 [1937].)

Where the trustee advances its own funds to meet interest payments, thus preventing the bondholders from learning of the obligor's default, it may be liable for any reduction in the value of the security which subsequently results. It has also been held in such a situation that the trustee is not entitled to assert a claim for reimbursement or share *pro rata* with the bondholders in a subsequent sale of the property. Similarly, it has been held that where the controlling stockholder of the obligor, engaged in marketing its bonds, personally advanced money to pay coupons to prevent notice of default, such coupons are paid and not purchased, and are not entitled to either priority or equality against the obligor's assets.

As has already been noted, where there is a paying agent for the obligor's securities other than the trustee, such paying agent is now under a duty to notify the trustee in case the obligor defaults in any installment of principal or interest when the same falls due.

Most indentures provide that the trustee may, at its sole discretion, advance moneys for the payment of taxes, insurance, rentals under leases, or other items for preserving the trust estate. It is also provided that to secure such advances the trustee shall be entitled to a lien on the trust estate prior to the lien of any bonds issued under the indenture. This type of advance, however, is exclusively for the purpose of preserving the trust estate or to prevent the creation of a prior lien thereon. It is to be distinguished from the type of advance referred to above, which prevents security holders from learning of a serious default.

In the case of advances by the trustee to preserve the trust estate, the trustee is now required under the Trust Indenture Act to give notice within ninety days of the making of any such advance if the amount of advances remaining unpaid aggregates more than 10 per cent of the principal amount of indenture securities outstanding. The trustee must also include in its annual report to security holders a report of any advances made by it which remain unpaid on the date of the report, if such advances remaining unpaid aggregate more than one-half of one per centum of the principal amount of the indenture securities outstanding on such date.

There is some inconsistency in the Trust Indenture Act provisions in this regard. As noted, the report sections require notice of advances only when they aggregate certain specified minimum amounts. Section 311, however, appears to protect the trustee's lien and right to prior repayment only with respect to advances which have been reported to security holders, regardless of amount. Also, it is unlikely that the trustee would make advances unless the obligor had defaulted. Notice of such default would have to be reported, unless it were withheld for the reasons permitted by the indenture. If such reasons are sufficient for withholding notice, the trustee should not be penalized by losing its lien or right to prior repayment. It is likely that the omission in Section 311 is an inadvertence and the trustee would be protected if it complied with the specific requirements for reporting outlined in other sections of the act. If such a situation arises, however, these provisions should receive the careful attention of the trustee and its counsel.

It is very important that the trustee be given a broad discretion in the matter of withholding notice of default and that it be protected in the exercise of such discretion. The security holders are entitled to prompt notice if their security or their investment is prejudiced, and the trustee should be prompt in notifying them of any serious default. As indicated, such notice is mandatory in the case of a default in payment of principal or interest. The primary objective of all parties, however, should be to prevent a default or to remedy the situation. If this is possible, then too hasty action in publicizing the default can cause irreparable damage. The trustee should always have sufficient time to explore the possiblity of curing a default or of working out some arrangement to prevent a serious loss of security holders.

The duty to act with a high degree of care embraces responsibility for withholding as well as giving notice in appropriate situations. In a doubtful or borderline case, notice should be given. All facts should be investigated promptly and weighed carefully. Whatever the conclusion of the administrative officer, it is recommended that the final decision in each case be made by the trust committee or, if there is none, by the executive committee or board of directors of the trustee.

The Trustee and the Indenture
Remedial Provisions

While under modern practice with certain special exceptions, recourse is seldom made to the specific remedial provisions set forth in the indenture, it is desirable to describe briefly the general principles applicable to their use.

(1) *Trustee's Discretion as to Remedy.*—Subject to the right of a majority of the indenture security holders to direct the time, method, and place of conducting any proceeding for any remedy available to the trustee—which exists under most modern indentures, the trustee has a broad discretion as to the particular remedy to be pursued. As long as it acts in good faith and not in a wholly unreasonable and arbitrary manner, a court of equity will not interfere with the trustee's exercise of discretion. This is true even though the trustee may have a conflicting interest. Likewise, the trustee will not be liable for any error of judgment made in good faith by a responsible officer, unless it can be shown that the trustee was negligent in ascertaining the pertinent facts.

Although the trustee's powers are strictly limited by the indenture, a court of equity may find implied powers or responsibilities or, in a particular situation, may authorize the trustee to perform acts which it would otherwise have no power to perform. Thus, in a case where depressed economic conditions had rendered it impossible for the obligor to perform a covenant in an indenture secured by real estate bonds relating to the maintenance of certain value ratios, and where the only alternative was foreclosure, the trustee was permitted to enter into a working agreement with the obligor permitting the latter to retain possession. (*Vid.*, N.J. National Bank & Trust Co. v. Lincoln Mortgage & Title Guaranty Company, *et al.*, 105 N.J. Eq. 557, 148 Atl. 713 [1930].) In another case where the security consisted of various collateral, the court held that it had the power to authorize the trustee to secure a loan on the collateral and make a distribution to security holders rather than dispose of it at a forced sale. (*Vid.*, Seigle, *et al.* v. First National Company, *et al.*, 338 Mo. 417, 90 S.W. (2d) 776 [1936].)

In pursuing a course of action not specifically authorized or permitted by the indenture, however, the trustee should endeavor to secure authority of a court or permission of a majority of the security holders. If it endeavors to act on its own without authority, even though in good faith and in an honest effort to preserve the security for the bondholders, it may be liable for any loss resulting from its action.

(2) *Rights Incident to Other Remedies.*—The first two remedies enumerated above are included primarily for the purpose of enabling the more adequate enforcement of other remedies.

The first of these is the right of acceleration of the maturity of the indenture securities. This right is given to the trustee alone and, frequently, to a specified percentage of the indenture security holders acting without the trustee. The purpose of the provision is to enable conversion of the company's obligation into a matured debt so that foreclosure or other proceedings may be undertaken to the same extent as if there had been a principal default. If the indenture does not contain such a provision, the trustee may not be able to foreclose, in the event of a default in interest, except to the extent of past due interest. This would necessitate successive actions until maturity of the principal debt. It is therefore important that every indenture contain an acceleration clause.

Another provision which was included in some indentures, and is now required to be included in all qualified indentures, is that giving the trustee the right to recover judgment in its own name in the event of a default in the payment of principal or interest. Since the trustee's duties relate primarily to enforcement of the security and the security holders themselves own the debt, a serious question arose as to the extent of the trustee's rights in the absence of such power. Some courts have held that on foreclosure the trustee could not recover a deficiency judgment in the absence of such a provision.

(3) *Rights of Entry, Sale, and Foreclosure.*—Some of the powers given the trustee in case of default are seldom exercised. One of these is the right of entry and possession until the default is cured. The theory underlying the right is prevention of mismanagement of the property and the diversion of the rents and profits therefrom to purposes other than the paying of interest and principal on the indenture securities. The theory is that the trustee should be able to take possession, receive the rents and profits until all defaults are cured, and then return the property in good condition to the mortgagor. Although such a procedure might be feasible in the case of a real estate mortgage, it is not practicable in the case of the usual industrial or utility mortgage where management is highly specialized. Receivers are sometimes appointed at the request of an indenture trustee, but this is usually an incident to foreclosure or other judicial remedy. Where a trustee is in possession pursuant to such a provision, however, it has all the rights of a mortgagee in possession and is accountable to the mortgagor only after all payments required by the indenture have been made to the bondholders.

Another remedy seldom pursued is that of sale without judicial proceedings. It is usually impossible for an outright sale of the property to be made to an independent purchaser, and sale of the properties is therefore only an incident to some form of reorganization proceedings, and actually is unnecessary under existing provisions of the bankruptcy statutes. This power has been used in particular situations, such as under a railroad equipment trust agreement. It also may be of value where the trustee holds marketable collateral securities. Except for such situations, however, the power of sale does not provide an effective usable remedy.

One of the important rights on default, which is necessarily an incident to the conception of the indenture as a mortgage, is the right of foreclosure. Prior to enactment of Sections 77 and 77B to the bankruptcy act, this was the most important remedy available and was used frequently to accomplish an effective reorganization. For this reason courts customarily found sufficient power invested in the trustee to initiate foreclosure proceedings, even where the indenture provisions were not clear or seemed to qualify the right. For example, when the only provision was an authorization for the trustee to foreclose on request of a specified percentage of bond-holders, it was held to have the right to do so on its own initiative.

As an incident to foreclosure proceedings or other remedies, an application should be made for appointment of a receiver for the benefit of the indenture trustee and the security holders. This is important in connection with provisions relating to assignment of rents and profits. The usual indenture is so drafted that the indenture trustee has no right to rents or profits until it takes possession. It has been held that a provision stating that an event of default would act as an automatic assignment of rents and profits is valid and enforceable. In any case, however, it is desirable to apply for appointment of a receiver and the segregation of rents and profits for the benefit of the trustee and bondholders.

One of the problems which arose in connection with foreclosure proceedings was the trustee's right to bid in the property. Where no such power was granted, the trustee's rights have been held to be limited to the taking of such steps as would lead to a cash distribution to bondholders, and therefore no right to purchase the property could exist. Other courts have held that such a power could be implied or, if not expressly given, could be authorized by the court. Unless expressly required by the indenture, the trustee cannot be compelled to bid in the property. Where the trustee bids in the property, it has an implied power to resell it for the best price obtainable.

INHERENT DIFFICULTIES
OF DEFAULT ADMINISTRATION

Having considered the various indenture provisions relating to default, it might be well to summarize the essential problems which face the trustee on default and the difficulty in dealing with them effectively.

While it is essential to include the broad remedial provisions in indentures, one of the unfortunate consequences is the false sense of security created in the minds of individual security holders. As has been emphasized, the real security for holders of securities is the "going concern" value of the obligor and the income and profits realized from operation of its business. The indenture covenants constitute a strong deterrent and if the business is profitable, the obligor is most concerned to see that no default occurs so that it may remain in the undisturbed possession and enjoyment of its properties. If the business becomes unprofitable, this "going concern" value and hence the bondholders' real security is depleted. The obligor is unable to meet its obligations and the realizable value of the property, as distinguished from its value in the operation of the business for which it was intended, is usually insufficient to discharge such obligations. This is particularly true when the default occurs during a period of general economic depression, or when the industry of which the obligor is a part is undergoing strain or depressed conditions. These are economic facts. They are the risks which each investor must personally evaluate, and no contract provisions can afford such investor complete protection against them.

A serious indenture default will usually be accompanied by a general inability of the obligor to meet its obligations or by insolvency. Where such a situation exists, the obligor can protect itself against the strict enforcement of indenture remedial provisions by filing a petition in bankruptcy or for reorganization. This in fact is what usually occurs. The trustee is then enjoined by the court from instituting or continuing any proceedings for enforcement of the indenture provisions.

Of even greater significance than the rights, powers, and remedies available to the trustee, are those which it does not have, either by express limitation or by the absence of a grant. The provisions customarily included which have become more or less standard are derived from traditional common law remedies which were developed in relation to small, readily identifiable properties having inherent intrinsic values. They were not designed for large industrial properties devoted to corporate rather than individual use. They contemplate some form of liquidation and sale, which in most cases is undesirable and impractical.

Even were it possible to enforce the remedial provisions according to the letter of the contract, this is seldom desirable, at least during the initial phases of most defaults. What is called for is some form of co-operative working arrangement to enable the obligor alone, or in conjunction with its major creditors, to endeavor to resolve its financial problems. It is in this area that the trustee is almost without power or authority to act effectively. It is true that action can be taken with the support and consent of certain percentages of the indenture security holders, but the delay necessarily involved as well as the occasional harassment by individual or minority groups of holders is unfortunate. As a result, the trustee must frequently walk a rather devious path. As suggested previously, further obstacles may have been created by the imposition of a stricter standard without a concurrent grant of broader authority.

Whether an indenture trustee should be given additional or broader powers is debatable. It is certain that such a grant would be resisted by trustees themselves unless adequate provisions for their protection in the exercise of discretion were included, as well as assurance that their expenses and appropriate compensation would be paid. Most corporate trust departments are not staffed to make the detailed studies and investigations called for, and employment of experts would be necessary in most cases.

Such a grant of power would also involve a delegation of authority which traditionally has been reserved to security holders themselves. Some authority for dealing with the situation during an interim period until security holders could be organized would be desirable, if accompanied by appropriate immunity and protective provisions, but it is doubtful that authority in excess of this should be granted.

In general, the powers granted to the trustee relate solely to the strict enforcement of the contractual rights under the indenture. To the extent that the obligor can be compelled, through judicial proceedings or otherwise, to perform its covenants and obligations under the indenture, or to the extent that a sale or foreclosure under the indenture is indicated and can be effected, the trustee has requisite authority.

Since the usual corporate mortgage involves important and necessary operating properties, liquidation such as is contemplated by sale or foreclosure is seldom feasible. Security holders will usually realize more through a reorganization or readjustment of the obligor's capital structure than through liquidation, even if the latter were permitted. Accordingly, where a major default occurs, the object of most proceedings is the reorganization of the financial structure of the obligor.

While the authority of the trustee in these proceedings is usually sufficient to enable it to take all preliminary steps, there are strict limitations on its rights to represent the security holders. A reorganization or recapitalization can generally be effected only where the security holders are willing to accept other securities of the reorganized company in satisfaction of their claims. This normally involves some compromise of claims.

The trustee has no power or authority to make such a compromise on behalf of the indenture security holders, or to accept anything but cash in satisfaction of their claim. The trustee has no title to, or interest in, the debt secured, except to the extent that it may recover judgment against the obligor as an incident to enforcement of the security. The debt secured cannot be compromised or discharged except by appropriate judicial decree or with the consent of the security holders themselves. Unusual circumstances may justify an exception to this general rule. In United States v. Freeman (USDC, SDNY, 1/25/60) the court held that indenture trustees had power and authority to consent to a compromise settlement binding on bondholders. The case involved a liquidation proceeding following a terminated unsuccessful effort to reorganize a railroad under Section 77. One of the powers of the trustees was the right to take possession, operate the properties, and pay taxes and other proper charges superior to the lien of the mortgage. Although the trustees were not in possession and had been specifically enjoined from enforcing indenture remedies, the court found that since the amount realized on liquidation was less than the claims alleged to be prior to the indenture lien, the trustees had a right to enter into an agreement compromising all claims, and that "this right of the trustees to assent on behalf of the bondholders was unquestioned."

In view of the limitations on the rights and powers of the trustee, it is important to consider the rights and powers of indenture security holders, both individually and collectively. This will be done in the next chapter before dealing with the problems involved in bankruptcy and reorganization proceedings.

13

Rights of Security Holders

THE PRIMARY PURPOSE of the indenture is to afford protection to the holders of the securities which are issued thereunder. The covenants and remedial provisions are of no avail unless ample power of enforcing them is given. In the previous chapter we considered the rights and duties of protecting such security holders' interests as are placed in the trustee. It was indicated, however, that these rights are not all-inclusive but are limited to those expressly granted. Therefore it is important to consider the rights which the security holders have with respect to the indenture, the enforcement of the provisions thereof, and the claims represented by the securities which they hold.

These considerations present a difficult question, and one which remains to be resolved adequately and satisfactorily. It is important to bear in mind always a distinction which has already been made. The obligation of the company to pay principal and interest on the individual securities runs directly to the security holders themselves. The ownership of the debt represented by the obligation rests in each individually. As a general principle, no one should be permitted to amend, modify, prejudice, or deal with such debt without the consent of the owner thereof.

The difficulty arises when it is necessary to distinguish between the claim of an individual holder, which may be represented by only one of many thousands of obligations identical in terms, and claims under the indenture which secures the entire debt represented by all such obligations outstanding. From the viewpoint of the obligor and the trustee, the debt secured by the indenture is a single obligation and is dealt with as such.

The rights, duties, and responsibilities of the trustee relate to enforcement of the security provisions of the indenture which secures this entire debt. Its right to sue and recover judgment for the debt is in furtherance of such enforcement. While it owes a duty to each individual holder, its primary responsibility is to security holders as a class, and it cannot permit the claim of an individual holder to prejudice the rights of the holders as a group.

Also, during the life of a bond issue the obligor accounts to the trustee with respect to its duties and obligations under the indenture. One of the advantages to an obligor of the indenture-trustee device is that it has only one entity with which to deal on most problems which arise. While most companies endeavor to provide any reasonable information requested by an individual holder, they cannot for practical reasons deal with many thousands of such holders individually.

A distinction should be made between holders of obligations issued publicly and holders who acquire an entire issue through "direct placement" negotiations. In the latter case, besides executing an indenture with the trustee, the obligor enters into a separate "purchase agreement" with each purchaser of a part of the debt. In these agreements the purchasers usually require filing of periodic financial and other information directly with them. These rights, however, are acquired under separate agreements with the obligor and not under the indenture. In many cases, these rights are also "personal" in that they are not transferred on sale of the obligations to a subsequent purchaser.

While in relation to enforcement, many of the rules which would apply to holders of a publicly distributed issue would also apply to holders under direct placement contracts, in the following pages we will be concerned only with the former.

RIGHTS PRIOR TO DEFAULT

Information and Disclosure Provisions

Adequate protection of the investor's interests involves factors over and above enforcement and remedial provisions of the indenture. He is entitled to have complete information as to the obligations offered him for purchase. He is entitled to the opportunity to be kept reasonably informed of developments which may affect his security so long as he continues to hold it. He is also entitled to know his rights in the event that action is required to enforce the claim represented by his security.

One of the basic purposes of the Securities Act of 1933 was to require full disclosure of information relative to new securities being issued publicly. The provisions of this act have been enlarged by the Trust Indenture Act which requires filing of copies of the indenture in connection with registrations of new securities. Summaries of important provisions of the indenture must be included in the registration statement. Pertinent financial and other information contained in such statement, including summaries of the indenture provisions, must be incorporated in the prospectus pursuant to which sale of the securities is made. Each purchaser must be delivered a copy of the prospectus so that the investor now has available all pertinent information on which an intelligent decision can be made.

The security itself refers to important sections of the indenture, particularly any which impose limitations on the rights of the holder. If further information is desired, the trustee will always make a copy of the indenture available for the holder's inspection or advise such holder as to the contents of particular sections which are of concern.

While not directly related to the individual security holder, the activities of the Securities and Exchange Commission under the Securities Exchange Act of 1934 and the subsequently enacted federal securities acts are designed to afford protection to security holders generally. Rules and regulations of the national securities exchanges, the National Association of Security Dealers, and other groups have the same purpose.

A great deal has thus been done and is being done to prevent fraud and sharp practices and to afford individual investors adequate information on which to make intelligent decisions. The investor must personally assume some initiative and responsibility for his or her own protection. If an investor hasn't the time or ability to do so, one solution would be to seek professional assistance in the management of his or her financial affairs.

Reports of the Obligor and the Trustee

Each obligor which has any security listed on any national securities exchange is required to file with the Securities and Exchange Commission, with each such exchange on which any securities are listed, and with the trustee under any indentures of such obligor, periodic financial statements and other reports. All such reports are public information and are available for inspection by any security holder. Copies may also be obtained from the commission upon payment of a small fee to cover cost of reproduction.

Each qualified indenture must also contain a provision requiring the obligor to transmit to indenture security holders such summaries of such reports and other information as the commission may prescribe by rules and regulations. No such rules or regulations have been issued, therefore this provision is currently inoperative. Many companies, however, endeavor to forward to known holders of their debt securities copies of annual reports forwarded to stockholders. It is probable that almost every obligor would do so if specifically requested by a security holder.

The trustee is now under a duty to submit periodic reports to security holders under indentures qualified under the Trust Indenture Act. These reports must be submitted at intervals of not more than twelve months. While these reports must necessarily be general, they are required to set forth: (1) statements as to the continued eligibility and qualification of the trustee; (2) the character and amount of any advances made by it, as indenture trustee, which remain unpaid on the date of the report and for reimbursement of which it claims, or may claim, a lien or charge prior to that of the indenture securities, on the trust estate, or on property or funds held or collected by it, if such advances remaining unpaid aggregate more than one-half of one per centum of the principal amount of the indenture securities outstanding; (3) any indebtedness owing to the trustee in its individual capacity and the security therefor, if any; (4) the property and funds physically in possession of the indenture trustee; (5) any release, or release and substitution of property under the indenture, and the consideration received therefor, not previously reported; (6) any additional issue of indenture securities not previously reported; and (7) any other action taken by it in the performance of its duties under the indenture which in its opinion materially affects the indenture securities or the trust estate.

We have previously considered notices which the trustee must give as to events of default under the indenture. There may be omitted from the annual report, however, notice of any default being withheld pursuant to appropriate indenture provisions and for the reasons previously discussed.

In addition to its annual report the trustee must also submit special interim reports as to important transactions. Other than reports of default, these include:

(1) A brief report of the release, or release and substitution of any property subject to the lien of the indenture, and the consideration therefor, if any, if the fair value of such property is 10 per cent or more of the principal amount of indenture securities outstanding on the date of the release. Such report must be transmitted to security holders within ninety days after execution and delivery of the release.

(2) A report as to the character and amount of any advances made by the trustee pursuant to the indenture, for which it claims or may claim a lien on the trust estate prior to that of the indenture security holders, if the amount of all advances remaining unpaid aggregates 10 per cent or more of the principal amount of indenture securities outstanding. This report also must be transmitted within ninety days.

Bondholder Lists

Prior to the advent of the all registered corporate bond issue, the trustee was always confronted with the absence of accurate information as to the holders of indenture securities. This information is of great importance in connection with the taking of any remedial action under the indenture.

The obligor is now required to furnish to the trustee, at intervals of not more than six months, all information coming into its possession, or that of its paying agents, as to the names and addresses of security holders. The trustee is also required to retain any such information which it may receive in its capacity as paying agent. The usual indenture provision is that all such information will be preserved by the trustee until a new list is received and prepared (which is done in connection with payment of the next maturing interest installment), and that the previous list may then be destroyed. The purpose is to keep such information in as current a form as possible.

In the case of debt obligations which are outstanding in bearer form, the only way that current information can be obtained as to the names of the holders is in connection with collection of the semi-annual interest coupons. The only difficulty is that very little information is actually obtained in this way.

At the time these sections of the Trust Indenture Act were being considered in Congress, the Internal Revenue Code required all bondholders to file ownership certificates when collecting their coupons for interest. These were filed with the U.S. Treasury Department and gave it a means of checking reports of interest income on income tax declarations. While these reports were merely transmitted to the treasury department by paying agents, they would have provided a basis on which almost complete information as to security holders could have been obtained. Current treasury regulations do not require filing of these certificates. Accordingly, this former source of information is gone.

Since most coupons are presented to the New York paying agents for collection, where such an agency is provided, the collection procedure in effect, as described in Chapter 9, does not provide for names of individual holders to reach the paying agent or the trustee. The only information actually obtained is that of the collecting agent which presents the coupons. In most cases, therefore, the list of holders obtained in this manner is of little practical value.

Where the company or the trustee desires to communicate with security holders in connection with a specific matter, such as a bondholders' meeting, an amendment to the indenture, or other special matter, a procedure has been developed whereby substantial information can be obtained in connection with the collection of interest coupons. This is done through use of a special form of Memorandum Certificate of Ownership (see Exhibit 11, Chapter 9). If notified at least thirty days in advance of an interest payment date, the paying agent can prepare and deliver to the collecting agents a supply of such certificates with the request that they be completed and submitted with the interest coupons. This is an effective procedure and can provide a fairly complete list of holders as of the particular date.

Another difficulty with this method of obtaining information is that it can be done only when interest is being paid. Once a default in interest occurs, no further coupons are presented. This is the time when the trustee is most in need of information and the source is no longer available. Once a default occurs, there is usually a great deal of speculative activity in the obligations, so that any list of holders previously obtained, even though relatively accurate at the time, quickly becomes obsolete.

The most accurate list of holders is that obtained from the registration records. Whether the security be fully registered, or registered as to principal only, the holder is assured of receiving all reports which the trustee submits to security holders. Of more practical importance, such holder is promptly notified of any redemption call which affects his or her holdings.

Where the holder of a bearer instrument does not wish to have such security registered, another alternative is now provided. The holder may advise the trustee of such holdings and request that his or her name be placed on file as the holder of particular securities. The trustee is required to maintain such name on file for a period of two years. In acknowledging any such request, the trustee should call attention to the two-year limitation and suggest filing of a renewal request on or before a particular date.

While the trustee is required only to mail copies of reports to the holders on this special list, most trustees treat it in the same manner as lists of registered holders. This is a very good practice, and it is suggested that copies of all redemption notices or other material of special interest to security holders be sent to all holders on the two-year list maintained by the trustee.

Unfortunately, few holders of bearer securities have taken advantage of the provision which enables them to place their name on file with the trustee for the purpose of receiving reports and other information. This may be due in large part to ignorance of this right. Trustees are urged to call security holders' attention to this privilege whenever an appropriate opportunity is afforded.

Annual reports of the trustee and reports submitted by it as to occurrence of events of default are required to be submitted to all known holders of indenture securities. This includes the list obtained from the obligor, the list maintained by it as paying agent, the list of registered holders and the special two-year list. Interim reports as to releases or advances by the trustee are required to be submitted only to registered holders and holders on the special two-year list. As a practical matter, however, any such interim reports are usually submitted to all holders, regardless of the source from which information was derived.

Access to Confidential Information

Information as to names and addresses of security holders is of importance to the obligor and to the trustee. On occasion it may also be of importance to other security holders. While this is particularly true in the event of a default or a threatened default, it may be important in relation to other proposed transactions. For example, certain holders may oppose a proposed amendment to the indenture and desire to organize other holders in opposition thereto. Where they feel that their rights may be prejudiced by any proposed action, they should be permitted to communicate their opposition and the reasons therefor to other holders.

This right is recognized by the requirement that qualified indentures contain a section conforming to the provisions of Section 312(b) of the Trust Indenture Act. This section provides that three or more holders of the indenture securities may petition the trustee and state their desire to communicate with other holders of indenture securities. If such holders can establish by reasonable proof that they have been holders of indenture securities for six months or longer, the trustee must afford to such applicants all information in its possession as to the names and addresses of security holders. If the trustee elects not to make such information available to the applicants, it may inform them as to the number of holders on the list maintained by it and the approximate cost of mailing the proxy or other information desired to be mailed by the applicants. Upon request of the petitioning security holders and payment of such costs, the trustee is required to mail copies of the proxy or other information to all security holders known to it. If it determines that mailing of such information would not be in the best interests of security holders it must, within five days after receiving the proxy or other material, file with the Securities and Exchange Commission and the applicants copies of the material submitted, together with its reasons for its belief that mailing of such material would not be in the interests of security holders. The act provides for a hearing by the commission and for a finding either sustaining or rejecting the trustee's contention. If rejected, the trustee must mail copies of such material with reasonable promptness to all security holders known to it.

The trustee is protected with respect to disclosure of information or mailing of any material in accordance with the provisions of the statute or the order of the commission.

A more difficult problem is sometimes presented when a security holder requests information as to affairs of the obligor which is in possession of the trustee. Theoretically, security holders entitled to any information in possession of the trustee which may affect their security. Occasionally, however, a particular holder may have ulterior motives, not related to such position as a security holder, for requesting such information. One such instance might be the purchase of a bond by a competitor of the obligor, or someone associated with a competitor, for the purpose of obtaining access to confidential information in the trustee's possession as to the obligor's affairs.

This is a difficult decision for the trustee. It has the right to inquire into the reasons for any request. Should the motive of the applicant appear questionable, the trustee should withhold access to the information until either it receives the obligor's approval or the applicant establishes such right, as a security holder, to the requested data.

Amendments to Indenture

Quite frequently it is necessary to amend the indenture by an appropriate supplement. Most amendments can be made by agreement between the obligor and the trustee without reference to or approval of the security holder. The most common amendments of this kind are the following:

(1) To create and provide the terms of additional series of securities authorized by the indenture to be issued;

(2) To mortgage or pledge under the indenture specific property or additional property as security, and to provide the terms and conditions upon which such property may be dealt with by the trustee, consistent with other provisions of the indenture;

(3) To modify, amend, or add to the provisions of the indenture in such manner as to permit the qualification thereof under the Trust Indenture Act of 1939;

(4) To add to the covenants and agreements of the obligor;

(5) To evidence the succession of another corporation to the obligor, and the assumption of the securities and the covenants and obligations of the obligor by such successor corporation;

(6) To cure any ambiguity, or any defective or inconsistent provision of the indenture, so long as the rights of the security holders are not adversely affected.

While amendments of the type above described do not adversely affect any substantive rights of security holders and so could be made without express authority therefor in the indenture, it is desirable and good practice to include such authority in every new indenture. This obviates the possibility of any objection being raised thereto.

At times it is considered necessary or desirable to make other changes or amendments to the indenture, or eliminate specific provisions thereof, which may affect a substantive right of the security holders. In the absence of indenture authority, such change could not be made without the consent of all of the security holders, or of all holders whose rights might be affected.

It is therefore of great importance to include in the indenture a section setting forth the manner in which such changes may be made, and the authority required. It is customary to permit such modifications with the consent of the holders of two thirds of the principal amount of the securities outstanding, excluding any securities held by or for the account of any obligor. The indenture should set forth in sufficient detail just how such consent is to be evidenced and the manner in which proof of security holdings is to be made. Here again it is desirable, rather than spelling out such requirements in detail, to permit the trustee to make rules and regulations covering such administrative matters.

It is well to provide for delivery to the trustee of executed consents within a specified period, or in the alternative, to permit modification of the indenture by vote of security holders at a formal meeting called for such purpose. In the latter event, provision should be made for voting by proxy. Where securities are outstanding in bearer form, notice of the proposed meeting should be made by publication sufficiently in advance. In addition, whether or not required by the indenture—and except for registered holders it is proper for technical reasons for the indenture not to so require —the trustee should mail copies of the notice to all security holders on the lists maintained by it.

Even though the obligor may be able to obtain the required consents without a formal meeting or approach to all security holders, the trustee should insist that notice of the proposed amendment be published or otherwise communicated to all holders. This will appraise everyone interested of the indicated change and afford them an opportunity to express their opinion thereon.

When the trustee has received the required consents, it is then authorized to join in the proposed amendment.

Certain provisions should not be subject to change or amendment without consent of all holders, or at least of those who may be affected. Such matters would include extension of the time for payment of principal or interest on any securities; reduction in the rate of interest; modification of any sinking fund or purchase fund; altering of the rights of holders of some securities without similar altering of the rights of other holders; or reduction of the percentage of the holders required to consent to any future amendment, to waive any default, or to waive compliance with any provision of the indenture.

Limitations on Rights of Individual Holders

Every indenture should contain limitations on the right of individual holders to institute an action to enforce the security provided in the indenture. One of the basic reasons for appointing a trustee is to make it the agency for the enforcement of the security holders' rights as a class. To permit individual security holders to bring suit for the enforcement of their individual security as soon as default occurred would prejudice the rights of the other security holders, as well as subject the obligor to an unnecessary multiplicity of suits.

The usual provision is that no individual holder can institute a suit to enforce the security provided in the indenture, or otherwise, unless after demand on the trustee by the holders of a specified percentage of the indenture securities and offer of indemnity, the trustee refuses or neglects to take action. The percentage of security holders usually required to make such a demand is 25 per cent, although this may vary. Holders purchase their securities subject to the provisions of the indenture, and such a provision restricting suits by individual holders has been enforced by the courts, even where it was established that it was impossible to secure the necessary percentage to make demand on the trustee. It has also been held that without showing compliance with the indenture provisions, a bondholder could not institute a suit for the foreclosure of the mortgage, or for an accounting for breach of trust on the trustee's failure to foreclose; apply for the appointment of a receiver for the mortgaged property; accelerate the principal of the bonds; or institute suit for the breach of a sinking fund provision.

Such restrictions on a holder's right of action are strictly construed, however, and must be clearly set forth in the bond or debenture itself. Accordingly, in one case where the only reference to the indenture in the bond was for the description and nature of the security, it was held that the bondholder's right of individual action could not be defeated by a restrictive provision in the indenture. Also, it has been indicated that such restrictions would be limited to suits for collection of the bonds or enforcement of the security, and that a bondholder could maintain an action to restrain impairment of the property by waste, deterioration, or destruction. In another case a corporation had an issue of bonds outstanding when all of its property was taken over by another corporation for cash, debenture shares, and stock. The cash and debenture shares were applied toward the reduction of the corporation's liabilities, including purchase and retirement of bonds. When all liabilities except $1,300,000 of bonds had been paid, and the corporation had $31,000,000 of cash and debenture shares remaining, it proposed to distribute $26,000,000 to its stockholders. A suit by bondholders for an injunction was sustained despite the fact that the corporation had $5,000,000 left for application to its bonds and that no demand had been made on the trustee. The court held that a bondholder had an inherent right to protect his security. (*Vid.*, Hoyt, *et al.*, v. E. I. du Pont de Nemours Powder Company, *et al.*, 88 N.J. Eq. 196, 102 Atl. 666 [1917].)

Where the necessary percentage of holders has made demand on the trustee and the latter has taken no action within the time required, suit may then be instituted by the holders themselves. If the trustee has instituted action for foreclosure, or for enforcement of any of the other remedies, an individual holder cannot intervene in the proceedings as a matter of right.

While the Trust Indenture Act neither requires nor prohibits restrictions on an individual holder's suits for enforcement, it authorizes the inclusion in indentures of a provision designed to prevent "strike suits" by individuals. This provision authorizes any court, in its discretion, in any suit for the enforcement of any right or remedy under the indenture, or in any suit against the trustee for any action taken or omitted by it as trustee, to require the filing by any party litigant of an undertaking to pay the costs of such suit, and provides that the court may, in its discretion, assess reasonable costs, including reasonable attorneys' fees, against any party litigant in such suit, having due regard to the merits and good faith of the claims or defenses made by such party litigant. The provision is not applicable to any suit instituted by a holder or holders of more than 10 per cent of the indenture securities outstanding or to any suit by any holder for principal of, or interest on, the security on or after the respective due dates expressed in the security.

Suit for Principal or Interest

Although provisions restraining suits by individual holders to enforce the indenture have been generally upheld, a different question is presented where the suit is for payment of the principal of, or interest on, the security.

Since the right to sue for principal or interest is regarded as an inherent part of the contract, any restriction on such right must be clearly and unambiguously set forth. The restriction must not only be included in the indenture, but must clearly appear on the face of the bond. A provision on the face of a bond that all rights of action on the bond, except as otherwise provided in the indenture, were vested in the trustee was held sufficient to prevent an individual bondholder's suit for principal, although a mere reference to the indenture for a description of the property mortgaged and the nature and extent of the security was held insufficient to incorporate such a restrictive provision.

Where the trustee has brought suit to foreclose the mortgage and has recovered judgment for the entire debt, this is held to merge the bondholders' rights and bar subsequent individual suits. The provision giving the trustee or bondholders the right to accelerate maturity is a right incident to enforcement of the remedies and does not give an individual holder the right to sue for principal following such acceleration.

It is clear that the indenture provision requiring demand on the trustee relates only to enforcement of the remedies and does not restrain an individual's right to sue for principal at maturity of such bond. Even though a substantial majority of the holders have consented to an extension of maturity, a nonassenter may still bring suit at the regular maturity. It has been indicated, however, that in such a case judgment could not be enforced by levy against any of the property mortgaged.

Most indentures expressly recognize the right of an individual holder to sue for principal or interest as the same matures, and this is mandatory in indentures qualified under the Trust Indenture

Act. In order to protect the holders as a class and facilitate temporary readjustments, there is permitted to be included a provision authorizing the holders of not less than 75 per cent in principal amount of the indenture securities outstanding to consent to the postponement of any interest payment for a period not exceeding three years from its due date. This consent will bind all holders. With this one exception, however, the indenture must provide that the right of any holder to receive payment of the principal of, or interest on, his security on and after the respective due dates expressed in such security, or to institute suit for the enforcement of any such payment, cannot be impaired without such holder's consent.

The only qualification on this absolute right is that the indenture may provide that such suit cannot be maintained if the institution or prosecution thereof, or the entry of judgment therein, would result in the surrender, impairment, waiver, or loss of the lien of the indenture upon any property subject to such lien.

Collective Action by Security Holders

(1) *Right to Direct Proceedings.*—The restrictions customarily placed on actions by individual holders do not apply to action by security holders as a group. Where the indenture provides that the trustee cannot be compelled to take action except on demand of a specified percentage of security holders, a demand by such percentage can compel the trustee to take action, or will give the holders themselves the right to do so.

A provision may be included in qualified indentures giving the holders of a majority in principal amount of the indenture securities outstanding, the right to direct the time, method, and place of conducting any proceeding for any remedy available to the trustee, or of exercising any trust or power conferred upon the trustee under the indenture.

Although this provision is not mandatory, it is a desirable one, and should serve in most cases for the better protection of the security holders' interests. The right given to a majority to control the trustee's action should greatly assist the trustee in determining the proper remedy to be pursued. Since the trustee is now subject to the prudent man standard after default, in a doubtful case it may well accelerate the principal and institute suit for foreclosure or file a petition in reorganization in order to protect itself against a charge of negligence for failing to take action. In many cases it might be possible to prevent bankruptcy or reorganization by delaying such proceedings. Since the trustee is protected in acting or refraining from action in accordance with the direction of a majority of the security holders, co-operation by the holders may serve to prevent hasty suits, or will contribute to determination of the proper remedy to pursue and the appropriate time and method for instituting suit.

(2) *Waiver of Default.*—In addition to the right to direct the time, method, and place of conducting proceedings for enforcement, a majority of the indenture security holders may be given the right to waive any past default and its consequences under the indenture, other than a default in principal or interest. Such waiver will be binding on all holders.

This provision can be extremely helpful in working out a readjustment plan where waiver of existing defaults is essential and consent of all holders could not be obtained. Such waiver could also apply to past sinking fund or purchase fund installments, even though extension of maturity, change in interest rate, or other prospective substantive change in the indenture could not be made.

Any such change requiring modification or amendment of the indenture can only be accomplished with the consent of the percentage of the holders required by the indenture. As previously indicated, this would not include extension of principal, reduction in interest, or change in future sinking fund requirements.

(3) *Removal of Trustee.*—Another remedy available to security holders, acting collectively, is removal of the trustee. The indenture will customarily provide that the trustee may be removed, and a new trustee substituted, by the action of a specified percentage—usually a majority—of the indenture security holders. Where a new trustee is appointed pursuant to such action, the court will not disturb the discretion of the security holders and must recognize the new trustee so appointed.

Instances where exercise of this remedy would be beneficial would be the trustee's neglect or refusal to take remedial action, or the existence of some conflicting interest which would make appointment of a successor advisable.

The right may not always be an unmixed blessing, however. In one case a group of holders acquired a majority of the bonds for the purpose of obtaining control of the obligor in default and using such control for purposes not related to protection and enforcement of their rights as security holders. The trustee, with the rights of the minority in mind, refused to accede to the demands of this group for particular action. It was removed pursuant to the indenture and a new trustee appointed, which joined in the action of the majority. The right of removal by the requisite percentage of holders is absolute.

Problems arise if there is not an appropriate indenture provision, or demand by the requisite percentage cannot be obtained. Where a trustee refused to comply with an order of a court in a foreclosure proceeding, it was held that it could be removed at the suit of an individual bondholder. A trustee will not be removed, however, if minority holders merely disagree with its policy, or by reason of the fact that it is a general creditor of the obligor.

(4) *Protective Committees.*—As a practical matter, the organization of security holders in such a manner as to secure unanimity of a majority to direct or assist the trustee is not an easy task. The principal advantage lies in the ability to obtain consents and permit some form of voluntary readjustment in cases where default is not too serious, and where bankruptcy and reorganization can be avoided.

The delay necessarily involved, however, means that the trustee must determine for itself the initial steps which must be taken and must proceed to the initiation of such action.

The historical way in which bondholders have been organized was through creation of protective committees. A small group, usually representing the more substantial holders, would form a committee, select a depositary, and request all holders to deposit their bonds pursuant to an agreement which gave the committee broad powers of representation. This arrangement was time consuming and expensive. As will be discussed in the succeeding chapter, it was an essential in connection with equity receivership proceedings.

With the amendments to the bankruptcy act permitting corporate reorganizations, actual committee depositary arrangements have fallen into disfavor. The customary practice today is for the committee to request proxies or powers of attorney authorizing it to represent assenting holders. The difficulty with this arrangement is that there is no way of establishing, at a given moment, just how many bonds the committee represents.

The trustee represents all the security holders and must always be alert to the interests of the minority. Accordingly, it should not endeavor to organize a committee or to identify itself with it, even though a majority of the securities may be represented thereby.

14

Bankruptcy and Reorganization

A CORPORATION may become bankrupt either through insolvency or by reason of an inability to pay its debts as they mature. When such a situation develops, a major default under the indenture results. The powers customarily given the trustee are indenture remedies. These contemplate the actual liquidation of the business of the obligor and sale of the properties mortgaged or pledged for the benefit of the security holders.

Actual liquidation, however, is seldom possible or desirable. Despite the loss in security values that may accompany filing of a petition in bankruptcy, it is usually in the interest of security holders, as well as obligor companies, that the latter's capital structure be readjusted and its business continued on a solvent basis. The object of most proceedings, where a major default has occurred, is some readjustment or reorganization of the obligor's affairs, brought about through an equitable compromise of the rights and claims of security holders and other creditors.

Reorganization may be accomplished either through a voluntary compromise between the obligor and its creditors, or through the process of a judicial arrangement or reorganization. Where the affairs of the obligor are undergoing only a temporary strain and it is basically solvent, every effort should be made to achieve some sort of voluntary adjustment. As indicated in the preceding chapter, indentures may now contain provisions permitting certain percentages of security holders to waive a past default, or even to compromise claims for interest for a limited period of time.

Permanent voluntary adjustments are difficult of accomplishment, however, unless the security holders are few and easily accessible. Under ordinary circumstances the rights of an individual holder cannot be changed without his express consent. Where a permanent adjustment in the terms of securities is required, it is usually necessary to have recourse to some form of judicial proceeding.

Much has been written on the various bankruptcy and reorganization statutes, and neither time nor space will permit a detailed discussion of this subject matter here. Most indenture administrative officers will at some time be faced with the very serious problems involved in these proceedings, and a brief review of the principal statutory provisions and the position of the indenture trustee in such proceedings may be beneficial.

JUDICIAL ARRANGEMENTS

To avoid the expense and delay of a major reorganization, an effort has been made to provide mechanics to assist in bringing about what in effect are forms of voluntary adjustments. These are incorporated in Section 20b of the Interstate Commerce Act and Chapter XI of the Bankruptcy Act.

Section 20b applies to railroad corporations and the proceeding is conducted entirely before the Interstate Commerce Commission. Under this section any security or securities of a corporation may be modified, extended, or exchanged for other securities. This applies to both debt and equity securities. The Interstate Commerce Commission may impose such conditions on the plan as it determines to be just and reasonable. If such plan is consented to by the holders of 75 per cent or more of each class of securities affected, and the imposed conditions are met; and the plan is approved by the commission, it is binding on all holders of the classes affected. Although not used extensively, these proceedings have in the past been carried out simply and expeditiously.

Chapter XI of the Bankruptcy Act is designed to permit voluntary arrangements for other types of corporations. It is much more limited in scope and is intended more for situations where a limited number of individual creditors is involved than for adjusting terms of indenture securities. As it is a bankruptcy statute, the proceedings are conducted before a federal district court and the conditions which would warrant the filing of a petition in bankruptcy must be shown. Only unsecured indebtedness may be adjusted under this chapter. The debtor is required to file a plan showing how it proposes to deal with its unsecured indebtedness, and it is desirable for the consent of all or a majority of the creditors of each class to be obtained before the filing of the petition. The arrangement will be confirmed if the court finds that it is fair and equitable; that it is for the best interests of creditors; and that it has been accepted by a majority of the creditors of each class, holding a majority in amount of claims of each class. While secured indebtedness cannot be dealt with in such an arrangement, the court may, for cause shown, enjoin enforcement of a lien during the pendency of any such proceeding.

Proceedings under either Section 20b or Chapter XI may be initiated only by a debtor.

JUDICIAL REORGANIZATIONS

Despite the desirability of voluntary readjustments or arrangements, the measures now available are inadequate to provide the necessary relief where a severe financial crisis is involved. Recourse must therefore be had to a more drastic reorganization. This may be done either through equity receivership or through reorganization under the Bankruptcy Act.

EQUITY RECEIVERSHIP

Prior to the enactment of Sections 77 and 77B of the Bankruptcy Act in 1933 and 1934, there was no statutory authority for reorganization as opposed to liquidation of a debtor corporation. Since liquidation was impossible in many cases for various reasons, the necessary result was accomplished through resort to an equity receivership proceeding.

This proceeding was an ingenious device which was developed by the federal courts. It used old equity forms which had been developed for the liquidation of property of a debtor for the benefit of creditors, but to accomplish the reverse effect. The result was to preserve the corporate property intact and to rearrange the liabilities of the debtor.

The proceedings were generally instituted by the filing of a voluntary petition by the obligor, or a general creditors' petition, resulting in the appointment of a general receiver of all the property of the obligor company. Under its general equity power, the court would enjoin all individual suits by creditors and the filing of any additional suits. All matters relating to the debtor were thus centered in the court.

The extensive development of the "protective committee" took place in connection with these proceedings and was actually essential to their successful culmination. Committees would be formed for each class of securities of the obligor company. A depositary would be selected and security holders would be requested to deposit their securities, receiving in return a certificate of deposit which could be negotiated in the same manner as the original security. Committees usually took title to the deposited securities and acted under deposit agreements which gave them very broad powers.

After formation of the various committees, subsequent proceedings were carried on largely by their representatives. Questions of lien priorities, formulae for segregation of earnings, and other matters were settled by negotiation or were litigated. The reorganization plan was worked out through a compromise of the various creditor representatives. Once agreement was reached, the plan was submitted to the court for approval.

One of the real difficulties encountered was in dealing with minorities, or with those refusing to deposit their securities with a committee. This problem was resolved by a judicial sale of the properties to a new corporation formed by the reorganization committee representing various creditor interests. The deposited securities would be conveyed to the new corporation in exchange for the new securities in the appropriate proportions provided in the plan. Sale of the properties of the debtor was made at public auction after the court had fixed a minimum or "upset" price. Payment was accomplished in large part by use of the deposited securities taken at the proportionate share to which they were entitled in the reorganized company. A limited period of time was always provided nonassenters to deposit their securities and participate in the reorganization. Their only alternative was to take their proportionate share of the cash value of the sale determined by the upset price. Despite the fact that the upset price was usually set very low to facilitate a successful reorganization, many security holders still failed to take advantage of the opportunity of receiving new securities of potentially greater value than the cash.

Every effort was made to keep the cash requirements of the reorganization plan as low as possible. Even so, substantial amounts of cash still had to be provided to pay off nondepositors, and in some cases, holders of prior claims who refused to accept anything less in settlement. A substantial portion of such cash requirements was frequently provided by conserving the cash income of the company during the receivership period. In addition, sufficient new senior securities of the reorganized company might be sold to provide the amount required. Another very common practice was to offer junior lienholders or stockholders, who would otherwise not participate in the plan, an opportunity to preserve their stake in the company by subscribing to stock. The funds thus raised were used to complete the purchase price of the properties and to pay the expenses of the proceeding.

The development of the equity receivership form was largely in connection with railroad organizations, although it later came to be used extensively by other types of business corporations.

While in general the equity receivership was successful in accomplishing the essential purposes intended, there were a number of disadvantages which needed correction:

(1) Where the debtor's property was located in more than one federal judicial district, it was necessary for ancillary proceedings to be initiated in each such separate district. This was time consuming and expensive. Where a number of subsidiary corporations were involved, which was particularly true in the case of large railroad systems, a number of separate proceedings had to be undertaken.

(2) The necessity for a judicial sale of the properties frequently involved difficult problems.

(3) One of the most difficult problems was that involving treatment of dissenters. There was no way in which they could be compelled to participate. Those who failed to do so because of ignorance or inadvertence were often accorded harsh treatment. Professional dissenters sometimes had a field day, and the fact that their efforts were often successful made subsequent proceedings more difficult.

(4) There was usually a great deal of collateral litigation during the course of the proceeding.

(5) The plan finally agreed upon frequently resulted in overcapitalization of the reorganized company. This was especially true in the period preceding enactment of the Interstate Commerce Act with the requirement for approval of all new security issues by the Interstate Commerce Commission.

(6) Finally, consummation of the reorganization seldom provided a permanent solution. Each decade seemed to produce a new

wave of equity receiverships, many of them involving the identical companies or their reorganized successors.

SECTION 77 PROCEEDINGS

In an effort to cure some of the imperfections in the equity receivership arrangements, Congress in the mid-thirties added certain sections to the bankruptcy statutes to provide for statutory reorganizations. These were not bankruptcy statutes in the true sense since they provided for reorganization rather than liquidation of the assets of the debtor. They were in effect an effort at codification of the essential features of the former equity practice.

The first of these statutes was Section 77, first enacted in 1933 and substantially amended in 1935. It was designed to provide for reorganization of railroad corporations, a number of which were then in equity receivership.

Section 77 effected a number of improvements in the former practices and also gave certain powers to the bankruptcy court, the exercise of which by the equity courts had raised some questions of constitutionality. The necessity for ancillary proceedings was eliminated, the single court being given full jurisdiction over the debtor, all its property wherever located, and all its creditors. It was no longer necessary to go through the formality of a judicial sale of the property. Most importantly, dissenters could now be dealt with without the necessity of raising substantial amounts of cash to pay their distributive shares. If the plan was approved by two thirds of the creditors and stockholders of each class affected, it was binding on dissenters and they could be forced to accept the same securities of the new company allocated to other holders of their class under the plan. This particular provision was further liberalized by the 1935 amendments. Requirement for approval was changed to holders of two thirds of the claims of each class actually voting on the plan. It was further provided that even though the required two-thirds approval was not obtained, the plan might still be confirmed if the court found that rejection of the plan by a particular class was not reasonably justified.

The procedure contemplated may be described briefly. If a petition is filed, either by the debtor or the required number of creditors, the court appoints a trustee or trustees for the property of the debtor. The trustee so appointed is directed to submit a plan of reorganization within six months, although this period is always extended. When a plan is submitted to the court, hearings are held and the plan is submitted to the Interstate Commerce Commission. The commission assigns the plan to one of its examiners who holds extensive hearings and submits a report to the commission. Then the commission submits an approved plan to the court (or it may report that no reorganization is feasible). After further hearings, the court may either approve the plan as submitted or make modifications. If the latter, it must be referred back to the commission and the procedure is repeated. When both the commission and the court approve the plan, it is referred back to the commission for submission to creditors and stockholders (if they are found to have an equity in the property) for voting. The votes having been tabulated, the plan is then referred back to the court for confirmation. Following confirmation, reorganization managers are appointed who undertake the preliminary work necessary to its consummation. During this period, applications for allowances of expenses and compensation are filed and hearings thereon are held by the commission. The latter is given the authority to fix maximum limits for such expenses and allowances. These are referred to the court which may approve them or reduce them further. Finally, an order is entered directing consummation of the plan and the proceeding is terminated.

Experience has shown that in operation, Section 77 has fallen far short of the expectations of its framers.

One of the most objectionable features is the time now required to consummate a reorganization. One of the objectives of the act was to facilitate a speedy reorganization, but the reverse has been accomplished. The shortest period of time for any proceeding under Section 77 has been four years, and most have taken from ten to fifteen; several have required over twenty years. One proceeding which was commenced as an equity receivership in 1932 and became a Section 77 proceeding in 1941, was not concluded until 1961.

A number of reasons for this delay could be cited, but the principal fault seems to be the substantially concurrent jurisdictions of the reorganization court and the Interstate Commerce Commission, and the procedures which each has established for carrying out its respective functions under the act. The result has been a constant shuttling of the plan between the two bodies and an unnecessary and time consuming procedure each time this is done.

Another major problem has arisen from what in effect has been the substitution of the dictates of the commission for the results achieved by negotiation among representatives of security holders and creditors. Under the equity receivership process, the plan was usually the outcome of extensive negotiation among various creditor interests. While this caused delay and litigation, the result achieved was in most cases more equitable to the various classes of claimants than that of the Section 77 proceedings. While the former practice did at times induce unfortunate overcapitalization, plans approved by the commission and confirmed by courts over objections of dissenting creditors in Section 77 proceedings have wiped out substantial values and have left the affected security holders no recourse whatever. One major carrier, after consummation of its plan, was able through earnings to retire all of its bonded indebtedness and preferred stock within a few years, despite the fact that the former stockholders had been found to have no equity in the property and their securities were declared worthless. Another road so improved its position that it was able to pay off its accrued charges and have the proceeding dismissed. Subsequently, the stock of this company, which the commission had found to be worthless, sold for several hundred dollars a share.

The position of dissenting creditors has been substantially weakened by the provisions giving the court power to confirm a plan even though it was not approved by the requisite percentage of holders. This has made it very difficult for security holders to dissent from arbitrary action by the commission.

Another concept which has developed under Section 77 proceedings has been the paramount importance accorded the "public interest," as opposed to the interests of creditors and stockholders. Railroads, of course, are companies affected with a public interest, and one of the principal functions of the commission is to see that the public interest is not prejudiced by arbitrary action of a carrier. It is submitted, however, that if the modern concept of "public interest" requires subsidization of a carrier's affairs, such subsidy should be provided by the public and not by the carrier's security holders. During the pendency of a Section 77 proceeding, creditors are enjoined from realizing on their security. The primary objective of the court, and the court appointed trustee, should be to provide protection to their rights until a fair and equitable reorganization can be brought about. However the reverse may be the case. In one notable proceeding, over the repeated objections of the indenture trustees during a fifteen-year period and despite statements of the commission that no plan of reorganization was feasible, the court refused to authorize a petition for abandonment and liquidation, asserting that its obligations to the shippers (who were largely nonexistent) and the employees would never permit it to authorize termination of service. Instead, and again over repeated objections of the indenture trustees, it authorized continued cannibalization of the line's fixed property and the bondholders' security to pay operating expenses. When the proceeding was finally terminated and the remaining properties sold, the monies realized were insufficient to pay administrative expenses incurred by the court appointed trustees during the proceedings, despite the fact that substantial amounts might have been realized by the security holders, even on a salvage basis, had they been permitted to foreclose when it first became apparent that reorganization was impossible.

Finally, a word should be said about the general scope of allowances to parties to the proceedings, which are now made by the court within the limits fixed by the commission. One of the criticisms directed against the former equity receivership proceedings was the great expense involved, and an element of this expense was the fees and allowances made to attorneys and other parties. This criticism was justified in some cases, but the results of the present procedure are unfortunate. Because of the many intricate problems involved, conduct of these proceedings requires the best talent available, yet the standard of compensation now allowed attorneys who appear is in many cases less than the amount charged by these firms for the work of junior associates. Even so, attorneys are treated handsomely in relation to the fees allowed other parties, including indenture trustees. Lawyers do appear before the court and the commission, and there is some opportunity to appraise their contribution. Yet corporate reorganizations are largely economic undertakings, requiring at many points appraisal of earnings, trends, and other economic factors and the exercise of astute business judgment. Most of the work is done outside the hearing room, and much of it by individuals who never appear before the court. Aside from the proceedings themselves, the trust estate must continue to be administered, and much work has to be done in relation to the securities and to security holders, a great deal of it not susceptible of exact time measurement. Even a nominal allowance for this work, accumulating over a period of fifteen to twenty years, appears large when a petition is finally filed. As a result, these proceedings are very expensive, and an indenture trustee can consider itself fortunate if it is allowed more than 15-20 per cent of its actual costs in time and effort. One of the best ways of achieving better results in reorganization would be the adoption of a system whereby professionals who render expert and competent assistance would be compensated adequately for the contribution rendered. For those who are required to perform a continuing administrative or professional function, this should be on a current basis as distinguished from compensation related to formulation and adoption of a plan.

CHAPTER X PROCEEDINGS

Section 77B was added to the Bankruptcy Act in 1934 to provide for a substantially similar procedure for the reorganization of nonrailroad corporations which could not file under Section 77. In 1938 this section was repealed and the present Chapter X substituted.

The proceedings under Chapter X are in many respects similar to those under Section 77. A trustee may be appointed, or the debtor may be continued in possession. The trustee is required to file a list of the creditors of each class and of the stockholders, and a statement of the property, liabilities, and financial condition of the debtor, the operation of the business, and the desirability of the continuance thereof. The court must also fix a time within which the trustee is to prepare and file a plan. Upon the filing of the plan, the court must conduct hearings thereon, at which time any creditor or stockholder may appear and file objections or amendments thereto. After the court has approved a plan, it must be submitted to creditors and, unless the debtor is found to be insolvent, to stockholders. On its acceptance by creditors holding two thirds of claims of each class, and by a majority of the stockholders (if they are entitled to participate), hearings are held on confirmation of the plan. If two thirds of any class of creditors will not accept the plan, adequate provision must be made for the realization by creditors of such a class of the value of their claims. If the court finds that the provisions of the plan provide such protection, the plan may be confirmed despite the failure of two-thirds approval.

The role which the Interstate Commerce Commission plays in Section 77 proceedings is delegated to the Securities and Exchange Commission under Chapter X, with a few significant differences. The plan must be submitted to the commission and cannot be approved by the court until the commission has submitted its report thereon, or has advised the court that it will not file a report, or until the time fixed for filing of such a report has expired. One significant difference from Section 77 is that under Chapter X, the Securities and Exchange Commission may intervene in the proceedings, and thereafter is deemed a party for all purposes, except that it may not appeal from any orders entered.

In practice, the commission not only intervenes in all Chapter X proceedings but also becomes a very forceful party in interest. Frequently, it has virtually usurped the function of the court and the court appointed trustee. The theory of the commission's participation was to provide the court with the objective viewpoint of an expert administrative body. Since the plan submitted is substantially the product of the commission staff, it is questionable how objectively it may view its own handiwork, or the criticisms and objections filed by interested creditors. Despite the excellent contributions made by the commission staff in many instances, representatives of creditor interests are generally relegated to a secondary position.

Viewed in the most favorable light, the statutory reorganizations have fallen far short of realizing the objectives intended. They have delayed rather than accelerated consummation of plans. The resulting loss to the real parties in interest has been far greater than is necessary. Despite the acknowledged good faith of the administrative agencies involved, it is questionable whether substitution of their judgment for that of the real claimants has been beneficial to debtors or creditors or to the public interest.

THE TRUSTEE AND SECURITY HOLDERS IN REORGANIZATION PROCEEDINGS

The rights and functions of indenture trustees in connection with reorganization proceedings have not been clearly defined. While they are recognized as representing the indenture security holders, such rights of representation are strictly limited. In general, any matter relating to the security, lien, or priority of the indenture securities is a matter in which the trustee is primarily interested and in which it should be vigilant. On the other hand, it has no power or authority to compromise the claim of the security holders and, accordingly, the extent to which it may properly participate in the formulation or advocacy of a plan which effects such a compromise is questionable.

In equity receivership proceedings, the indenture trustee often took an active role. Quite frequently its right of foreclosure under the indenture was used to effect a sale of the property at the established upset price. Also, it participated in litigating questions of lien, the equity of segregation formulae, and other matters. Despite the existence of various committees, it was usually recognized by the court as the principal representative of the indenture security holders.

For the reasons previously discussed, formation of security holders' protective committees was an essential part of the procedure, and actual negotiation looking toward formulation of a plan was carried on largely by these committees. The trustee usually worked closely with the committee. This was particularly true in connection with all litigation initiated by the trustee.

Protection of minority interests was always a problem. Usually they had no representative other than the trustee, and their position in connection with a plan was almost always adverse to that of the majority represented by the committee. For that reason, although it endeavored to co-operate with the committee on most matters, the trustee maintained a position of independence and refused to be identified with the committee.

The right of the indenture trustee to be heard on all matters arising during the proceedings has been specifically recognized in both Section 77 and Chapter X. The indenture trustee may file a petition against a debtor under Chapter X, and while not so authorized specifically, this right undoubtedly exists under Section 77. It also may intervene in any such proceeding as a matter of right, and is entitled to receive notice of all important matters arising during the proceedings.

The specific provisions of these statutes as to the rights of the indenture trustee have not enlarged its authority to represent individual security holders. They have recognized the importance of the trustee as an agency for the representation of the security holders during the proceedings, but the importance of representation by the security holders themselves has also been recognized and emphasized. Under Section 206 of Chapter X, any creditor has the right to be heard on any matter arising during the proceeding. The importance of the exercise of independent judgment by individual creditors is illustrated by Section 212 of this act, under which the court is empowered to disregard any provision in a trust indenture or deposit agreement by which the trustee or a committee purports to represent security holders; and by Section 176, which invalidates any proxy, power of attorney, or other authorization to accept a plan on behalf of individual holders until the plan has been submitted to the holders by the court.

This emphasis on the individual holder, however, has not minimized the importance of collective action by security holders through committees. The right of any creditor to be represented in a Chapter X proceeding by a committee is specifically recognized in Section 209. Because of the complexity of the usual reorganization, and the lack of information available to an individual holder, as well as the substantial expense involved, it is impractical for most individual holders to appear personally in the proceeding. In addition to facilitating conduct of the proceedings by having the various classes of creditors represented by committees rather than by a number of individuals, an objection which may be raised will be more persuasive if it is entered collectively by a large number of a particular class. A committee will also be able, as a rule, to intervene in the proceedings, a privilege which offers a much greater opportunity for participation than the general right of individual holders to be heard. If anything, the importance of collective action has now been increased by reason of the fact that acceptance of a plan by two thirds of the creditors of any class will bind dissenters. Therefore, a dissenting minority now has more at stake and should organize to protect itself. Since the activity of these committees is now subject to court supervision, security holders should be better protected in surrendering their right of individual action to a committee.

The following are suggested as general guides to indenture trustee administrative officers in connection with reorganization proceedings. The circumstances of each individual case should be controlling, but these suggestions should apply in most situations:

(1) Despite imposition of the prudent man standard of conduct and an understandable inclination of the indenture trustee to pro-

tect itself by court proceedings, filing of a petition for reorganization by an indenture trustee should be the last step to be taken. Experience has demonstrated that with a few exceptions, such proceedings have resulted in substantial delays and losses to indenture security holders. Every effort should be made to work out with the obligor and, to the extent possible, with a majority of the security holders, an interim arrangement whereby the business can be continued and the rights of security holders protected. Filing of a petition in bankruptcy or reorganization should be regarded as an act of desperation and resorted to only where no other means are available for protecting the inherent rights of the indenture security holders.

(2) Where a petition is filed by the debtor, or by other creditors, the trustee should intervene promptly so that it will receive notice of all matters presented to the court and will have the right to be heard on any matter.

(3) Where the indenture is a lien on the principal fixed properties of the obligor and grants the trustee right to income after a default, a petition should be filed promptly praying for segregation of all income for the benefit of the trustee and the indenture security holders. This is important as it may seriously affect the rights of the security holders under the plan when it is presented, or the right of the trustee to object to the disposition of accumulated income during the proceeding.

(4) The reorganization trustee will probably present a petition for a general order authorizing it to sell or dispose of specific items of property without release from mortgage indentures. The indenture trustee should insist that there be included in the order approving this petition, a provision that the proceeds of any sale shall be held subject to the same liens and priorities as existed on the property disposed of, and shall be used only for capital purposes. On petition for approval of individual sales under such general order, the indenture trustee should require presentation of appropriate evidence as to the sufficiency of the consideration for any such sale.

(5) Every petition filed in the proceedings should be examined carefully. A majority of these will deal with routine administrative matters and will require no action or statement of position by the trustee. The objective should be to maintain the priority lien position of the indenture on the debtor's property until a reorganiza-

tion is consummated. Any proposed action which seems to affect such a position should be examined carefully, and if it appears likely to prejudice such a position, it should be opposed vigorously.

(6) The trustee's primary responsibility is to the maintenance and preservation of the bondholders' security. The trustee should initiate any action which seems appropriate or necessary for the protection of the security. In particular, it should endeavor to prevent the diversion of the proceeds of sale or liquidation of any of its security to purposes not of direct benefit to security holders.

(7) Any petition by the court trustee for authority to incur debt or to issue trustee's certificates should be examined carefully. These obligations will constitute a lien prior to any pre-bankruptcy obligations. If a substantial amount of prior indebtedness is created, the security holders' position in the subsequent reorganization may be weakened.

(8) Where a number of different lien positions are involved, as is frequently the case in railroad reorganizations, it may be necessary for the court trustee to prepare segregation formulae for the allocation of earnings and expenses among the various segments of the line subject to different lien priorities. Since under Section 77 the new securities issued on reorganization must bear a direct relationship to prospective earnings, development of proper formulae for allocation of such earnings is frequently one of the most important activities during the entire proceeding. Accordingly, the trustee should participate actively in all discussions and hearings relating thereto. This is a matter for experts, and in an appropriate case the trustee is well advised to employ expert assistance to support its case.

(9) While committees to represent security holders' interests directly are usually of great importance, the trustee should never endeavor to organize a committee or take any active part in such organization. This is of particular importance in Chapter X proceedings where the statute contains specific sections relating to activities of committees. If the indenture trustee is in possession of lists of security holders, these should be delivered to the court trustee or filed in court, and access of individuals endeavoring to form committees should be to lists on file with the court. The trustee should not make such information available directly except with the approval of the court.

(10) Once a committee has been organized and has intervened in

the proceeding, the trustee should endeavor to work closely with it on all matters relating to protection of the security holders as a class. In most situations the interests of the trustee and the committee will be identical. Under the statutory provisions, the interests of the unrepresented security holders is usually the same as those represented by the committee, since all will now participate to the same extent and in the same manner under the plan finally approved. In the normal situation, therefore, no position adverse to the committee is necessary for protection of the minority.

The trustee should always bear in mind, however, that it represents *all* the security holders. While co-operating with a committee in every way possible, the trustee should never surrender its position of independence or prejudice its right to take a contrary stand. This is particularly true where the principal holders represented by a committee are interested in issues other than the indenture securities.

(11) The administration officer should make certain that every department of the bank is aware of the pending proceedings, and is familiar with the statutory prohibition against any dealing in securities represented in the proceeding by the trustee. This is governed by Section 249 of Chapter X. While no similar provision appears in Section 77, it should be assumed that the same care should be exercised.

(12) The trustee should take an active interest in all matters relating to preparation and adoption of a plan. Many trustees, conscious of their lack of authority to compromise the claims of security holders, have taken the position that negotiations on a plan are a matter for the security holders and their committees, and that the trustee should play a passive role. Such an attitude is shortsighted and unrealistic. It is true that indenture trustees cannot make a commitment binding on their security holders; nor can anyone else. This is a matter for individual holders who must be given the right to express their approval or disapproval by vote once a plan is approved. The indenture trustee has no right to vote on a plan, but it should feel free to participate to the same extent as other parties, including committees, in all discussions leading to agreement on a plan. Participation will not foreclose its right to object to confirmation of a plan which appears to it unfair or inequitable, or which its security holders subsequently reject.

Under normal circumstances, the indenture trustee should not itself endeavor to prepare and file a plan. The only authority for it to do so is contained in Section 170 of Chapter X which refers to situations where the debtor is continued in possession and no court trustee is appointed. This should not limit the trustee's participation, however, since the court trustee will be delighted to file any plan which appears fair, equitable, and feasible, regardless of its source.

(13) One important duty which the indenture trustee should perform is the filing of a proof of claim on behalf of all indenture security holders. Express authority to do so is usually included in most indentures, but the trustee undoubtedly has implied authority even in the absence of such a provision. Under Chapter X, the indenture trustee is specifically authorized to file a blanket proof of claim. By reason of a provision that only holders who have filed individual proofs of claim may vote on a plan, such proofs are mailed with ballots to all security holders at the time votes are solicited. This procedure, however, should not influence the indenture trustee against filing a blanket claim, as many security holders will not vote and hence will not record their individual claims.

(14) The trustee should insist that the final order of the court directing and providing for consummation of the plan contain a specific discharge of the indenture and the trustee. If this is done, the cancelled indenture securities may be properly disposed of by the distribution or exchange agent appointed by the reorganization managers and the court, without being returned to the trustee for cancellation and discharge. Unless this is done, the trustee may find itself called upon to perform a great deal of unnecessary detailed work for which it will receive no compensation.

(15) Chapter X contains an express authorization for the court, in directing consummation of the plan, to set a period of time, not less than five years, during which all claimants must present their securities or claims for exchange. At the expiration of this period the estate is closed and all unexchanged securities become void. Any property left in the hands of the exchange agent becomes the property of the reorganized company. This is an important provision and is usually contained in all final orders of reorganization proceedings, the court being deemed to have such authority by

reason of its exclusive equity jurisdiction, even in the absence of express statutory authority. Failure to so provide may mean that an estate may never be closed.

(16) Where a debtor has been through a previous reorganization without provision for a final termination of an estate, a current proceeding provides an opportunity to secure an appropriate order and dispose of remaining property which may be held for exchange for old securities still outstanding from the previous reorganization. At the time of entry of the final order in the current proceeding, an effort should be made to secure court authority for terminating remaining matters in all previous proceedings.

(17) Where the proceeding is one of foreclosure or liquidation rather than reorganization, an order setting a limited period within which claimants must present their securities to receive their distributive share of the proceeds should still be obtained. Since in this situation there is no reorganized company to receive the balance of proceeds, a procedure which has been used successfully is to provide for a second *pro rata* distribution among holders who, during the period provided, did present their claims and receive the initial distribution. This enables the indenture trustee to close the estate within a reasonable period of time, and is the most equitable disposition that could be made of the remaining funds. It is essential, however, that such a method of distribution be incorporated in the initial order for distribution. In one case where this was attempted by a subsequent order, a state successfully intervened and claimed a vested interest in the remaining funds under an abandoned property law. Where provision is contained in the initial order for complete distribution of all proceeds, no such rights can vest in the state.

15

Specialized Trusts and Agency Appointments

IN THE PRECEDING CHAPTERS, we considered the more important duties and responsibilities of trustees under the customary indenture and private placement contract. Even these will vary however, because of differences in types of financing, the nature of the security, particular indenture provisions, and other factors. In general, such differences will constitute matters of detail rather than a change in basic functions.

From time to time, a bank performing the corporate trust function will be called upon to serve in a somewhat different or more limited capacity. Four of the more significant of these trusts and/or agency appointments are discussed below.

EQUIPMENT TRUSTS

A special form of contract has been developed for the financing of the purchase of equipment by railroads, and since 1970, for the financing of aircraft by the major airlines.

The basic concept of the equipment trust is ownership of the equipment by the trustee during the life of the loan. The obligations are in the form of equipment trust certificates, executed by the trustee, which represent a *pro rata* interest in the rentals and other proceeds received by the trustee through lease of the equipment to the user corporation. The proceeds received from sale of the certificates are used to purchase the equipment, and a lease thereof is executed by the trustee to the user corporation. This is a net lease calling for payments of rental over an 8 to 15 year period sufficient to pay all interest and principal on the certificates. In the case of railroads, the certificates mature serially and the obligations are retired more rapidly than normal depreciation on the equipment. Since the corporation (or as more recently seen, an institutional investor) will provide equity in an amount equal to 20-30 per cent of the purchase price of the equipment, and since most of such equipment is considered salable, these obligations command a ready market and usually a better price than the credit of many railroads or airlines alone would warrant.

In addition to its obligation to make the rental payments under the lease, the user corporation executes a guaranty on each certificate which runs directly to the certificate holder.

Normally, administration of these trusts is somewhat easier than the average trust indenture, although the initial documentation tends to be more complex and very special problems are created if a default or equipment loss occurs under the lease.

CONSTRUCTION AND BOND FUND TRUSTS

Although occasionally an indenture will require administration of a construction fund in connection with a new bond issue, as part of the other duties of the trustee, the type of trust considered here is somewhat unique. It may occur in connection with a revenue bond issue of a state or municipality, or a public or quasi-public body, created for a special purpose. Power districts, sewer districts, turnpike commissions, and similar entities are typical examples. Since the security for the bonds issued consists of the revenue to be derived from the project to be constructed, the bond proceeds are required to be segregated and held in trust solely to pay the construction costs of the project.

The function of the construction fund trustee is to hold such proceeds, make investment thereof in such manner as to provide the greatest return consistent with the requirement for paying them out over a predetermined period, and disburse the funds and the income thereon for the construction cost of the project. Disbursement is made against certifications by the project engineers as to actual expenditures made or obligations incurred for construction purposes. While the trustee is entitled to rely on these certifications, it should check them in sufficient detail to satisfy itself that the expenditures listed are of the type properly chargeable against the construction monies.

One very important consideration in establishing a construction fund is to provide for a revolving fund in a sufficient amount to take care of ordinary day to day disbursements for a reasonable period of time. This permits all miscellaneous disbursements to be included in one certificate at monthly or other periodic intervals, at which time the revolving fund is replenished.

Once the project has been completed and an appropriate certificate to this effect received, the duties of the construction fund trustee are finished. Any disbursed funds are usually turned over to the bond fund trustee and used to retire a portion of the debt.

In addition to a construction fund trustee for a revenue project, it is also necessary to designate a bond fund trustee. These may be separate institutions or one trustee may be designated to perform both functions.

The duties of the bond fund trustee relate solely to receipt and disbursement of the revenues of the project once operation commences. Varied types of special funds are usually created to provide for operating expenses, maintenance, bond service, reserves, and major replacements, additions, or extensions to the project. The revenues are received directly by the trustee and allocated to each fund according to the formula set forth in the indenture. The funds are then disbursed for the proper purposes either according to a predetermined schedule or against certifications of the proper officials of the district, commission, or authority.

A bond fund trustee has no power of enforcement or other rights in the event of default or insufficiency of the revenues. Should the revenues or other payments due be withheld wrongfully, it could undoubtedly bring suit to recover them. Its duties, however, relate solely to the revenues or other funds which are provided to be paid to it. It is not a representative of the bondholders for purpose of enforcement.

MUNICIPAL TRUSTS AND FISCAL AGENTS

Although not strictly within the purview of this book, most banks which offer professional corporate trust services are also involved in acting in an agency capacity for states and municipal issuers, primarily as paying agent. In addition, the accounting and destruction service for these obligations, introduced in the mid 1950's is becoming accepted by an increasing number of such issuers.

The increase in the availability of such appointments, together with the interest of banks as major purchasers of tax-exempt obligations has resulted in an accentuation of an area of conflict between the corporate trust fraternity and certain investment bankers and underwriters of these obligations. Underwriters are interested in the marketing of new issues and a number of them have urged issuers to delegate to them the right to name the trustee and paying agents for each issue. They argue that in view of the demand for tax-exempt obligations among commercial banks, the award of a corporate appointment to the largest purchaser enables them to secure advance commitments and results in a saving to the issuer through a reduction in the underwriters' "spread" or commission. While this may be true in certain instances, the accuracy of this argument as applied generally is open to question. In any event, it should be obvious that the aggregate demand for tax-exempt obligations is not increased, to the extent that any commercial bank purchases bonds solely to obtain a corporate appointment, the funds which would have been used for purchase of other obligations are used up. Investment needs and portfolio requirements should be the factors which determine bank purchases and not collateral considerations such as these. This is particularly true when one considers that the gross fees for a paying agency appointment represent less than one basis point in terms of interest costs.

There are even more compelling reasons for issuers to refuse to yield to any such demands. The services of a corporate trustee or agent require professional competence. While in theory any commercial bank should be able to make payment of an obligation, much more is involved in the service of a professional paying agent, just as there is much more involved in the practice of law than copying forms from a book. The advantages to an issuer in establishing and maintaining a continuing relationship with a qualified and experienced fiscal agent are substantial. In addition to the advice and assistance which can be rendered by such an agent, efficient and uniform accounting services can be provided, which is not true if there are multiple agents. Servicing costs also tend to be reduced as charges are normally determined by volume. Marketing is a short term consideration, whereas the trustee or agent designated will represent the issuer for many years. Their selection should be based on the quality of services rendered, and the issuer should retain complete control over its agents at all times.

One innovation in the form of the bond itself is the imprinting of the customary legal opinion on the bond. Prior to 1959, a separate legal opinion was rendered, many purchasers requiring a copy of the opinion as a condition to the purchase. As the result of increasing storage problems for institutional investors and the need for referring to opinions on older issues, the Investment Bankers Association recommended that the opinion be printed on the bond form. This recommendation has been accepted by most of the law firms involved and most new issues now have the opinions so imprinted.

The widespread acceptance of corporate bond issues in fully registered form only has as yet had no significant impact on tax-exempt obligations. A number of problems exist which are not present in the corporate issue, including the use of serial rather than term bonds; the requirement of a legal opinion sufficiently identifying the obligation; legal and budgetary problems in many jurisdictions; and the likelihood of more trading activity.

While these problems can and should be resolved, the general acceptance of the $5,000 coupon bond has, among other reasons, postponed the search for other solutions. There is however, a growing demand for bonds in registered form by the traditional purchasers of tax-exempt obligations, as well as by individual investors who are accustomed to receiving corporate securities (both equity and debt) in such form.

It is probable that developments in the securities industry since 1970, and the ever increasing attention by the federal government toward reporting of "investment income" may, during the next several years, accelerate the change toward all registered tax-exempt issues. A further trend, already in process for equity issues, will be the immobilization of the certificates themselves through the use of "book-entries" by the agent of the issuer and/or the use of regional depositories.

16

In Conclusion

THE WHOLE SPECTRUM of the corporate trust function, including the administration of the trust indenture contract, has been undergoing an evolutionary process for almost a century. The changes however, have been most evident since 1939 and especially during the past ten years. In the case of the indenture instrument, it has been able to be adapted quite readily to new modes and types of capital debt financing.

There is every reason to believe that this evolutionary process will continue, and probably at an accelerated rate. Certain areas which need further development and refinement are apparent although exactly how (and how soon) this will come about is not completely clear.

One way which may cause some of these changes to evolve is a project which has been undertaken by the American Law Institute. This project is designed to propose a new Federal Securities Code for adoption by the Congress. It is intended to revise the laws relating to securities distributions and markets, investment advisors, trust indentures, investment companies, and utility holding companies. Among the existing securities laws being reviewed is the Trust Indenture Act.

The essential function of the trustee is to administer the contract between borrower and lender. It cannot and should not undertake to rewrite the contract, nor should it assume responsibilities or powers not granted to it. It must live with the contract for a great many years, however, and every effort should be made to see that the indenture is so drawn, and that the rights and powers of the trustee are sufficient, to enable it to discharge its functions properly and with due regard to its fiduciary responsibilities to both obligor and indenture security holders.

More flexibility is needed in connection with pre-default administrative activity. The trustee should not be permitted to waive or ignore any indenture covenant, as this would do violence to the basic nature of the contract. In drafting particular indenture provisions, however, a greater degree of judgment or discretion might be granted the trustee. It should be better equipped to fit indenture language to changing circumstances and unusual situations so that the essential purpose of the contract could be carried out.

Without changing or diminishing the basic rights of individual security holders, an effort should be made to find some way to resolve the problem created by an indenture default, particularly one which does not or should not lead to an immediate petition for reorganization. The prudent man standard of conduct has been established as a result of the charge that the fault was a lack of due care on the part of trustees. To the extent that some trustees may have been guilty of this charge, the fault is remedied. The basic problem, however, is lack of clear and unquestionable authority for the trustee to act in many situations in a manner it deems to be in the best interests of the indenture security holders. Such action need not mean immediate pursuit of the drastic indenture remedies or recourse to other judicial proceedings.

Experience has shown that the reorganization provisions of the Federal Bankruptcy Statutes, as embodied in Section 77 and Chapter X, have not afforded the relief that was intended. Substantial revision of these statutes is overdue. One change should be in the direction of enlarging and improving procedures for voluntary adjustments. Where a major readjustment of capital structure is required, paramount jurisdiction should be lodged in the bankruptcy court. The function of the federal regulatory agencies should be limited and clarified. The right of representatives of security holders and other claimants to participate actively in the negotiations leading up to a plan is of foremost importance and should be recognized. Finally, a way should be found for properly compensating those who are necessary parties to the proceedings.

Another area to which it is hoped increasing attention will be paid is in draftsmanship of the indenture. Due to pressure of time or other work, or because they are too wedded to established forms, many lawyers engaged in this practice use far too much scissors and paste and too little original thinking when preparing the basic financing documents. The result is an effort to fit each new debt issue into a pre-established pattern rather than an endeavor to adapt the indenture contract and other documents to the purposes and objectives of the particular financing. A great deal of subsequent expense and effort, as well as considerable embarrassment at times, might be saved by more careful attention during the drafting process.

It is also clear that the future of the corporate trust industry will be effected by several trends which have become more evident since 1970. Among the more important of these are the increased financing demands of municipal and other public and quasi-public issuers; the expanding role of federal regulatory authorities such as the Federal Reserve Board and the Securities and Exchange Commission; the rapid development of the depository concept to immobilize the debt certificate itself (which in turn will ultimately lead to the virtual elimination of the certificate as a means of evidencing ownership of a bond); and the tendency of the more mature corporations to resort to special purpose unsecured financing rather than using the traditional open-end mortgage, as well as the use of provisions designed to attract the smaller investor.

A noteworthy example of this last trend is the floating rate issue which pegs the interest rate for each six month period to a rate 1 per cent or more above the average rate on three month U.S. Treasury discount bills. An added inducement is a provision permitting holders to redeem their holdings (or a part thereof), at par, on any interest payment date, after a two year period from the original issuance of the issue; provided that the option is exercised not less than thirty days preceding such interest payment date.

Index